VOYAGES IN ENGLISH

VOYAGES in English

Carolyn Marie Dimick

General Editor

Jeanne M. Baker
Maria Byers
Carolyn Marie Dimick
Joan I. Rychalsky

Authors

Loyola University Press Chicago

CONTRIBUTORS   Michael Lipkin
                   Sylvia Foust

PROJECT EDITORS   Janet Battiste
                   Kathleen Schultz

DESIGNER   William A. Seabright

ISBN 0-8294-0562-3 Teacher's Edition

ISBN 0-8294-0563-1

Preface

In every grade, language development challenges teachers and students to explore their world through the spoken and the written word. Language in all its aspects is essential to the development of the individual on a personal as well as a social level. Language is a vehicle for expressing wonder and delight, a tool for exchanging ideas, a medium for transmitting information, and a resource for bridging the differences among peoples of other cultures. These are the ultimate goals of language and the underlying philosophy of *Voyages in English*.

The revised *Voyages in English* is designed to include the major areas of the language arts curriculum: writing, grammar, correct usage, mechanics, dictionary and library skills, speaking and listening skills, and literature. These areas should not be considered separate and distinct from one another. For purposes of instruction, the skills are often taught in isolation, but the challenge of the teacher is to see that the areas are integrated and that the students begin to perceive the parts of the language arts curriculum as a whole. Finally, students should view the entire language arts program as an essential tool for building competency and success in other curriculum areas.

Before teaching the material contained in *Voyages in English,* the teacher should become acquainted with the format of the book. There are two distinct sections in the textbook: writing and grammar. Neither section is meant to be taught in its entirety at one time. Familiarity with the chapters in both areas will enable the teacher to move with ease between the two sections. For example, when working with the students in the proofreading stage of the writing process, the teacher will discover areas of weakness in correct usage and mechanics. At this point, it is recommended that the teacher turn to the lesson in the grammar section that corresponds to that particular area of weakness and teach the concept within the context of the writing activity. When teaching an area of grammar such as adjectives, the lessons on word substitution, sentence expansion, or descriptive writing provide an effective way of integrating grammar and writing. The correlations are many, and at all times the instructional goal should be integration, not isolation.

Developing good writing skills is essential at every grade level. The teacher should read the section entitled "The Writing Process" and become familiar with the components of the writing process. Students enjoy writing and should be engaged in the process as frequently as possible. **MORE TO EXPLORE** (grades 7–8) and **WRITE AWAY!** (grades 3–6) are an extension of the activities in each writing lesson. They may or may not be completed depending upon student ability to handle the extra material. Some students will need the challenge, others will not.

SHARPENING YOUR SKILLS (grades 7–8) and **PRACTICE POWER** (grades 3–6) provide a writing or skill-extension activity following each grammar lesson. In some cases, it is simply writing sentences or completing a review exercise; in others, it involves writing a brief paragraph or poem. With teacher assistance, the students should be led to realize the importance of integrating grammar, correct usage, and mechanics with writing skills.

The **CHAPTER CHALLENGE** at the end of each grammar chapter is a paragraph designed to incorporate all the skills the students have learned in the chapter. Identification of various grammatical structures is more difficult in paragraph form than in isolated sentences. In most cases, it should be teacher directed and not used as a testing tool.

The full page **ILLUSTRATION** that opens each chapter has a lead question that is designed to be a springboard for class discussion. Many of the illustrations have a connection with the chapter that follows, but some may be more appropriately used with other text material. The ideas explored through the illustrations can often become the subject of a poem or composition; therefore, having an overview of all the illustrations in the text is helpful so that at *anytime* throughout the year *any* photograph or art reproduction can be used as a basis for a writing activity. Although poems and compositions are encouraged, in simpler ways students can write different kinds of sentences about the picture: declarative, interrogative, etc. A simple sentence about the illustration can be expanded by words, phrases, or clauses, all of which could include various types of figurative language or, in the upper grades, the use of verbals.

WRITING CORNER (grades 6–7) provides more activities in the area of writing. It moves away from the structure presented in the writing chapters, and permits the students to explore other creative writing styles. In a few instances, these activities deal with research skills and with techniques helpful in practical classroom writing.

The selections from literature in **CREATIVE SPACE** are meant to be enjoyed first and then analyzed. For most students, they open up new writing possibilities; therefore, using literature as a model for students' original work is to be encouraged. Likewise, teachers creating original pieces of writing along with the students is a way of helping them see the challenge, effort, and satisfaction involved in the writing process.

The **TEACHER'S GUIDE** sets the objectives and presents directives for initiating each lesson. The teacher's guide in part 1 (grades 5–8) includes an **ENRICHMENT** section that provides a challenge for the better students. This should be used at the discretion of the teacher. The teacher's guide in part 2 contains an extended application for many of the exercises. This will aid the teacher in making as thorough use of the exercises as possible. The lessons within the chapters are not necessarily meant to be taught in one day. Many will require two or three days of instruction. The pacing of this instruction depends upon class as well as individual needs.

It is hoped that *Voyages in English* will provide students with a thorough knowledge of the English language and lead them to a greater appreciation for the gift that language is. A textbook can only accomplish so much, but coupled with a teacher's own love of language and attentiveness to its many nuances and subtleties, it can be a vehicle for growth and development in all areas of the curriculum.

The Writing Process

Exploring and discovering meaning through written language should be a part of every child's educational experience. Schools should place a high priority on developing writing skills, allowing teachers and students the freedom and time to foster the writing process within the curriculum. When the process is begun in the early school years, children have no fear or anxiety about writing. Instead, they often find it an exhilarating and happy experience. There is a sense of satisfaction in knowing a piece is well-written and has expressed exactly what the author intended to say.

Although much research is yet to be done regarding the composing or writing process, most authorities would agree that the process can be separated into four major divisions: prewriting, writing or drafting, revision, and editing. No division is isolated from the other. Writing is a cyclic process and thus implies that all divisions overlap, allowing the writer to wander in and out of all stages during the writing process.

The **PREWRITING** stage is the preliminary activity that goes on before the writer begins an actual draft. Observing, discussing, note-taking, reading, journaling, interviewing, brainstorming, imagining, and remembering are a few of the pre-draft experiences. In this stage, the writer zeros in on a subject, narrows it, and makes decisions about audience and purpose. For whom is the composition being written? Why is it being written? What form should the writing take? This stage is where a great deal of enthusiasm is generated. Interaction between student and teacher helps attest to the value of what the student is going to write. Students should be encouraged to share their ideas so that they can hear their thoughts, which ultimately lead them to be selective about their choice of material, make associations, and evaluate their information.

The student writer next moves into the **WRITING** stage, which is the creation of a first draft. Getting the information down on paper is the essential part of this stage. The writer should be encouraged to keep the ideas flowing without worrying about sentence structure or correct usage. There should be an effort to complete the piece from beginning to end at one sitting. Keeping up the momentum is important so that all ideas are on paper. The first draft is the visible form of what went on in the prewriting stage. It allows the writer to see what shape the work is taking. Students in this stage should be encouraged to write without making corrections, and to write on every other line so as to provide room for revision.

One of the most difficult, yet most vital areas, is **REVISION**. Here the student takes time to look at the work again and again. First drafts are rarely well-organized or cohesive. Vocabulary needs development, sentences need variety, and ideas need clarification. All this takes more than one revision, and students should be encouraged to write as many drafts as necessary.

It is at this stage of the writing process that teacher/student interaction is paramount. When trust has been built up, students will readily share their work. The teacher can act as a guide by asking essential questions: What are you writing about? Is there more you can say about your subject? Have you said it the best way you can? What is the part you like best? least? Deleting, adding, and rearranging ideas are essential to the revision process.

Students should be taught to look for specific things in examining their own work: Is the beginning sentence effective? clever? Is there a sentence that states the topic? Is there enough sentence variety? Are strong action verbs used? Does the ending sentence draw everything to a close? Since peer response is important, students should ask these questions when critiquing one another's work as well. The more feedback from students and teacher, the better the revision will be. Language at this point can be exciting and challenging. Trying to get the right word in the right place at the right time is the challenge of revision.

EDITING is the final stage before publication. It is here that students must look to the correctness of their piece. Punctuation, spelling, capitalization, and correct usage are important if the audience is to believe what the author is saying. All students should be taught the importance of proofreading and should be encouraged to do much of it on their own. But frequently the author gets caught up in content (which is not the domain of editing) instead of being attentive to mechanical details. To avoid this, it is often helpful to have another student edit the work. Some expert editors can be assigned in the classroom to help students who have difficulty in this area. The teacher can also control the editing process by naming the specific areas to be edited, making certain that all students are checking out four or five areas of concern.

It is important to note again that writers wander in and out of the various stages. Many times, one begins to revise even while writing a first draft. Frequently, it is necessary to return to a prewriting stage in order to gather more information or to think through an idea. Bits of editing are done while revising. No student should be locked into writing stage by stage.

Finally, students are ready to publish their work. All work should be as perfect as possible for publication. The audience has the right to demand that finished pieces be comprehensible and stylistically correct. But all publication is not meant for the teacher. Parents, principals, other students, and the community are all appropriate audiences. If the audience receives the work well, then the student has learned much from becoming totally involved in the process of writing. Student joy is teacher joy. The satisfaction that comes from a good piece of writing is immeasurable. The hard work is well worth the effort!

Contents

Part II   Grammar, Correct Usage, Mechanics

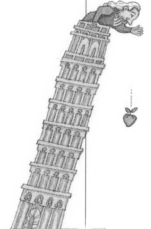

XVII

Exploring Our Language

Part I

Written and Oral Communication

Chapter 1

Building the Paragraph

Lesson 1 Selecting and Narrowing a Topic

A topic is the idea about which a paragraph or a composition is written.

The first step in writing is to decide on a topic. Do you think choosing a topic is difficult? Actually, it is easier than you might imagine. Professional writers usually find topics from their experiences and interests, and you can choose your own topics the same way. You probably will be surprised at how many topics there are for writing!

The best way to find a topic is to *brainstorm* for ideas. Think about some of your interests and about experiences you have had. Then take out a sheet of paper and write down ten topics that come to mind. For example, some of your topics might be "trips," "movies," "sports," or "friends."

As you look over your list, you will see that some of the items are things that are familiar to you. Others are things you like, but about which you need to learn more. Write the headings "Things I Know About" and "Things I Like (But Need to Learn About)" on a sheet of paper and put each topic you listed under the appropriate heading.

Everyone likes to share ideas. If you were in this picture, what thoughts would you be sharing?

The planet Saturn

For now, concentrate on choosing things familiar to you as paragraph topics. Suppose one of the topics you listed was "trips." That is such a big topic it would be difficult to know where to begin. So before you start to write, you must *narrow* the topic "trips" to one specific idea. That specific idea will become the topic of your paragraph.

Look at the two examples below. What happens to each topic?

> *Topic*: Trips
> *Narrowed topic*: A class trip
> *Narrower topic*: Our class trip to the planetarium
> *Specific idea*: How I got lost in the planetarium

> *Topic*: My neighborhood
> *Narrowed topic*: My block
> *Narrower topic*: People on my block
> *Specific idea*: My best friends on my block

Activity A

In each list below, a topic is narrowed down to a specific idea. However, the items in the list are out of order. Number them in the correct order as follows:

> *topic* (1)
> *narrow topic* (2)
> *narrower topic* (3)
> *specific idea* (4)

1. Movies
   Why _____ is my favorite movie of the year
   Movies I like
   Movies I liked this year
2. Soccer
   My soccer team
   Sports
   How my soccer team almost won the championship
3. Houses of the Algonquian Indians
   American Indians
   The Algonquians
   Indians of our area

4. Why I liked *The Left Hand of Darkness*
   The Left Hand of Darkness
   Science fiction books
   Books
5. How I learned to do a cartwheel
   Stunts I learned in gymnastics class
   Gymnastics
   My gymnastics class
6. Some good advice from my older sister
   My family
   Families
   My older sister
7. American history
   Zebulon Pike
   Exploration of Zebulon Pike
   Famous explorers in American history
8. Piano
   Music
   My first piano recital
   Learning to play the piano

Zebulon Pike

Activity B

Narrow each of the topics below to one specific idea. Write each specific idea as a statement.

1. Computers
2. Clothes
3. Food
4. Parties
5. Games

Write Away!

Think of three topics about which you would like to write. Narrow each down to a specific idea. Then discuss with another student what you might include in a paragraph about that specific idea.

Lesson 2 Writing Topic and Beginning Sentences

Topic Sentences

A topic sentence states the specific idea of a paragraph. It is often the beginning sentence.

Has anyone ever asked you "What was that movie about?" If you answered that it was about alien beings coming to earth or about how Egyptians built pyramids, then you have given the specific idea of the movie. When you write a paragraph, it is important to tell the reader your specific idea. The specific idea is expressed in a *topic sentence*.

Here are three topic sentences. What information do you think would be included in each paragraph?
1. Stickball is becoming a popular sport in our neighborhood.
2. My bedroom looks like a miniature zoo.
3. A shower of popcorn signaled my first real cooking disaster.

Now find the topic sentence in the following paragraph.

> Lively monkeys chattered nonstop as they swung about in their roomy cages. Puppies whimpered and made little barks when anyone approached them. Melodious songs came from the quivering throats of sleek canaries, and monotonous chirps were produced by baby chicks. From their perches overhead, brightly colored parrots squawked as if they were determined to be heard above the din. The pet shop we visited last week was an orchestra of competing sounds.

In the paragraph above, the topic sentence is the last sentence. The specific idea is "the noises in a pet shop." The topic sentence states the specific idea. All the other sentences in the paragraph give details about that idea.

The topic sentence is often—but not always—the first sentence in a paragraph. In the paragraph you have just read, the writer put the topic sentence last. All the sentences in the paragraph lead up to the topic sentence. The writer might also have put the topic sentence first to let the reader know the location of the noises immediately. If you had written this paragraph, where would you have put the topic sentence? Why?

Activity

Find the topic sentence in each of the following paragraphs.

1

Making quilts is a traditional American art. It dates back to the days of the American colonies. A quilt results when two layers of cloth are stitched together with a soft stuffing between them. American pioneers often stitched many pieces of colorful cloth together in their quilts. Because all the sewing was done by hand, making a quilt took a long time. To speed the process, pioneers would join in quilting bees. Families would sew quilts in the afternoon, and they would eat and dance in the evening. Quilts were valued by pioneers as warm bed covers and as shields from cold drafts. Their quilts are still valued by Americans today—mostly for the beauty of the quilts as colorful, original works of art.

Traditional American Quilts

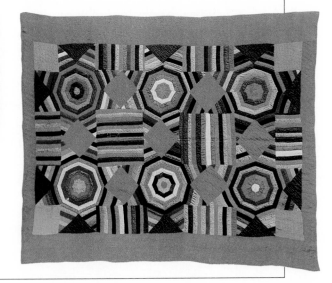

2

I felt unsure, but I decided to try anyway. I took a firm grip on the sticks. My first attempt ended with a "plop" and splatter. I looked around to see if anyone in the restaurant had noticed, but no one had. I practiced moving the sticks until I felt more comfortable with them. Gathering my courage and determination, I tried again and managed to get a piece of vegetable into my mouth. My first experience at using chopsticks in a Chinese restaurant started out shakily but ended in success.

3

Why is a porcupine a porcupine? Why is a hippopotamus called by such a strange, hard-to-spell name? The variety in the origin of animal names is almost as varied as the animals themselves. Some animals are named after places. Shetland ponies are named for islands near Scotland. Some animals are named after people. The Doberman pinscher, a large, smooth-coated dog, is named for Ludwig Dobermann, the German who first bred the dog. Some names describe the animal. Often, however, these names are in foreign languages. For example, *porcupine* comes from Latin words meaning "pig with thorns." The Greek words "river horse" make the word *hippopotamus*. Check your dictionary or other word books to learn more about how animals get their names.

Beginning Sentences

A good beginning sentence introduces the topic and tries to interest the reader in the paragraph.

Whenever you write, you are writing *to someone*. You may be writing a composition for your teacher, a note to your parents, or a letter to a friend. You want to make sure that your audience will be interested in what you write. To create interest, you should write a good *beginning sentence*. A good *beginning sentence* will *introduce the topic of the paragraph, arouse the reader's curiosity*, and *encourage him or her to read on*.

Sometimes a beginning sentence may be written as a simple topic sentence, which tells the specific idea of the paragraph.

The day finally arrived for our trip to the wax museum.

Sometimes a beginning sentence may be written in a more interesting and creative way. Such a sentence may still give the specific idea of the paragraph.

How many famous people would greet me on my journey through the halls of the wax museum?

The first example tells the reader that the paragraph will be about a trip to the wax museum. The second example gives the same information, but it does so in a more creative style. The writer uses an interrogative sentence and colorful language so that the reader will want to continue reading to discover more about the famous people in the wax museum.

Below is an example of each kind of beginning sentence. Either one could be used at the beginning of a paragraph about fossils. What is the difference between the two sentences?

Topic sentence: Fossils are records of the distant past.
Creative sentence: Fossils are a kind of ancient photography that captures life as it was millions of years ago.

Here are two more beginning sentences. Think about how they are different and what each one tells you about the topic.

Topic sentence: Autumn is my favorite season.
Creative sentence: When leaves turn to red and yellow and a cool wind blows, I anticipate some of my favorite things—apple picking, the World Series, and jack-o-lanterns.

Activity A

Tell whether the beginning sentences below are simple topic sentences or creative sentences.

1. The family gathered together for Thanksgiving.
2. Will a typical lunch of the future be a "hamburger" tablet?
3. Wow! I never thought all this could possibly happen to me in one day.
4. Christmas is always a great deal of fun.
5. I watched the rain making patterns on my window and wondered if she would find shelter out there.
6. Len's face beamed as he surveyed the delicious dinner spread before him.
7. Owning tropical fish can be a fascinating hobby.
8. Zoom! Our spaceship sped like lightning through the vast empty space of the galaxy.
9. "Oh, no!" Anita cried. "I forgot to study for the math test."
10. An astronaut's training is very difficult.

Activity B

Below are five simple topic sentences. Each expresses the specific idea, or topic, of a paragraph. Try writing a creative beginning sentence to go along with each topic sentence. If you do not know enough about a topic, use your imagination.

1. Last year my family took a trip to New York City.
2. Cars of the future will be longer and sleeker.
3. Life was an adventure for King Arthur's knights.
4. My friend Sally had a huge insect collection.
5. Buildings shook as an earthquake rumbled through the city.

Activity C

Supply a beginning sentence for each of the paragraphs that follow. Be sure to write one that is interesting and gives a hint of what the paragraph is about. Decide whether you want to write a simple topic sentence or a more creative sentence. You may write two sentences to begin a paragraph if you need to.

<u>1</u>

_____

My uncle and I sat at either end of the canoe and paddled, and my little brother Jimmy sat in the middle. Jimmy was content to sit still and watch the world go by until he spied a frog resting on a floating log. I saw what he was going to do and shouted, "Jimmy—no!" It was too late. Jimmy reached out to grab the frog, the canoe tipped over, and we all tumbled into the lake. Although it was a frightening moment, luck was with us. We fell onto a sandbar where the water was shallow, and we were safe. I didn't see the frog again, but I'm sure that wherever it went, it was laughing all the way.

2

The typical cowboy of the late 1800s was a short, rather ordinary-looking man. He rarely, if ever, shot his gun, got into barroom fights, or chased desperadoes. Much of his time was spent on long and hazardous cattle drives, where blankets and some extra clothing were all he could bring along. Often, there was not even a tent in which to sleep. If he was injured on the drive, he was likely to be left behind. It was a hard life, and very different from the way we picture it today.

3

Each day I feed him, clean his cage, and let him fly around the house. If he lands on my arm, I say "Hello" in the hope that he will learn to say the same to me. Taking care of Petey is not much trouble, but yesterday I was careless and left a window open. I saw a flash of brightly colored feathers, and Petey was gone. It was such a shock that at first I stood perfectly still. Then I raced to the window and peered anxiously in every direction. There was no sign of Petey anywhere. I turned sadly away and started to walk across the room when suddenly I heard "Hello." Spinning around, I saw Petey perched on the windowsill. He had come back on his own—and announced his arrival!

Write Away!

Write a simple topic sentence for each of the topics below. Then write a more creative beginning sentence for each topic. If you do not know enough about one topic, use your imagination.
  1. The flight of monarch butterflies south for the winter
  2. My favorite ride at the amusement park
  3. Food that astronauts eat on space flights
  4. Winning a contest
  5. The day I disappeared

Lesson 3 Writing Supporting Sentences

Supporting sentences give details that explain the topic.

You have already learned how to choose a topic, narrow it, and write an interesting beginning sentence. After you write your beginning sentence, you will want to tell more about your topic. *Supporting sentences*, or middle sentences, tell the important details. Each supporting sentence adds information and carries the idea of the paragraph forward.

Read the paragraph below. Notice how the supporting details develop the idea expressed in the topic sentence.

A Useful Plant

The whole life of Egypt seemed to depend on the papyrus plant. The young shoots were eaten, and the juice was made into a drink. Weavers learned how to twist its fibers into a kind of cloth, and shoemakers made shoes of its bark. Boatmakers tied bundles of it together to make small canoes and even larger boats. Out of its stems were made utensils for the house. Last, but not least, paper was made from it! Is it any wonder that the Egyptians valued papyrus so highly?

The topic of the paragraph is "the usefulness of the papyrus plant." The beginning sentence explains that life in Egypt depended on this plant, and the supporting sentences provide the details that show this. The supporting sentences do not tell what the plant looked like or how it was grown. Instead, they keep to the topic and explain how the plant supplied things needed for life.

Papyrus

The diagram below is a *word map* that describes the paragraph about papyrus. At the center of the word map is the topic of the paragraph. Around the center are the supporting details. You may want to draw a word map before you write a paragraph. A word map is a useful tool to help you organize your ideas and decide what details to include.

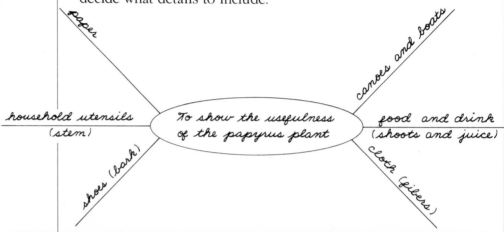

paper

canoes and boats

household utensils (stem)

To show the usefulness of the papyrus plant

food and drink (shoots and juice)

shoes (bark)

cloth (fibers)

A painting illustrating a noble Egyptian family's use of the papyrus plant.

12

Activity A

Read the specific idea in each circle below. Then complete the word maps by giving four supporting details for each topic.

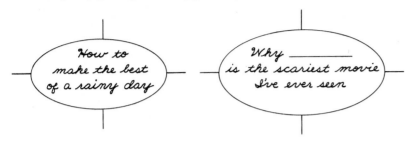

How to make the best of a rainy day

Why _____ is the scariest movie I've ever seen

Activity B

Write a beginning sentence for each topic in activity A. Then complete the paragraph, putting your supporting details in order and adding any additional information you think the reader might need to know. Remember to keep to your topic! Read your paragraph and decide if it makes sense and reads smoothly. If not, move sentences and words around to improve it. Reread your paragraph one more time.

Write Away!

Choose any two of the five topics below. Make a word map with four to six details for each topic. Then choose the word map that has the most ideas and write a paragraph using the word map as a guide. Write a good beginning sentence and supporting sentences that give the details. Put the sentences in the order that seems most logical to you.

1. How to roller-skate
2. Why _____ is my favorite _____
3. An afternoon in the year 2050
4. A punishment I really deserved
5. The best adventure of my life

Lesson 4 Writing Ending Sentences

An ending sentence draws the paragraph to a close.

In lesson 3, you wrote some paragraphs with beginning sentences and supporting details. Perhaps you added a sentence at the end to express your opinion or to sum up the ideas in the paragraph. You might have done this simply to bring your paragraph to a smoother conclusion. If you did, you were writing an *ending sentence.*

An ending sentence, besides just bringing the paragraph to a close, may do several things.

An ending sentence may give a last fact or detail.

> An old red cloth thrown over the cage soon silenced the bird.
>
> Suddenly, the diver emerged from the glistening blue-green water with a handful of gold coins.

An ending sentence may tell what the writer thinks or feels.

> After that experience, I'll never hike in shorts and tennis shoes again.
>
> Now I know that joining the neighborhood swim team was a good idea.

An ending sentence may also draw together everything in the paragraph.

> With all these uses, it is no wonder microwave ovens are part of the modern kitchen.
>
> The magician's fast-paced tricks left Jonathan wide-eyed with amazement.

Activity A

Choose the ending sentence that would best complete each of the paragraphs described below. Explain the reason for your choice.

1. Gary is writing about how he sold the most candy in the candy drive at school and won a prize for his efforts. Which of the following sentences would be an ending sentence that expresses Gary's feelings about the contest?
   a. When the teacher announced a candy drive, I just groaned.
   b. This is the most exciting thing that ever happened to me!
   c. Finally, I sold twenty boxes to my favorite aunt.

2. Tina has just finished writing about a collection of stories by Rod Serling. She is ready to draw the ideas in her paragraph together. Which of the following sentences would be an ending sentence that would do this?
   a. Everyone interested in mystery and suspense should sample a Rod Serling story.
   b. I can't believe I read the whole book in one sitting!
   c. Are you hooked on stories about strange happenings?

3. Hanna is writing a paragraph about her first experience waterskiing. Which sentence could end the paragraph and give a detail?
   a. Waterskiing will be part of my summer activities from now on.
   b. If my little brother could water-ski, so could I.
   c. I let go of the ropes and collapsed into the water, ready to take up the challenge once again.

Activity B

Supply a good ending sentence for each of the following paragraphs. Think of one that is interesting and will really wrap up the story.

1

The flap-flap-flapping noise attracted my attention, so I gazed across the park. What a surprise to see a man in blue jeans and a floppy old top hat juggling silver-colored clubs. Before long, I learned about this unusual young man. He had spent the winter at clown school in Florida where he studied such skills as magic, juggling, gymnastics, and mime. He had not yet found a job as a professional clown, but each evening he came out to practice his new craft. Day by day, more people gathered to watch. _____

2

"I'll never make any friends in this new neighborhood," I thought, as I bounced a ball against the brick wall. The block seemed deserted, and I missed my old friends. As the ball thumped against the wall, I noticed someone standing near me. A dark-haired, freckle-faced girl was watching me. She seemed to be wondering who I was. I didn't know what to say, but suddenly I had an idea and flipped the ball over to her. "Nice catch," I said. _____

<u>3</u>

Shortly after the Civil War, American theatergoers watched a young actress named Belle Boyd give dramatic readings about the adventures of a Confederate spy. It was more than just an act, however, since Boyd had really led the life of a Civil War spy. By the age of seventeen, she was watching the Northern army move through her native South and sending coded messages to Southern leaders. Northern soldiers captured her three times, but each time she was released. One of her guards even fell in love with her, and the two were married.

Write Away!

Here are five topics for paragraphs. Write an ending sentence for each paragraph and explain what purpose or purposes the ending sentence serves.

1. My worst injury
2. A troublesome neighbor
3. A surprise birthday party
4. An unexpected friend
5. If I could live in another time . . .

Lesson 5 Paragraph Unity

Paragraph unity means that all the sentences in a paragraph are related to the specific idea.

In the previous lessons, you wrote some paragraphs. Then you reread your paragraphs to see if they made sense. What does it really mean for a paragraph to make sense? For one thing, it means that all the sentences are related to the topic.

Sometimes when you reread a paragraph you have written, one or two sentences just do not seem to belong. These *misfit sentences*, which are not related to the topic, must be taken out. Read the following paragraph and note how one sentence interrupts the thought. Which sentence does not belong? Why is it a misfit?

"Can this thing really play music?" I thought as Willie handed me his electric guitar. It wasn't hollow like other guitars, and when I plucked a string, there was no noise. Willie said that he would explain to me how an electric guitar worked. Willie's group is called the "Soul Rockers." He plugged the guitar in, and when I plucked the string again, there was a rich, loud sound. "The strings don't really make the music," he explained. "When you play a string, it gives an electrical signal to the amplifier and to the loud speaker. That's where the music comes from!"

Activity A

Each list below has a topic and four supporting details. In each list, one detail does not fit. Find the misfit details and replace them with ideas that fit the topics.

1. Hurricane safety tips
   a. Board up your windows.
   b. Keep a supply of food in the house.
   c. Make sure you have candles.
   d. Tornadoes are also dangerous.

2. Why sixteen-year-olds should be allowed to drive
   a. They can run family errands.
   b. They will vote in two years.
   c. They should be responsible by that age.
   d. They may need a car for dates and parties.

3. Why every family will want to own a robot
   a. It can do household chores.
   b. The word *robot* means "work."
   c. It can be a companion.
   d. It can help with homework.

4. My Halloween costume
   a. Jessica dressed as a witch.
   b. I dressed as an astronaut.
   c. I was supposed to be Sally Ride.
   d. My costume was shiny and silver-colored.

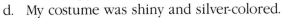

Activity B

Read the following paragraphs and find the misfit sentences. Explain why each misfit is not related to the topic of the paragraph.

1

I saw quite an unusual sight last week. A wrecking crew was scheduled to remove a large old building. I had previously seen many buildings being torn down. For those buildings, a wrecking ball was used to knock down the building piece by piece. Wrecking equipment can be quite expensive. The process was slow but fascinating. The event last week was quite different. People like me were allowed to watch—but from a safe distance. The crew placed explosives throughout the building. These were then set off, and the building collapsed straight down. It was all over in less than a minute. The process was fast—and fascinating.

2

"Help me," yelled the frightened man from the pool. A large man, weighing maybe two hundred pounds, was in the deep water and could not stay afloat. The lifeguard ran to the side of the pool. She was a girl of about fifteen and weighed no more than one hundred pounds. She wore a red and white swimsuit and a striped bathing cap. I didn't think she could save such a big man, but she worked quickly. She threw him the nearest kickboard and said, "Calm down. Relax. Just hold the board and kick to the nearest side of the pool." Her method worked, and the man kicked safely to the side. She had learned her lifesaving lessons well.

3

The first known valentine dates back to 1415. Then a French noble who was imprisoned in England sent one to his wife in France. By 1750, it had become a custom in England and America to tuck valentines into doors. These early valentines were made by hand and were not signed. By 1850, valentines were made by machine, and over three million were sold in the United States. Although valentines of this time were machine-made, decorations were often added to them by hand, and these valentines are considered among the most beautiful ever produced. They often had frilly lace borders, flowers, and colorful pictures added to them. Valentines were just one example of the beautiful arts of the 1800s. By 1900, postcard valentines with humorous messages were popular. These are not unlike some of the valentines we send today.

Old-fashioned Valentine Card

Write Away!

Choose any one of the narrowed topics from activity A and write a short paragraph. You may add new supporting sentences and make changes in the ones that are already written. Create an interesting beginning sentence, keep the middle sentences unified, and write an effective ending.

Old-fashioned Valentine Card

Lesson 6 Creating a Title

A title is the name that is given to any piece of writing.

The title is the first part of your paragraph, composition, or story that the reader will see. Sometimes the title helps a reader decide whether to read on or not. Do you think a story called "Building a Boat" would interest you? Would you want to read an article called "Whales"? *Perhaps* you would, but wouldn't titles like "Modern-Day Vikings" and "Underwater Giants" spark your interest a bit more?

Titles are fun to create. There are several different approaches you can take to writing titles. Sometimes titles tell the specific idea of the paragraph, such as "Danger: Sharks!" What do you think that paragraph is about?

Other titles give just a hint of what is in the paragraph. The title "A Narrow Escape" sounds exciting. It makes you ask yourself these questions: From what situation must the main character escape? How will he or she accomplish this?

Still other titles are more creative, such as the titles of C. S. Lewis's novels *That Hideous Strength* and *The Lion, the Witch, and the Wardrobe* or of Mary Stewart's novel *The Crystal Cave*.

Notice that most titles are short and that each important word begins with a capital letter. The words *a, an, the,* and *and* are capitalized only when they are the first word of the title.

Activity A

Each of these five topics has two possible titles. Which title do you think is better for each topic? Give the reason for your choice.

1. Getting lost on a camping trip
   a. Lost in the Woods
   b. A Quick Lesson in Survival
2. Your first experience at cooking
   a. Pancakes—I Think!
   b. An Unsuccessful Meal
3. Hitting your first home run
   a. The Crack of the Bat
   b. I Hit a Home Run
4. Using a pen with evaporating ink
   a. A Disappearing Note
   b. For Your Eyes Only
5. Moving to a new city
   a. Destination: Atlanta
   b. My Family Moves to Atlanta

Activity B

Reread the paragraphs on pages 5 and 6 or pages 9 and 10. Create an interesting title for each.

Write Away!

Here are five topics. Create an interesting title for each.

1. Learning to dance
2. A woman who becomes a police officer
3. Watching a big fire
4. The first day of spring
5. Watching a new music video on television

Writing Corner 1
Journal Writing

Do you ever write for yourself—just to express your ideas? A journal is a special place for writing about yourself and the things that interest you.

In your journal, along with your own ideas and feelings, you might include favorite poems or song lyrics, pictures, and interesting facts. You can share your journal with your friends, family, teacher, or classmates. You might want to keep your journal just for yourself.

A journal can be helpful in your schoolwork. It can include topics and ideas for writing assignments. Journals are often kept by writers. In them, writers record events and ideas that they will use later. You can do the same thing. You might even carry your journal with you and jot down what you observe during the course of a day. You will find that the more you write, the easier it will be to write and the more you will enjoy writing.

Here is an entry from a student's journal.

What a long winter! Sometimes I feel as if I am in hibernation. This might be a nice thing for a bear, but not for me. I've noticed that I've been grumpier lately, but today there is a new feeling in the air. The birds are chirping and the bushes are showing some green fuzz. There are lots of worms on the ground. The birds have their eyes on these wriggly creatures. (I wonder if _I_ could eat a worm!) Crocuses and snowdrops are in bloom and I'm glad this spring breeze is milder than the cold wind that's been blowing. I would like to go to the park and fly a kite.

Such a journal entry might give you an idea for a poem like the following.

> It's time for bears to yawn and stretch
> To open their eyes, look outside, and watch
> Birds chirp and chatter
> Trees and bushes turn green
> Worms rise and squirm
> Crocuses and snowdrops bloom
> Winds warm and play
> Kites bob and jerk
> Because it's finally SPRING!

★ Buy a spiral notebook, and begin to keep your own journal. Here are some ideas about which you might like to write.

> My idea of the perfect day/friend/meal
> The most difficult thing I have ever done
> The best/scariest/funniest thing that has ever happened to me
> My favorite place/season/movie/hobby/music
> I wish I could meet . . .
> I wish I could learn to . . .
> What I think life as a doctor/zookeeper/TV star would be like
> What would happen if there were no TV
> What would happen if I could be in two places at once
> What would happen if I could change places with Mom or Dad
> A country that I would like to go to and why

Word Study 1

Prefixes

A prefix is a syllable (or syllables) added to the beginning of a word that changes the meaning of that word.

You already know many prefixes. If your teacher tells you to *re*write a paragraph or *re*read a story, you know that the prefix *re* tells you to do something *again*. If a task is *im*possible, the prefix *im* tells you the task is *not* possible. Notice that a prefix is always followed by a *root*. The prefix will give the root a new meaning.

Here is a list of prefixes. Study them carefully.

Prefix	Meaning	Example
bi	two	bicycle
co	together	copilot
dis	not	disapprove
micro	small	microcomputer
mini	small	miniskirt
non	not, without	nonstop
over	above, too much	overcook
re	again	reunite
tri	three	triangle
uni	one	unicycle

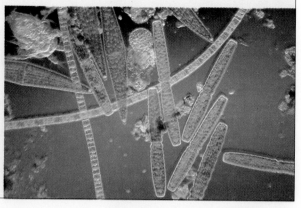

Green algae magnified through a microscope

Activity A

Copy the chart below, and fill in the missing parts. The first one is done for you.

	Prefix	Root	New Word	Meaning
1.	re	trace	retrace	trace again
2.	_____	load	_____	to load too much
3.	_____	_____	microwave	small electric wave
4.	non	returnable	_____	_____
5.	mini	van	_____	_____
6.	_____	lateral	_____	two-sided
7.	_____	satisfied	dissatisfied	_____
8.	tri	color	_____	_____
9.	co	_____	cowinner	_____
10.	_____	_____	unisyllabic	with one syllable

Activity B

Complete each sentence with the correct word by adding a prefix from the list to the word at the left.

grown   1. The field was _____ with bushes and weeds.

set   2. Because of the electrical failure, we had to _____ the clocks.

bike   3. If I had a _____, I could ride to school every day.

sense   4. Humorous poems are often called _____ poems.

cycle   5. I remember riding a _____ when I was very small.

operate   6. If this project is to succeed, everyone must _____.

corn   7. There was a picture of a _____ in the mythology book.

scope   8. In science class, I spent fifteen minutes looking through a _____ at different kinds of leaves.

agreed   9. "Strike three," yelled the umpire, but the batter _____.

weekly   10. Jamie receives the magazine every two weeks. It must be a _____ subscription.

Chapter 2

Refining Your Writing Skills

Lesson 1 Expanding Sentences

You can expand a sentence by adding adjectives, adverbs, and phrases that help to give the reader a clearer picture.

Adding Adjectives and Adverbs

Sometimes you may decide that a paragraph you have written is dull and uninteresting because it fails to give the reader a clear *picture*. Sentences in such a paragraph can come to life, if you add colorful and expressive adjectives and adverbs.

If you write *The lanterns swayed*, for example, your sentence is not very specific. You could add adjectives and an adverb to make the sentence read, *The colorful Chinese lanterns swayed rhythmically*. Now the reader gets a clearer picture!

Study this example. Note the words that are added to the second sentence.

> The tightrope walker balanced herself.
> The daring, graceful tightrope walker balanced herself effortlessly.

The writer has added

> the adjectives *daring* and *graceful*
> the adverb *effortlessly*

Lighting a lantern helps you see more clearly. Can the words you use when you write help you to see your ideas more clearly? How?

Activity

These ten sentences could use improvement. Whenever you see this symbol, ∧ (called a caret), put in one or more adjectives or adverbs.

1. The ∧ rain fell ∧.
2. The ∧ hikers ∧ walked through the ∧ forest.
3. The ∧ pirates ∧ boarded the ∧ ship.
4. ∧ bees swarmed ∧ over the rose garden.
5. The puck flew ∧ past the ∧ goalie.
6. The ∧ campfire blazed ∧.
7. The artist did a(n) ∧ painting.
8. I bought a(n) ∧ frozen yogurt.
9. Two ∧ shadows ∧ emerged from the ∧ spaceship.
10. The ∧ frog leaped ∧ from the log.

Adding Prepositional Phrases

You have seen how adjectives and adverbs can make your sentences come to life. Prepositional phrases are another helpful tool that you can use.

Look at this sentence again.

The colorful Chinese lanterns swayed rhythmically.

You could also add a prepositional phrase to make the sentence read

The colorful Chinese lanterns swayed rhythmically *in the light breeze*.

With the addition of a prepositional phrase, the picture becomes even clearer.

Study the example below. Note the phrases that are added to the second sentence.

The graceful, daring tightrope walker balanced herself effortlessly.

The graceful, daring tightrope walker in a red leotard balanced herself effortlessly on the wire above the crowd.

The writer has added

the phrase *in a red leotard* after a noun
the phrases *on the wire* and *above the crowd* after the verb

Activity A

The sentences below are not very specific. Add a prepositional phrase or phrases to each sentence to give a clearer picture.

1. The Frisbee landed.
2. Doug dribbled the ball.
3. The river overflowed.
4. The drums boomed.
5. The snow drifted.
6. Cactus grew.
7. The scuba diver floated.
8. Crowds of people stood.
9. The lion crouched.
10. The rocket rose.

Activity B

Expand the following sentences. Add colorful adjectives, adverbs, and phrases. Try doing this activity in two steps: first add adjectives and adverbs, and then go back and add prepositional phrases where you think they are needed.

1. David was a keyboard player.
2. He wanted to start a rock group.
3. He knew that John and Eddie were guitar players.
4. They agreed to join the group.
5. The next member was Josh, a drummer.
6. David heard a singer named Maggie.
7. He asked Maggie to join, and she agreed.
8. The group got together and practiced.

Write Away!

Make this dull paragraph come alive by adding interesting adjectives, adverbs, and prepositional phrases. If you need to, you may also change other words in the paragraph.

The canoe moved along the Amazon River. The three explorers and their guide gazed at the rain forest. The forest looked like a green wall. Monkeys and other animals made noises. Above, birds flew. Fish and crocodiles swam nearby. The explorers saw snakes on the shore. The explorers wanted to reach their destination.

Lesson 2 Combining Independent Clauses

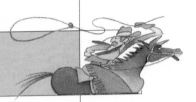

You can add variety and length to a paragraph by combining independent clauses.

In lesson 1 of this chapter, you learned to expand and enliven sentences by adding adjectives, adverbs, and phrases. You can also expand sentences and add variety to paragraphs by connecting independent clauses (which are really simple sentences) with *coordinate conjunctions*. Below are the most common coordinate conjunctions and the special purpose that each serves. As you read the sample sentences, notice what kind of punctuation you must use to connect two independent clauses.

Coordinate Conjunction	Special Purpose
and	*And* connects two ideas that are similar or that happen together. *Bernard and Darnell went to the movie theater, and they saw an exciting western.*
but, yet	*But* and *yet* connect clauses that have opposite or contrasting ideas. *Bernard had a lot of homework, but he went to the movie anyway.*
or	*Or* suggests that there is a choice. *Darnell could stay home to watch his favorite TV program, or he could go to see the movie.*

Activity A

Choose the best coordinate conjunction to combine the following pairs of sentences. Explain each of your choices.

1. Liza likes to play the saxophone.
   The orchestra leader wants her to try the clarinet.
2. I rode over to the bike repair shop.
   It was closed.
3. Enrique reads many detective stories.
   Sometimes he even writes a mystery of his own.
4. Ballets tell a story.
   The dancers do not speak any words.
5. After high school, you can go to college.
   You can find a full-time job.
6. The test seemed very easy.
   I got a low grade.
7. Tony is an excellent shortstop.
   He is a good hitter.
8. Delia wants to be a nurse.
   Sheila wants to be one, too.
9. Sugar can give you energy quickly.
   It can also cause your teeth to decay.
10. Marti must practice each day.
    She won't make the field hockey team.

Activity B

Here is a paragraph of short sentences for you to revise.
Combine at least two pairs of sentences by using coordinate
conjunctions. Expand as many sentences as you can with
adjectives, adverbs, and phrases. If you need to, you may change
other words in the paragraph.

One of the most famous cowboys was a black man. His
real name was Nat Love. People called him Deadwood Dick.
Love was born a slave in Tennessee in 1854. He was freed
when he was fifteen years old. Then Love had a choice. He
could work on his father's farm. He could go west and
become a cowboy. Love decided to become a cowboy. He
worked on cattle drives for twenty years. His riding ability
was exceptional. His roping was unmatched. He even won a
contest among cowboys in Deadwood, South Dakota. There
he got his nickname. As Love grew older, he wanted to tell
his story. He wrote his autobiography. He called it *The
Adventures of Nat Love, Better Known in Cattle Country as
Deadwood Dick.*

Write Away!

Write three sentences for each coordinate conjunction: *and*,
but or *yet*, and *or*. Then, to prove that you have connected
independent clauses, take the coordinate conjunction out of
each sentence and see if you have two simple sentences.

Lesson 3 Revising Rambling and Run-on Sentences

Sentences that contain too many ideas to be clearly understood must be divided.

Rambling Sentences

In the previous two lessons, you have learned to lengthen sentences in two ways: by adding adjectives, adverbs, and phrases, as well as by connecting independent clauses. However, do not let "longer is better" become your motto for writing. A well-written paragraph usually has sentences of varying lengths. Some of the sentences in a paragraph may become *too* long and complicated. Often the reader cannot tell where one idea ends and another begins. To improve a rambling sentence, divide it into two or more sentences. Notice how the following rambling sentence can be broken down to form a few clearer sentences.

Rambling Sentence

Rebecca was watching her favorite television program, which is a show about a group of young scientists, and today's story was especially interesting because it was about scientists who discovered a "caveman" who had never had contact with modern society and who was found walking across the Golden Gate Bridge, and he was as confused about how he got there as the scientists were about finding him.

Improved Sentences

Rebecca was watching her favorite television program, a show about a group of young scientists. Today's story was especially interesting. It was about scientists who discovered a "caveman" who had never had contact with modern society. The "caveman" was found walking across the Golden Gate Bridge. He was as confused about how he got there as the scientists were about finding him.

Activity A

Improve these rambling sentences. You may add or change words to make your improved sentences read smoothly.

1. In 1985, a massive earthquake jolted Mexico City, killing thousands of people and destroying millions of dollars worth of property, and groups across the United States immediately began sending medical aid and money to the battered city because they hoped to save lives and help the homeless.

2. This was my best summer ever because my family spent the entire month of August in Wisconsin where we rented a cabin that was on a lake and we could swim, row our boat, windsurf, dive off a raft, or just lie in the sun on the sandy shore.

3. William Penn was a Quaker and he believed in the people's right to practice their religion freely and so he founded a city in Pennsylvania and he called this city Philadelphia, which means "brotherly love."

4. The forests of the world are one of its most valuable resources but they are disappearing and we should do what we can to protect them because it would take many years to replace them when they are gone.

5. The telegraph was invented by Samuel F. B. Morse and the first message sent across the wires read, "What hath God wrought!" and it was flashed from Baltimore to Washington.

6. My neighborhood is near the airport and when planes fly directly overhead, the noise is deafening and we can hardly hear each other speak, so last week a group of neighbors went to visit the mayor to see if she could arrange to have the takeoff and landing patterns changed.

7. The pampas are grassy plains covering a large area in Argentina in South America, and the humid eastern pampas do bear some crops but the dry western ones support only livestock, and the pampas are well known as the home of the gaucho, the Argentine cowboy.

8. Two teenage Frisbee "experts" toss their disk every summer day in a vacant lot on Foster Avenue and I enjoy watching their long, arching throws and their almost impossible one-finger or behind-the-back catches and many other people are likewise entertained.

9. Copper is a strong, tough metal and it carries heat and electricity well and it has many important uses and among them is its use in wires of all kinds, including telephone, telegraph, and power lines.

10. Jennifer likes to read and she usually reads historical fiction but last week she read the science fiction novel *The Martian Chronicles* by Ray Bradbury and she enjoyed it very much and so she has decided to read more science fiction.

Activity B

Here is a paragraph for you to revise. Shorten the rambling sentences so the reader can understand the paragraph more easily.

Florence Nightingale was a British nurse who became famous for her work during the Crimean War in which Britain and France fought Russia, and she was the leader of a small group of nurses who had to care for hundreds of wounded soldiers but there were not enough medical supplies or hospital cots. Florence worked hard to organize the army hospital and get it cleaned up, and she demanded medical supplies from British leaders and every night walked the hospital halls to check on the patients. She even visited the battlefield where she caught a serious illness called Crimean Fever but she did not let her illness stop her work and said, "I can stand out this war with any man." Florence Nightingale's tireless, unselfish efforts saved many lives and set an example of organization, cleanliness, and hard work that are the basis of the nursing profession today, and all modern nurses should be thankful to her.

Run-on Sentences

Sometimes when you write, one sentence will run into the next. It is difficult to tell where one idea ends and the next idea begins. Often there is no punctuation between two thoughts or an incorrect mark of punctuation is used. This is called a run-on sentence. Look carefully at the following sentences:

A. Some people in the Sahara build their houses below the ground they dig twenty-five feet into the earth.
B. Underground, the people of the Sahara find water and shelter from sandstorms, it is also cooler there on hot days.

Each of the above sentences is a run-on sentence because there are two separate thoughts, but they are written as one sentence. In sentence A, there is no mark of punctuation. In sentence B, there is an incorrect mark of punctuation.

Can you tell where the first thought ends in sentence A? It ends after the word *ground*; therefore, a period should be inserted and a new sentence begun. Can you tell where the first idea ends in sentence B? It ends after the word *sandstorms*; therefore, a period should be inserted and a new sentence begun. When they are corrected, the sentences would read and look like this:

A. Some people in the Sahara build their houses below ground. They dig twenty-five feet into the earth.
B. Underground, the people of the Sahara find water and shelter from sandstorms. It is also cooler there on hot days.

A sand dune in the desert

Activity

Correct the following run-on sentences. Make sure the proper mark of punctuation is inserted between the different ideas.

1. A camel is a large desert animal it can travel long distances.
2. Camels can survive with little food or water they draw on the reserve in their "storage tank" for energy.
3. The camel's hump is a "storage tank" it stores water, not fat.
4. Some camels have one hump and some have two, it depends on what type of camel they are.
5. The Arabian camel has one hump the Bactrian camel has two humps.
6. Some Arabian camels, called dromedaries, are used for riding and racing, they can travel about ten miles an hour and about one hundred miles a day.
7. Camels do not like to work they are not so obedient as dogs and horses.
8. Camel's milk is used for drinking and for making cheese, it is so thick that it forms lumps in liquids.
9. The hair of the Bactrian camel can be woven blankets, tents, and clothing are made from this hair.
10. Camels are useful animals for those who live in the desert these people probably could not survive without them.

Write Away!

Look at sentence 2 in activity A for rambling sentences. Pretend that last summer was *your* best summer ever. Write four or five sentences about what you did. Write some short sentences and some longer (but not run-on) sentences.

Lesson 4 Choosing the Best Word

You can liven up a paragraph by using picture or precise words to replace lifeless words.

To become a skilled writer, you need to develop a strong vocabulary. If you reread a paragraph you have written and find some dull, lifeless words, you must search for more vivid *picture words*. Often a good picture word will be a *synonym* for the word it replaces. Compare the sentences in the left-hand column with those in the right-hand column. Do you see pictures in the sentences on the right that you did not see in the ones on the left? Do you find more precise words on the right? What are they?

A light appeared before me.	A light *flashed* before me.
The fire burned in the distance.	The fire *blazed* in the distance.
The water ran down the rocks.	The water *trickled* down the rocks.
Red leaves covered the ground.	*Crimson* leaves covered the ground.
I was awakened by a loud noise.	I was awakened by a *shrill scream*.
The dog ran into the traffic.	The dog *darted* into the traffic.

As you reread your writing, look for words that are dull and overused. To help you in thinking of new words to replace the dull ones, you might use a dictionary or a thesaurus. Some dictionaries give lists of synonyms after an entry. A thesaurus is a book of synonyms.

Activity A

"Polish" some words yourself. For each italicized word below, think of two other words that are more vivid or that express the idea more precisely. Use a dictionary or thesaurus for help.

1. A *bad* storm
2. A *pretty* painting
3. My *aim* in life
4. A *brave* knight
5. To *hold* a life preserver
6. A *big* glacier
7. A *fast* antelope
8. A *trip* down the Mississippi
9. An *interesting* dream
10. The *increasing* popularity of soccer

Activity B

1. Think of a vivid picture word to replace *move* in each example below. Then complete each sentence.
   a. The space shuttle *moved* …
   b. An old car *moved* …
   c. The supersonic jet *moved* …
   d. The lame dog *moved* …
   e. The lion *moved* …
   f. The last person to finish the marathon *moved* …
2. Describe each noise with a colorful verb.
   a. A crying baby
   b. A snake
   c. Two cats fighting
   d. A huge waterfall
   e. The crowd at a basketball game
   f. The people in a library
3. What adjective could be used in place of *old* if you were writing about the following?
   a. A grandfather clock
   b. A style of clothing
   c. A book
   d. A friend
   e. An Egyptian pyramid
   f. A running shoe

Write Away!

The following paragraph has a number of dull, lifeless words. Liven up the paragraph by substituting either a picture word or a more precise word for each word in italics. Use a dictionary or thesaurus if you need help.

As I *walked* through the park Saturday afternoon, I *saw* a *big* Indian totem pole. The pole itself was painted brown, but the faces *made* on it were *bright* reds and yellows. They were faces of people and of *odd* animals, both *funny* and *scary* at the same time. What an interesting thing to see in the middle of a *big* city!

Lesson 5 Using Similes and Metaphors

Similes and metaphors are comparisons of unlike things. Both can help you write more expressively.

You have learned how to enliven your sentences with colorful picture words. Another way to make writing vivid is with comparisons. Read these comparisons.

> The spiderweb, wet with dew, was like a piece of fine lace. The hang gliders were enormous colorful birds against the sky.

Notice how each comparison creates a clearer image. The first example is a *simile*, a comparison that uses the words *like* or *as*. Since lace is delicate and exquisite, the sentence gives a picture of a spiderweb as a delicate, airy work of art.

The second example does not use the words *like* or *as*. It states directly the hang gliders *were* birds. Such a comparison is called a *metaphor*. In this metaphor, the comparison with birds gives the reader a picture of a sky filled with brilliant flying objects. Vivid similes and metaphors help writers *paint pictures* in their sentences.

Sometimes a simile or a metaphor is overused. For example, have you ever heard the expression "as cold as ice" or "as happy as a lark"? Such overused similes and metaphors are clichés. In using similes and metaphors, be creative and avoid clichés.

Below is a list of comparisons describing white clouds, a stream, and fireworks. Can you tell which are similes and which are metaphors?

White Clouds

like scoops of vanilla ice cream
white elephants, whales, hippopotamuses in the sky
floating like parachutes

A Stream

a silver serpent
bubbling like soda pop
a shiny ribbon unrolling through the forest

Fireworks

bouquets of light
as bright as a million lightning bugs
popping popcorn in the sky

Activity A

Read these ten sentences and tell whether the comparison is written as a simile or a metaphor. Then name the two objects that are being compared and explain how they are different and what they have in common.

1. The giant redwoods are the skyscrapers of the forest.
2. The opposing fullback was as wide as a garage door.
3. To the astronaut, the earth was a huge blue-green ball.
4. The sun was a player in a game of hide-and-seek.
5. The corridors of the building are like a maze.
6. Dina's arrival brightened the room like a light bulb.
7. The last day of school crawled as slowly as a turtle.
8. When the skunk came out from behind the tree, Teddy ran like an Olympic gold medal sprinter.
9. The entire class was chattering like a bunch of monkeys.
10. Aunt Lou's face is an accordion of wrinkles.

Activity B

Complete the following sentences on a sheet of paper. If the phrase uses *like* or *as*, create a simile. If it does not, create a metaphor. Remember to use things that are unlike in your comparisons.

1. During rush hour, the cars move like _____.
2. When it is full, the moon is _____.
3. The water lilies cover the pond like _____.
4. The room on the cold winter morning was _____.
5. The creatures who emerged from the spaceship seemed like _____.
6. The hose lying on the grass was _____
7. The sound of the squeaking door is like _____.
8. As Julie looked down from the mountain, the city was _____.
9. After José ran a mile, he felt like _____.

Write Away!

Practice writing some of your own similes and metaphors. The paragraph below has none. Revise it by adding *at least* two similes and one metaphor. You may change or add sentences if you want.

Beth loves to ride her bicycle on the path by Lake Michigan. It is always an interesting adventure, full of wonderful sights. The lake is so wide that Beth cannot see across it. She likes the clear, sunny days when the water is bright blue. On windy days, the lake is choppy, and water splashes on the concrete path. Then Beth gets soaked, and her bike hisses as she rides over the wet concrete. Whenever she rides, she notices everything around her—joggers, skaters, swimmers, trees, bushes, and even the city skyline. When Beth is on the bicycle path, she feels happy and free.

Revising Your Writing

The skills that you have studied in this chapter will be very useful when you revise any piece of writing. Revising is an important part of the writing process. It involves rereading to correct and improve your writing.

Consider these general questions as you revise your work:
—Does my writing make sense?
—Will a reader be able to understand what I am saying?
—Do all the sentences develop the specific idea?

Also review the skills you have learned in this chapter as you revise.
—Do I need to lengthen sentences by adding information or combining ideas?
—Do I need to shorten rambling sentences or correct run-on sentences?
—Have I used precise, vivid words?

Finally, proofread your work. Check capitalization, punctuation, and spelling.

To indicate changes as you reread your work, you may want to use these proofreading symbols:

ᴧ	add	The giant panda ᴧ*may* become extinct.
ℒ	omit	The giant panda may ~~perhaps~~ become extinct.
≡	capitalize	≡the giant panda may become extinct.
/	lowercase	The giant Ᵽanda may become extinct.
∿	reverse	The gᴉaᴎt panda may become extinct.
¶	begin a new paragraph	¶ The giant panda may become extinct.

After you proofread your work, you may want to recopy it in order to hand in a neat, correct paper.

Study how the symbols used in the following paragraph show changes and corrections.

Penguins are ~~bizarre~~ *unusual* creatures. They are able to stand out in blizzards of below-freezing tempratures for weeks̥ they do not even have to eat a meal during that time. Their feathers provide them with insulation̦ Their fat provides them with food. Penguins cannot run nor fly They are able to walk clumsily on land. In water, however, these seabirds use their wings as as paddels to propel themselves. They swim *like Olympic champions* ~~very well~~ as they look for fish.

Writing Corner 2

Poetry into Prose

A poem and a paragraph can present the same ideas, but in very different ways. Both are fun to write, but each requires a different style of writing. Carefully read the poem below.

Fourth of July Night

Pin wheels whirling round
Spit sparks upon the ground,
And rockets shoot up high
And blossom in the sky—
Blue and yellow, green and red
Flowers falling on my head,
And I don't ever have to go
To bed, to bed, to bed!

Dorothy Aldis

Now read this paragraph.

Celebrating Independence!

The Fourth of July is one of the best celebrations of the year. The picnics and games in the afternoon are great fun, but the fireworks at night are the highlight of the day. When the time comes for this spectacular display, I grab a front-row seat. I love to watch the pinwheels swirling and the rockets shooting high above me. Their sudden cracking sound turns them into colorful flowers blossoming in the sky. The excitement goes on late into the night, and on this special occasion, everyone gets to stay up way past bedtime.

Which piece of writing uses fewer words but contains very vivid images? Which piece uses rhyme? Which piece uses mainly words that describe? You would be right if you said the *poem.*

Which piece of writing gives more information and uses more sentences? You would be right if you said the *paragraph*. This kind of writing is called *prose*. As you can see, prose is different from poetry.

You can express the *same thoughts* and *feelings* in prose and poetry but in a *different way*.

Here are two poems. One is about automobiles and the other about autumn leaves. Read each one several times and then discuss them in class.

Stop-Go

Automobiles
In
  a
    row
Wait to go
While the signal says:
      STOP

Bells ring
Tingaling
Red light's gone!
Green light's on!
Horns blow!
And the row
Starts
  to
      GO

Dorothy Baruch

Autumn Woods

I like the woods
    In autumn
When dry leaves hide the ground,
When the trees are bare
And the wind sweeps by
With a lonesome rushing sound.

I can rustle the leaves
    In autumn
And I can make a bed
In the thick dry leaves
That have fallen
From the bare trees
Overhead.

James S. Tippett

★ Choose the poem above that interests you more. What ideas of your own do you have about cars or autumn? Are they similar or different from the ones in these poems? Write a paragraph (prose) that uses some of the images from the poem along with your own ideas.

Suffixes

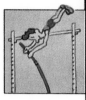

A suffix is a syllable (or syllables) added to the end of a root to create a new word. A suffix may change the part of speech of a word.

You use many words that have suffixes. On a lovely summer morning you might exclaim, "What a *beautiful* day!" On a very hot day, you might think, "I don't feel very *energetic*."

For each italicized word, a suffix is added to the end of a root to change a noun to an adjective. The suffix *ful* meaning "full of" is added to the root *beauty* to form *beautiful. Beautiful* is an adjective that means "full of beauty." The suffix *ic* meaning "relating to" is added to the root *energy* to form *energetic. Energetic* is an adjective that means "relating to energy."

Sometimes there is a spelling change when you add a suffix. In the word *beauty*, the *y* becomes an *i* before the suffix is added. In the word *energy*, the *y* is dropped, and an *e* and *t* come before the suffix.

Here is a list of some common suffixes. Study them carefully.

Suffix	Meaning	Example
ette	little	Annette, dinette
ful	full of	skillful
ic	relating to	athletic
ish	somewhat, like a	childish
like	resembling	catlike
some	the quality of	troublesome
th, eth	in the order of a certain number	sixth, fiftieth
y	full of	cloudy

Activity A

Copy the chart below, and fill in the missing parts.

Root	Suffix	New Word	Meaning
1. sorrow	ful	_____	_____
2. _____	ish	_____	like a fool
3. majesty	_____	_____	relating to majesty
4. mud	y	_____	_____
5. _____	_____	sixtieth	number sixty in order
6. child	_____	childlike	_____
7. _____	_____	lonesome	the quality of being alone
8. _____	ette	kitchenette	_____

Activity B

Complete each sentence with the correct word by adding a suffix from the list to the word at the left. Use the dictionary to check spelling.

tickle   1. I never knew Pat was so _____.

winter   2. It was a cold _____ day with the snow a foot deep.

grace   3. The _____ ballerina seemed to float on the stage.

five   4. Reading mystery stories is _____ on my list of favorite things.

life   5. The figures in the wax museum were very _____.

base   6. The book *How Things Work* gives a very _____ explanation of how astronauts communicate with each other in space.

adventure 7. Do you think that Huckleberry Finn was _____?

Paul   8. Even though _____ had never played touch football before, she proved to be an excellent pass receiver.

Chapter 3

Kinds of Writing

Lesson 1 Using Transition Words

Transition words help to make smooth connections between sentences and paragraphs.

A good writer knows how to take the reader through a series of connected ideas or events skillfully. The reader never has to wonder how two ideas or two sentences fit together. A good paragraph flows smoothly, and it has no gaps. One of the best tools for creating a smooth paragraph is the use of transition words, which show the relationship between two sentences or ideas.

Many transition words create a time relationship. When you write a paragraph or story, you often put events and ideas according to the *time sequence* in which they occur. Here are some connecting words that indicate time. They can help make your paragraphs read more smoothly.

afterward	later
at first	meanwhile
at last	next
at the same time	now
earlier	second
finally	soon
first	then
last	third

Bridges help shorten the distance between people and places. How would bridges bring people of other races and cultures together?

Read the sentences below, for example. On the left are five unconnected sentences. On the right, transition words have been added at the beginning of sentences 2, 3, and 5. The transition words are *First, Then,* and *Soon.* Adding transition words makes the paragraph flow more smoothly.

1. Paul couldn't decide what he wanted to be for Halloween.
2. He told us that he would be Dracula and wear his mother's old black cape.
3. He changed his mind and said he would be a pirate and wear one of his sister's earrings.
4. On Halloween, we noticed someone dressed as a ghost, completely covered in a sheet.
5. We recognized that it was Paul by his old orange sneakers.

   Paul couldn't decide what he wanted to be for Halloween. *First,* he told us that he would be Dracula and wear his mother's old black cape. *Then* he changed his mind and said he would be a pirate and wear one of his sister's earrings. On Halloween, we noticed someone dressed as a ghost, completely covered in a sheet. *Soon* we recognized that it was Paul by his old orange sneakers.

Activity A

Below are five sets of sentences. Rewrite the sentences in each set so they fit together smoothly. Use at least one transition word. Refer to the sample in the introduction of the lesson for help.

1. a. Using a microcomputer is not so difficult.
    b. You put in a diskette.
    c. You type in your information, or data.
2. a. Firefighters circled the blazing forest in small planes.
    b. "Smoke jumpers" parachuted into safe areas with their equipment.
    c. The fire was under control.
3. a. Miss O'Malley asked for Timothy's homework.
    b. Timothy looked through his English folder and his desk.
    c. He found his homework in his science folder.
4. a. Tiffany was listening to her records.
    b. She was trying to do homework.
    c. She realized that she had to choose one or the other.
5. a. There was a flash of light.
    b. There was a loud noise.
    c. The little shack was just a pile of rubble on the ground.

Activity B

Complete this paragraph on a sheet of paper by filling in information. You might imagine that you recently had a day that was filled with good or bad surprises. Notice how the transition words express a time relationship. When you are finished, read your paragraph aloud to hear how the transition words help make connections.

It all started when _____.
Next, _____. Later, _____
_____. Meanwhile, _____
_____. Then _____. Finally, _____
_____.

Write Away!

The paragraph below needs some transition words. Decide on the best ones to use (see the list on page 55), and then revise the paragraph. Add at least three transition words.

When Saundra invited Joe to go to the roller rink, Joe could not bring himself to admit that he had never skated. At the rink, Saundra put on her skates and began swiftly gliding along in time to the music. Joe rented a pair of skates. He thought it would be simple to teach himself to skate. He realized that he could move only a few feet before tumbling to his hands and knees. He swallowed his pride and called to Saundra for help. She laughed at how stubborn he had been and gave him a quick lesson. Joe was able to skate slowly and cautiously around the rink.

Lesson 2 Writing a Narrative Paragraph

A narrative paragraph tells a story. The paragraph usually tells about the events in the order in which they happened.

Narrative paragraphs should be familiar to you. You have probably heard narratives all your life, beginning with the stories your parents read to you as a child. Many of the short stories and novels you read now are also narratives. You even create narratives yourself in everyday conversations. If someone asks you, "What happened?" for instance, your answer is probably in the form of a narrative. You would tell the events in the order in which they happened.

Study the following example of a narrative paragraph from Walter Farley's novel *The Black Stallion*. In the paragraph, young Alec Ramsey and the stallion are trapped on a deserted island after a shipwreck.

> One night Alec sat beside his campfire and stared into the flames that reached hungrily into the air; his knees were crossed and his elbows rested heavily upon them; his chin was cupped in his two hands. He was deep in thought. The Drake had left Bombay on a Saturday, the fifteenth of August. The shipwreck had happened a little over two weeks later, perhaps on the second of September. He had been on the island exactly nineteen . . . days. That would make it approximately the twenty-first of September. By now his family must think him dead! He doubled his fists. He had to find a way out; a ship just had to pass the island sometime. Daily he had stood up on top of the hill peering out to sea, frantically hoping to sight a boat.

In the paragraph, Alec is thinking back on events that occurred since he arrived on the island. Notice the words that show time: *one night, by now,* and *daily.* How do they help to make the order of events clear?

Your own story might have a more simple time sequence, such as from morning to evening of one day. You could use the transition words that show time that you learned in lesson 1, or you could use other words or phrases that show time, such as *at noon, by one o'clock, by the end of the day.* Like the time words in the paragraph from *The Black Stallion,* these words help show the order of events.

There is another decision to make when you plan a narrative paragraph besides choosing appropriate connecting words. You must decide whether the narrator (the one who is telling the story) is a *character in the story* or an *observer.* Read the two sentences below and see if you can tell whether the narrator is *inside* or *outside* the story.
A. When lightning struck the tree, we all headed for cover.
B. When lightning struck the tree, the boys headed for cover.

Now reread the paragraph from *The Black Stallion* and answer the same question.

In a good narrative paragraph, the narrator is either a character in the story or an observer, but not both. The time sequence is clear by the use of transition words and time words. Most important, the events that the narrator tells must be interesting.

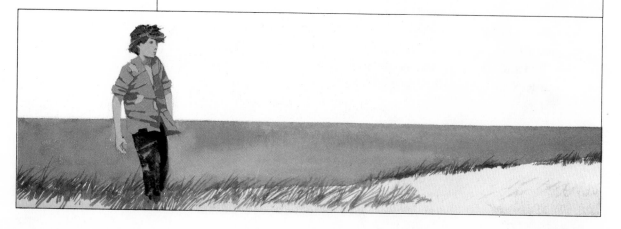

Activity A

Here are some events that could make up a narrative paragraph. On a sheet of paper, write the events in the correct order.

1. "Calm down; we'll work this out," said Jason's father.
2. Jason's parents decided to take the family to New Orleans for a month during the summer vacation.
3. "That's not fair—my friends and I are planning a bike trip then!" Jason exclaimed.
4. Jason's father suggested that Jason call his friends to see if they could make their trip at a later date.
5. "Let's all think of solutions," said Jason's mother.
6. He offered to help the boys choose a place to ride and take them there.
7. "And next time," said Jason's mother, "we'll include you when we make our plans."
8. They told Jason about it one evening at supper.
9. "Wow," said Jason, "that's a pretty good offer! I'm sure my friends will change their plans."
10. Jason and his parents talked over the problem for the next half hour.

Activity B

Here are some more events that are out of order. Put them in order in paragraph form, and add at least four transition words. Then review the paragraph to make sure it reads smoothly.

1. Everyone in the family was pleased to see such a delicious meal awaiting them at home.
2. With two overflowing pails in the basket of her bike, she took the ferry back to shore.
3. Last summer Bobby Jeanne and her family were spending the month of August at a seaside cottage in Maine.
4. Clever Bobby Jeanne had $11.25 to show for her skill at cooking on a budget.
5. For seventy-five cents, she bought a ticket to an island called Islesboro.
6. Bobby Jeanne had an idea, and she quickly rode her bike to the ferry landing.
7. "We'll be back from the beach at 6:30," she added as they left.
8. Once she was home, she steamed the clams and mussels, made some butter sauce, and chopped up vegetables for a salad.
9. One afternoon Bobby Jeanne's mother said to her, "Dinner is up to you tonight."
10. She rode to a little beach on the island where she knew she could collect plenty of clams and mussels.
11. She gave Bobby Jeanne $12.00 and said, "Whatever is left over, you can keep."
12. She dug for shellfish—clams and mussels.

Write Away!

Now write your own narrative paragraph. First, brainstorm for an idea. You could write about an unusual or interesting experience you have had. Then list the events as they happened. Finally, write them out as one paragraph. Make sure you use transition words to keep the paragraph flowing smoothly. Reread your paragraph and continue to revise it until you are satisfied with your work.

Revision: Time to Take Another Look

As you reread your narrative paragraph, ask yourself the following questions:
—Are all the events in correct time order?
—Did I use appropriate connecting words?
—Did I use strong verbs in my paragraph? (Don't count *is* or *was*. Avoid overusing these verbs.)
—Do I have some simple and some compound sentences? Try to have both long and short sentences.
—Did I write an interesting beginning sentence?
—Does the ending sentence draw my story to a close?
—Will a reader be able to understand my paragraph easily?

If you need to work on anything from the above list, *do it now*. *Delete* or *add* words. *Rearrange* ideas if necessary. After your revision, rewrite the paragraph and go on to proofreading.

Proofreading: Time to Look at Capitalization, Punctuation, and Spelling

λ	Add
$\mathcal{D}$	Omit
$\equiv$	Capitalize
$/$	Lowercase
$\cap$	Reverse
$\P$	New paragraph

—Did I begin each sentence with a capital letter?
—Did I indent the first word of the paragraph?
—Did I use the correct mark of punctuation at the end of each sentence?
—Do some transition words need a comma following them?

Start at the last word of the paragraph and read backwards to check for spelling errors. If necessary, rewrite the paragraph in your best handwriting.

Lesson 3 Using Your Senses in Writing

Writing can come alive when you use your senses—seeing, hearing, touching, smelling, and tasting.

To become a skilled writer, you must create *pictures* in the minds of your readers. You need to *show* them what you mean, not just *tell* them. One way to help create a picture is to describe things in terms of the senses: seeing, hearing, smelling, tasting, and feeling.

Read these two sentences and notice the difference between them. Which sentence just tells and which one shows? What do you see, hear, smell, taste, or feel? What words appeal directly to the senses?

The campfire blazed.

The huge, crackling campfire blazed a bright red in the dark forest clearing.

Study the sentences below. Notice how each appeals to a different sense.

Sight

The snow-white horses wore shining silver harnesses and were hitched to a brightly painted circus carriage.

Sound

The foghorn's deep piercing sound filled the harbor.

Touch

The youngster ran her hand over the sleek skin of the dolphin. Near its snout, she felt a few smooth hairs and a wiry whisker or two.

Taste

As I was heaping the juicy hot dog with mounds of succulent onions, hot green chilies, spicy mustard, tangy ketchup, and a slice of sour dill pickle, my mouth watered in anticipation.

Smell

A mixture of aromas flooded the outdoor market: the smell of fresh fish on one side and of strong cheese and exotic spices on the other.

Activity A

Make a chart like the one below. Brainstorm for different words that appeal to the senses to put in each column.

Sight	Sound	Taste	Smell	Touch
glistening	shrill	spicy	woodsy	scaly
blinding	thumping	salty	rancid	silky

Activity B

Write a one-sentence description of each item below. Include as many sensory impressions as you can.

1. A flag flying in the wind
2. The feel of a snake
3. A bowl of granola
4. A ride in a helicopter
5. The coldest day of the year
6. The skyline of a big city
7. An ice-cream cone
8. A snowstorm
9. Sitting next to a person who is smoking a cigar
10. An oil painting at the museum
11. A runner finishing a 100-meter sprint
12. A building under construction

Write Away!

Write five descriptive sentences about any *one* of the topics that follow. Use as many sensory details as you can. Try to create a clear picture in the reader's mind.

1. A walk through the zoo
2. An exciting amusement park ride
3. The cafeteria at school
4. A robot that directs traffic
5. A bicycle accident

Lesson 4 Writing a Descriptive Paragraph

A descriptive paragraph paints a picture with words.

A descriptive paragraph can be challenging to write. It is interesting to try to make the reader see things as you do, and it even frees *you* to observe more closely. Ideas for descriptive paragraphs can come from just about anywhere—from your own experiences or from your imagination. Read the descriptive paragraphs below from the novel *Sounder* by William H. Armstrong about a boy and his dog, Sounder. These paragraphs occur soon after Sounder was wounded by a sheriff's deputy.

> Suddenly a sharp yelp came from the road. Just like when a bee stung Sounder under the porch or a brier caught in his ear in the bramble, the boy thought. In an instant the boy was on his feet. Bruised foot and fingers, throbbing head were forgotten. He raced into the dark. Sounder tried to rise but fell again. There was another yelp, this one constrained and plaintive. The boy, trained in night-sight when the lantern was dimmed so as not to alert the wood's creatures, picked out a blurred shape in the dark.

[Sounder staggers home and crawls under the porch to nurse his injury. The boy can only go inside and wait.]

> Inside the cabin the younger children sat huddled together near the stove. The boy rubbed his hands together near the stovepipe to warm them. His bruised fingers began to throb again. His foot and his head hurt, and he felt a lump rising on the side of his head. If Sounder would whimper or yelp, I would know, the boy thought. But there was no sound, no thump, thump, thump of a paw scratching fleas and hitting the floor underneath.

To what senses do these paragraphs appeal? Give the words or phrases from the paragraphs that appeal to each of these senses. Describe one picture that either paragraph paints in your mind.

Activity A

From the list below, choose *one* person, *one* place, and *one* thing to describe. Then give as many sense impressions as you can for each one. For example:

A Bull

Sight: glossy, black, muscular
Sound: snorting, grunting, bellowing
Smell: earthy, sweaty
Feel: solid

1. *People:* an Olympic swimmer, a circus animal trainer, a salesperson in a fast-food restaurant, a rock singer, a flower vendor, a magician, a chimney sweep
2. *Places:* a forest, a cave, an empty movie theater, a crowded football stadium, a deserted house, an Eskimo ice house (igloo)
3. *Things:* a turkey, a space suit, a campfire, a new car, a scarecrow

Activity B

Choose any one of the three subjects you just described and write a descriptive paragraph of about six sentences. Use the sensory impressions you listed and any others that come to mind. Make sure that what you write follows all the rules for a good paragraph.

Write Away!

Using as many sensory impressions as you can, write a descriptive paragraph about this picture. What would you see, hear, taste, smell, and touch if you were actually in this scene?

Revision: Time to Take Another Look

As you reread your descriptive paragraph, ask yourself the following questions:

—What sensory impressions did I use in my paragraph?

—Could I paint a picture from my description?

—Did I use a simile or a metaphor in the paragraph?

—Did I write some long and some short sentences?

—Do I have a good beginning and ending sentence?

—Do the middle sentences add important information about the topic?

—Will a reader be able to understand my description easily?

If you need to work on anything from the above list, *do it now.* *Delete* or *add* words. *Rearrange* ideas if necessary. After your revision, rewrite the paragraph and go on to proofreading.

Proofreading: Time to Look at Capitalization, Punctuation, and Spelling

⋏	Add
ℯ	Omit
≡	Capitalize
∕	Lowercase
∿	Reverse
¶	New paragraph

—Did I begin each sentence with a capital letter?

—Did I indent the first word of the paragraph?

—Did I use the correct mark of punctuation at the end of each sentence?

Start at the last word of the paragraph and read backwards to check for spelling errors. If necessary, rewrite the paragraph in your best handwriting.

Lesson 5 Fact and Opinion

Facts can be proven. Opinions cannot be proven either true or false.

Read the following statements about a political campaign.
A. Yolanda Jones is the best candidate for mayor.
B. Yolanda Jones has lived in the city all her life, and she has supported many community projects in her five years on the city council.

Statement A is a statement of opinion. Other people may have a different opinion about the best candidate for mayor. Statement B expresses facts. It can be shown how long Yolanda Jones has lived in the city, and her voting record on community projects can be checked.

Statement A, the opinion, can be "supported" by statement B. Statement B gives a fact to show why Yolanda Jones might be the best candidate. One good way of supporting opinions is by using facts.

Now read the following dialogue from a debate over the best candidate for mayor.

RON: Clyde Baker is the best person for mayor. He has lowered city taxes, attracted new industries to boost employment, and built new hotels to accommodate tourists. Mayor Baker is one of the friendliest political leaders. He is always willing to talk to people about their problems. He's definitely the mayor our city needs.

RICK: Clyde Baker is the best person for mayor. He is one of the nicest, most pleasant persons you would ever want to meet. He is always trying to do what is best for the people. Mayor Baker is fifty-five years old, and both he and his wife are natives of this city. People seem happy and satisfied with Clyde Baker.

Notice how Ron uses both *fact* and *opinion* to support his view that Clyde Baker should be reelected mayor. What are the facts? Can they be proven? What are his opinions?

Notice how Rick also uses *fact* and *opinion* to support his view about Clyde Baker. What are his facts? Can they be proven? What are his opinions?

When you are trying to persuade someone to think as you do, it is important that the statements supporting your opinions be convincing. For example:

> This is an excellent novel. *It cost $14.95.*
> This is an excellent novel. *It recently won the Newbery Award.*

The supporting statement *It cost $14.95* is a fact, but the price of the novel does not make it excellent. The supporting statement *It recently won the Newbery Award* is also a fact. Winning a major book award, however, will more likely convince someone that the novel is excellent.

Reread the statements about Clyde Baker. Both Ron and Rick support Mayor Baker for reelection. Who provides more facts about the mayor's achievements? Why are Ron's statements more convincing than Rick's?

Activity A

Jill feels that the school gym should be open during the day in summer. Identify which of her statements are facts and which are opinions. Which of the five statements do you think is the most convincing?

1. Over fifty percent of the mothers in this area work. They need a safe place for their children to go during the day.
2. Children should be out of the sun during the afternoon.
3. The gym is the best place to play basketball games.
4. The gym is in walking distance of many children's houses.
5. It is one of the best places to spend an afternoon with friends.

Bill feels that the school gym should not be open during the day in the summer. Identify which of his statements are facts and which are opinions. Which of the five statements is the most convincing?

1. Children should be outside during the summer.
2. Each summer the number of adult volunteers to supervise recreational activities decreases.
3. The gym is equipped for only one game—basketball.
4. The younger children and older ones will not play together.
5. It would require extra personnel and tax money to maintain the gym.

Activity B

The first sentence in each pair is a statement of opinion. Tell whether the supporting sentence, the second sentence, is convincing or not convincing.

1. Speedy Airlines is the best airline.

   Its friendly service, on-time departures, and safety record cannot be beat.

2. For a class party, it is better to serve cupcakes than a sheet cake.

   Cupcakes bake faster than a sheet cake.

3. The town needs to build public swimming pools.

   This would provide a supervised recreational area for children.

4. Our class is the best in the school.

   We have some of the most popular students.

5. Ho-Bo's has the best food in town.

   The meals there are really cheap.

Write Away!

Each sentence below is an opinion. Choose any two, and write three strong supporting statements for each one.

1. Everyone should take a computer course.
2. Our soccer team is the best in the league.
3. Day-care centers are necessary in our society.
4. "The Right Wardrobe" sells the best clothes.
5. I should have a party for my friends.

Lesson 6 Writing a Persuasive Paragraph

A persuasive paragraph tries to influence the reader's opinion.

Writing a persuasive paragraph is like being in a debate—you want to prove that your opinion is correct. In writing a persuasive paragraph, you state your opinion in the topic sentence and provide supporting facts in the middle sentences. Save your best and most convincing facts for last. Conclude with a strong ending sentence that restates your opinion and explains how you have showed that it is a reasonable one.

Read this example of a persuasive paragraph.

(Topic sentence states an opinion.)

   I think our teacher should assign science fiction books as part of reading class. Science fiction is good literature, often more suspenseful and imaginative than other types of books. In science fiction, anything can happen. The fate of the universe might be at stake, a town might be caught in a time warp, or the human race might become invisible. Much that has been written in the past as science fiction has come true today, and much that is written today will probably be true in the twenty-first century. Is there a better way to learn about the future of our world? Most of all, students will never forget what they read, and they will want to read more. Science fiction plots are so clever that they will long be remembered and enjoyed. If teachers want their students to read, they should treat them to the best books of all— science fiction.

– (Supporting details)

(Ending sentence restates the opinion.)

Notice the clear, precise writing in the persuasive paragraph on the page before this one. Each sentence states exactly why the writer thinks that science fiction is good writing and should be used in school assignments. The writer points out that science fiction is imaginative and teaches about the future. All the sentences flow in a smooth and logical manner. An effective persuasive paragraph should cause the reader to think, "That's true. I never thought of it in that way before."

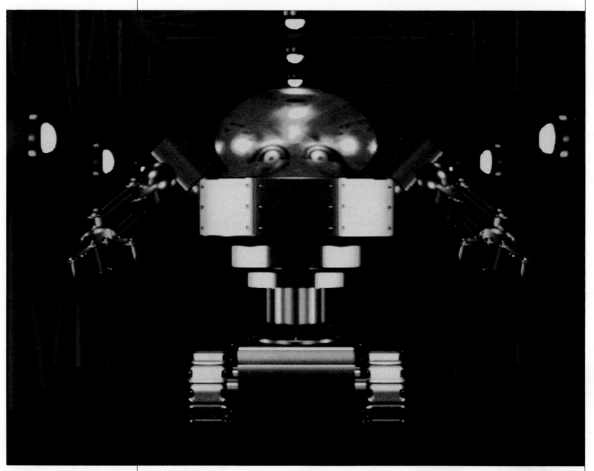

A Friendly Robot

Activity A

A good way to plan a persuasive paragraph is to state the opinion and then list a series of "becauses"—supporting arguments. For each topic below, give four details that favor the idea and four that oppose it. Model your answers on the example.

Example:

I. Recess should be longer
   A. *because* we would have more of a break from our studies
   B. *because* it would give us more time to relax or exercise
   C. *because* it would help us come back to our schoolwork feeling more refreshed
   D. *because* it would make the school day more enjoyable

II. Recess should not be longer
   A. *because* a longer recess might make it harder for us to get back to concentrating on schoolwork
   B. *because* we have enough time after school to relax and exercise
   C. *because* there is hardly enough time in the school day to get in all the subjects
   D. *because* school is a place for learning, not for relaxing or running around

1. Everyone should study a foreign language in grammar school.
2. Children under twelve should be able to enter all museums, movie theaters, and sports events free of charge.
3. A law should be passed that all bicyclists must wear helmets.
4. Schools should arrange more field trips for students.

Activity B

Choose one of the topics in activity A and write a persuasive paragraph. Model your paragraph on the one in the lesson.

Write Away!

Write a persuasive paragraph on one of the topics listed below.
1. There is a neighborhood festival near your house that lasts until ten o'clock at night. Persuade your parents to let you stay out later than usual.
2. Persuade other students that you should be the class president.
3. Persuade your teacher that radio headsets should be allowed in class.
4. You have heard both rock music and jazz. Write a paragraph explaining why one is better than the other.

Revision: Time to Take Another Look

As you reread your persuasive paragraph, ask yourself the following questions:

—Does the first sentence state my opinion?
—Did I use enough reasons to support my opinion?
—Is my last reason the strongest and best?
—Did I use exact words and not repeat ideas?
—Did I use strong verbs instead of *is* and *was*?
—Does the ending sentence restate my opinion?
—Will a reader be able to understand my paragraph easily?

If you need to work on anything from the above list, *do it now.* *Delete* and *add* words. *Rearrange* ideas if necessary. After your revision, rewrite the paragraph and go on to proofreading.

Proofreading: Time to Look at Capitalization, Punctuation, and Spelling

⋏	Add
ℒ	Omit
=	Capitalize
/	Lowercase
∩∪	Reverse
¶	New paragraph

—Did I begin each sentence with a capital letter?
—Did I indent the first word of the paragraph?
—Did I use the correct mark of punctuation at the end of each sentence?

Start at the last word of the paragraph and read backwards to check for spelling errors. If necessary, rewrite the paragraph in your best handwriting.

Writing Corner 3

Art into Writing

When you watch a sports event on television or a film recorded on a videocassette, have you ever seen action "frozen" in time? Artists who paint need skillful techniques to freeze action in their paintings. Study the actions frozen in these two paintings.

★ Choose one of the following two assignments to complete.
   A. Imagine that you are a person *in* one of the paintings. Describe the event that is taking place. Express your feelings about your part in what is happening.

B. Imagine that you could *rewind* or *fast forward* either of the two scenes in the paintings. Focus on what happens right *before* or right *after* the scene shown. Tell about the events from the viewpoint of one person taking part in it.

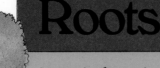

Word Study 3

Roots

A root is the main part of a word. Other words can be built from the root.

You have already learned to use prefixes and suffixes. Prefixes and suffixes are syllables that are added to a root. The root is the most important part of the meaning of a word.

For example, in the word *reopen*, the root is *open*. The word *reopen* means "open again."

Roots come from a number of different languages, but a great many come from either Latin or Greek. For example, *scope* is a root. It comes from a Greek word that means "watch." The prefix *micro* can be added to it to form the word *microscope*, a device for watching or viewing small things. Also, *scope* is a root in the word *telescope*, a device for viewing things that are far away.

Here are some common Latin and Greek roots and their meanings.

Root	Meaning
annu	year
geo	earth, surface
mis, mit	to send
phono	sound
sol	alone
vid, vis	to see

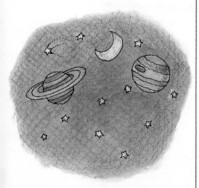

Activity A

Copy the chart below, and fill in the missing parts.

Prefix/Suffix	Root	New Word	Meaning
1. trans (across)	mis, mit	_____	to send across
2. tele (far)	_____	telephone	a device to send sound far away
3. logy (the study of)	_____	geology	_____
4. ion (the act of)	vid, vis	_____	_____
5. itude (quality of)	sol	_____	quality of being alone
6. al (relating to)	_____	annual	relating to one year

Activity B

Look at the words in column A. Try to determine the meaning of each word from the root. Match each word in column A with the correct meaning in column B. Once you have finished, use the dictionary to check your answers.

Column A	Column B
a. solo	1. the measurement of surfaces
b. mission	2. unable to be seen
c. geometry	3. task one is sent to do
d. homophones	4. a machine that reproduces sounds
e. invisible	5. an object sent or thrown
f. phonograph	6. a performance by one person
g. missile	7. a magnetic tape that reproduces both sounds and pictures
h. semiannually	8. words that sound alike but that have different meanings and spellings
i. solitary	9. occurring every half year
j. videotape	10. pertaining to being alone

Chapter 4

Learning More about Writing

Lesson 1 Taking Notes and Preparing an Outline

Taking notes and making an outline help you organize your ideas before you begin to write.

Taking notes and outlining are especially helpful when you are writing a factual composition, or *report*. Suppose you choose "earthquakes" as the topic of your report. You first need to read some books and articles about your topic. You also need to think of at least three questions you would like answered about the topic. Write each question at the top of a separate index card.

For a report on earthquakes, here are three possible questions:

1. What causes earthquakes?
2. Where do earthquakes occur?
3. What damage can they cause?

As you find answers to your questions, jot the answers down on the appropriate card. At the bottom of each card, write the *source* of your information. *A source is a book or article you may have read in order to gather information about your topic.*

Would words capture the beauty of this scene just as well as a photograph? What words would you use to describe it?

Scenes from the San Francisco
earthquake in 1906

Your index cards might look like this:

What causes earthquakes?

Earthquakes are sudden shocks to the surface of the earth. They occur when great pressure is put on rock. The rock begins to bend and fold. The pressure becomes so great that the rock splits and the earth moves. These splits are called _faults_.

All about Earthquakes, p. 11

Where do earthquakes occur?

Many earthquakes occur along fault lines. The lines usually are in areas where new mountains or trenches have formed, rather than on older, flat parts of the earth. Most earthquakes occur under the sea. Many occur along the circum-Pacific belt, along the edge of the Pacific Ocean.

Young Adult Encyclopedia, vol. 3, p. 75

What damage can they cause?

Buildings collapse, tidal waves form, and fires often break out. Thousands of people can lose their lives.

Earthquakes, p. 123

Your questions will become the main topics of your outline. Each main topic begins with a roman numeral followed by a period. The topics of the outline on earthquakes would be these:

    I. What causes earthquakes?
    II. Where do earthquakes occur?
    III. What damage can earthquakes cause?

Next you need to fill in two or more *subtopics* under each main topic. Each subtopic begins with a capital letter that is followed by a period. The subtopics should come from the material in your notes. Subtopics are the answers to the questions (main topics). The subtopics may be phrases or complete sentences.

    I. What causes earthquakes? (*main topic*)
      A. An earthquake is a shock to the earth's surface. (*subtopic*)
      B. Great pressure is put on rock. (*subtopic*)
      C. Rock splits and folds. (*subtopic*)
      D. The earth moves. (*subtopic*)
    II. Where do earthquakes occur? (*main topic*)

Once the outline is complete, you are ready to begin writing. Each main topic with its subtopics will be *one paragraph* in your report.

Early folk painting
of Telegraph Hill
in San Francisco

Activity A

Below is an outline about air traffic controllers. The outline is not numbered or lettered correctly. On a sheet of paper, rewrite the outline as it should be. Use the outline on earthquakes as a model.

A. Requirements for an air traffic controller
   1. College education
   2. Physical and mental tests
   3. Extensive training program
B. Job responsibilities
   1. Give directions to pilots
   2. Ensure on-ground safety
   3. Ensure in-flight safety
C. Working conditions
   1. Irregular working hours
   2. Constant pressure
   3. Feeling of accomplishment

Activity B

Below is a mixed-up outline for a report on dinosaurs. The main topics are labeled correctly, but the subtopics on the right are out of order. On a sheet of paper, write the outline correctly.

  I. What is a dinosaur?   Asteroid crash
     A.   When they lived
     B.   Definition
     C.   Change in plant life
  II. How did dinosaurs live?   Kinds of dinosaurs
     A.   Diet
     B.   Reproduction
     C.   Cooling of climate
III. Why did dinosaurs disappear?   Group life
     A.
     B.
     C.

Write Away!

The main topics of an outline about caves are given below. Put them in logical order, and then use an encyclopedia and other books to complete the outline. Compare your outline with that of another student.

What famous caves are in the United States?
What are caves?
What animals live in caves?

Lesson 2 Writing a Report

The composition you write from a factual outline is called a report.

Once you have organized your information in outline form, your report is nearly written. As you have learned, each main topic with its subtopics will be one paragraph in your report. Each subtopic provides a starting point for the supporting sentences of the paragraph. Of course, all of your details will not be in your outline. You can return to your notes to obtain facts to help develop your supporting sentences. In this way, you can put together a *rough draft* of your report.

Look at the following part of an outline on the topic "early Eskimos," and then read the first paragraph of the report. Notice how the paragraph tells about main topic I, "Who were the early Eskimos?" Each supporting sentence is one of the subtopics.

Early Eskimos
  I. Who were the early Eskimos?
    A. Hunters and gatherers from Asia
    B. Migrated to North America during the Ice Age
    C. Came over a land bridge connecting Asia with North America
    D. By 800 B.C., spread over the far north of North America

Today's Eskimos are the descendants of early hunting and gathering peoples who migrated to North America from Asia. These groups came during the last Ice Age, which was at its height about 20,000 years ago. At that time, a land bridge connected Asia and North America. Groups of hunters and gatherers moved across the bridge over many thousands of years, probably in search of animals to hunt. Early Eskimos were among the last groups to arrive, and by 800 B.C. they had spread over much of our continent's far north.

Activity A

The main topic and subtopics from the second part of the outline for the report on early Eskimos are below. The topic sentence for the second paragraph has been written for you. Complete this paragraph on a sheet of paper by including all the ideas listed as subtopics. Use an encyclopedia or other books to find additional facts.

II. How did the Eskimos survive their harsh environment?
   A. Built houses of sod or snow (igloos) for winter
   B. Made tents of sealskin or caribou skin for summer
   C. Ate food from environment—seal and caribou meat, fish, birds, some berries and roots
   D. Made clothes from skins of animals—seals, caribou, bear, and fox

Topic sentence: The Eskimos learned to meet the challenges of their harsh environment in many ways.

Activity B

Use the main topic and subtopics from the third part of the outline to write the third paragraph of the report. This time write a topic sentence on your own, and include a sentence for each subtopic. You may include other facts that are related to the main topic. The last sentence in this paragraph should sum up everything you have written and bring the report to a close. This will be the concluding sentence of your report.

III. What kind of social life did the Eskimos have?
   A. Lived in cooperative family groups
   B. No government needed
   C. Rules enforced and arguments settled peacefully

Write Away!

Choose a topic from either your social studies or your science class. Take notes from your textbook, library books, or an encyclopedia. Write an outline for a three-paragraph report on the topic. After you have finished the outline, write a report based on it. Be sure to develop your paragraphs carefully.

Revision: Time to Take Another Look

As you reread your report, ask yourself the following questions:

—Does each paragraph include the main topic and subtopics from my outline?

—Does the first paragraph have a beginning sentence that tells the topic of the report?

—Do the supporting details for each paragraph flow smoothly?

—Does the concluding sentence in the last paragraph sum up everything I have written?

—At the end of the report, did I list the encyclopedia or other books that I used?

—Does my report make sense?

If you need to work on anything from the list, *do it now. Delete, add,* or *rearrange* your ideas. After revision, rewrite the report and go on to proofreading.

Proofreading: Time to Look at Capitalization, Punctuation, and Spelling

⋏	Add
ℐ	Omit
≡	Capitalize
/	Lowercase
∩	Reverse
¶	New paragraph

—Did I begin each sentence with a capital letter?

—Did I use the correct mark of punctuation at the end of each sentence?

—Did I indent the first word of each new paragraph?

Start at the last word of the report and read backwards to check for spelling errors. If necessary, rewrite the report in your best handwriting.

Lesson 3 Writing a Story: Setting and Characters

The setting describes when and where a story occurs. Characters are the people and animals in a story.

Writing a *story* can be very enjoyable. The writer tries to entertain a reader by recounting an interesting set of events. The events do not have to be true. They can come partly, or completely, from the writer's own imagination.

The greatest challenge in writing a story is to capture and keep the reader's interest. A good way of doing this is to make the story seem real. You have already learned many skills that can bring a story to life. You have learned to use colorful words, similes, metaphors, and sensory impressions to create pictures in the reader's mind. You have also learned to write smooth narrative paragraphs with effective transition words. Now you will have a chance to use your skills of description and narration by writing a story.

One of the first steps in writing a story is to create a believable *setting*. A good writer tries to put the reader *into* the setting. Read this paragraph from Irene Hunt's novel *Across Five Aprils*, the story of a woman and her son during the Civil War years. How does the author's description make the setting seem to come to life?

> Ellen Creighton and her nine-year-old son, Jethro, were planting potatoes in the half-acre just south of their cabin that morning in mid-April, 1861; they were out in the field as soon as breakfast was over, and southern Illinois at that hour was pink with sunrise and swelling redbud and clusters of bloom over the apple orchard across the road. Jethro walked on the warm clods of plowed earth and felt them crumble beneath his feet as he helped his mother carry the tub of potato cuttings they had prepared the night before.

Once the story's time and place have been established, the author will try to describe the *characters* in a way that will arouse the reader's interest. In the following paragraph, the author introduces the character of Ellen Creighton. After reading the paragraph, tell what you feel about Ellen. What does she look like? What kind of life has she had?

She was a small, spare woman with large dark eyes and skin as brown and dry as leather. She had been a pretty girl back in the 1830's when she married Matthew Creighton, but prettiness was short-lived among country women of her time; she didn't think much about it anymore except now and then when Jenny's fourteen-year-old radiance was especially compelling . . . She had borne twelve children, four of whom were dead—perhaps five, for the oldest son had not been heard from since he left for the goldfields of California twelve years before; she had lived through sickness, poverty, and danger for over thirty years; the sight of a pretty face might bring a smile to her lips, but it was a thing of little value in Ellen's world.

Notice how the writer has included information about how Ellen looked, as well as facts about her life. A skilled writer can use descriptions of setting and character to make a story come alive and to capture the reader's interest.

Activity A

Create an interesting setting for any two of the items below. Write at least one paragraph for each. Remember to use the skills you have learned to try to "paint a picture" in your reader's mind.

1. A landing of creatures from another planet
2. Your living room decorated for a party
3. Swimming races at the local pool
4. A busy city street
5. A safari in Africa
6. Any setting of your choice

Activity B

Now think of one character for each of the two settings you have just created. Use colorful words to tell what the character looks like. For example, instead of "The guide had an interesting face," you could say, "The guide's tanned, weather-beaten face gave witness to his years of experience in the African bush." Next tell something more about the character. How does the character fit into the setting or scene? What are his or her thoughts or feelings?

Write Away!

Think of another character for a story, and then create a setting into which to put the character. Write at least two paragraphs. Remember to make the character and setting interesting, colorful, and believable.

Lesson 4 Writing the Plot

 The plot of a story is the series of events it describes.

Although setting and character are important, much of the pleasure of reading a story comes from following an intriguing *plot* as it unravels. As a reader, you want to know *what happens*. You may be surprised to learn, however, that the plot of most stories—a novel, a play, or a short story—will follow the same four steps outlined below.

1. *Introduction*: The setting and some of the important characters are presented. Setting and characters by themselves, however, do not make a story. In order for the action to begin, the main character must have a *problem*. There must be a situation in which *something needs to be done*. For example, think of a simple detective story. Something may be stolen or missing and the detective must find it. In a series of books by Donald Sobol, Encyclopedia Brown is a young detective who is often called upon to find missing objects. In one story, he is asked to recover a stolen giant watermelon.

2. *Development*: The problem or situation moves along and gets more complex. The main character may seek solutions or simply avoid the problem and suffer the consequences. Whatever happens, the problem is always central. In the detective story, for example, Encyclopedia Brown interviews the owner of the watermelon, gathers information, and looks for clues.

3. *Climax*: This is the high point of the story—the most interesting and exciting part. All the action up to now has led to this point. The reader finally discovers what really happened. In the climax of a detective story, the detective finds out who the thief is and often goes through an exciting and dangerous chase to catch the person.

4. *Conclusion*: In the conclusion, the problem is solved, but not always happily. There may be a sad or a surprise ending. In the conclusion of the Encyclopedia Brown story, he explains what clues led him to the thief. The reader discovers *why* the crime was committed—and the fate of the giant watermelon.

Activity A

Your library contains many good stories. Your reader in school has interesting ones, too. Read a story or review one that you have already read. When you have finished, summarize the parts of the plot by completing a chart that looks like this:

Title _____ Author _____

Introduction (Setting, Characters, and Problem) _____

_____

_____

_____

Development (Series of Events) _____

_____

_____

Climax (High Point) _____

_____

_____

Conclusion (Problem Solved) _____

_____

_____

Activity B

In lesson 3, you created a number of settings with a character for each setting. Choose your favorite and develop a plot by briefly answering the following questions. (Add more characters if necessary.)

1. What will the problem or conflict be?
2. How will the story develop? (List a series of events or ways the character goes about solving the problem.)
3. How will the story reach a climax?
4. How will the story end?

Write Away!

Use your setting, characters, and plot outline from activity B to write the first draft of a short story. Remember to use the skills you have learned to make the story interesting, lifelike, and believable.

Lesson 5 Making Characters Talk

Dialogue, or conversation, makes characters come alive.

Stories become more lifelike when characters speak to one another. Dialogue reveals the thoughts and emotions of the characters while also revealing important events in the story.

Read the following dialogue from a short story about a girl's clever attempts to get the autograph of her favorite rock musician. What does the dialogue reveal about Wendy and the musician's mother? What do you think will happen? (Wendy's friend is the narrator, the *I*. The *she* is Wendy.)

> I follow her to one of those telephones that connect the caller to hotel rooms. She dials a number. She waits. Then she says, "Craig the Cat, please." She looks at me. "I found him! Listen!" She tilts the receiver so that I, too, can hear what's being said. It's a strain, but I can hear.
>
> A woman is on the other end. "How did you find out where Craig the Cat is staying?" she asks. "The leak. I need to know where the leak is."
>
> "There isn't any. I'm the only one with the information. Please be nice. I want his autograph."
>
> "Who doesn't."
>
> "Help me get it, please. What are my chances?"
>
> "Poor to nonexistent."
>
> "Oh."
>
> "I'm his manager and, my dear, I'm his mother. I protect Craig from two vantage points. I keep a low profile. Now, how many other fans know where he's staying?"
>
> "None that I know of."
>
> "You mean you didn't peddle the information to the highest bidder?"
>
> "I wouldn't do that."
>
> "Maybe not, dear, but I'm tired of his fans. They tug at Craig's whiskers. They pull his tail. Leave him alone! I'm hanging up." Click.

To find out what happens with Wendy and the musician who dresses as a cat, read Marjorie Sharmat's "May I Have Your Autograph?"

Here are some points to keep in mind when writing dialogue.
1. Indent and begin a new paragraph each time a different character speaks.
2. Enclose the speaker's words in quotation marks.
3. Use commas to separate the name of the speaker from his or her exact words. For example: "Now that I think about it," said Billy with a grin, "maybe I will have some ice cream."
4. Remember to put the quotation marks *after* the punctuation that ends or interrupts the quote.

Activity A

Review the four points above for writing dialogue and rewrite this dialogue with the correct punctuation and indentation.

Ooooh, groaned Eric, as his father nudged him to wake up Wednesday morning, I feel terrible today. What's the problem? asked his father. My head is throbbing with pain, Eric complained, my stomach is upset, and all my muscles feel weak. Is that all? his father asked. I think I have a fever, too, Eric added. It's probably from playing football out in the snow yesterday. I got all wet and tired. That must be what did it. Well, said his father I guess you'll have to stay home from school today. Will you miss anything important? Oh, not much he replied just a small science test, and I think there might be a math test, too.

Activity B

Make the situations below come alive by creating dialogue. Have each person speak only once.

Example: A lifeguard speaking to a swimmer

> "Please don't run around the sides of the pool," cautioned the lifeguard.
>
> "Sorry," said Mark, "I was playing a game and I forgot."

1. A student talking with a teacher about a homework assignment
2. A person calling the janitor of the apartment building
3. A boy and girl talking about taking part in a fund-raising drive
4. A husband and wife as they see a baseball crashing through their window
5. Two people caught in an elevator during a power failure

Write Away!

Make up two situations like those in activity B, and write each situation on a separate piece of paper. Put your paper in a jar or box along with the papers of the other students. Pick out one piece of paper and write six interesting lines of dialogue for the particular situation.

Lesson 6 Writing about Characters from Books

Writing a description of a character from a book is one way of reporting on a book you have read.

In each new book and short story you read, you meet new people. Many are colorful and exciting individuals to whom you may become quite attached. These new friends sometimes have a great influence on your life. In fact, you might even want to share your book friends with your real-life friends. Your writing skills can help you do this when you create an interesting paragraph about a favorite book character. Read the following description of a famous detective you might meet in your own book adventures.

My name is Sherlock Holmes, and I reside at Number 221B Baker Street in nineteenth-century London, England. It is there that my clients come to see me, for I am a detective—a *master* detective, one might say. Many consider me the world's greatest sleuth. Perhaps you have seen me at work. I am quite tall and thin with a checked, two-peaked cap and an ever-present pipe that hangs over my chin. With my companion Dr. Watson at my side, I have solved numerous baffling mysteries, such as one eerie case involving the devilish "hound of the Baskervilles." On every case, I look closely at the clues and try to understand what they tell me. Next, I often set a trap to snare the evildoer. Invariably, Dr. Watson is amazed and perplexed at my solutions. "Elementary, my dear Watson," I always exclaim, as I describe my logical deductions from the available clues. Watson may remain confused, but he is always happy that the case has been solved and all is well—at least until the next crime is committed.

Notice how the writer "became" the character by using the pronoun *I*. Writing in the first person is one good way of sharing a character with others. Find the answers to these questions in the paragraph you just read.

1. Who is the main character?
2. When and where does this character live?
3. How does this character look?
4. What makes this character special?

Activity A

List interesting characters you have met in novels or short stories. Write a two- or three-sentence description of two or three of these characters.

Activity B

Copy the form below on a sheet of paper and write a first-person descriptive paragraph about one of the characters you listed in activity A. Use the sample description of Sherlock Holmes as a model.

Title _____
Author _____
Type of Book or Story _____
Introducing _____
_____
_____
_____
_____

Write Away!

Choose two more characters from the list you made for activity A. Use your imagination to describe a meeting between the two characters. The characters do not have to be from the same time or place. Use picture words and dialogue to make the conversation come alive.

Lesson 7 Writing a Book Report

A book report is a formal way of writing about a book you have read. The report includes a summary and a personal reaction.

In this chapter, you have learned to write a factual *report* by first taking notes, then putting together an outline, and, finally, turning your outline into a series of paragraphs. You have also learned to write a *story* by using colorful language to create an intriguing setting and characters and by constructing a plot that will hold a reader's interest. When you write a book report, you use all of these skills: you are writing a *report* that tells about a *story*.

A book report contains the following information: the book's title, the author, the kind of book it is, the names of the characters, a summary of the story, and your own personal reaction to the book. Read the model report on the next page about the novel *Johnny Tremain*.

Book reports like the model are useful for a number of reasons. A book report will help you remember the story and how you felt about it. Others who read the report can decide if they would like to read the book. Most important, writing a book report teaches you to *analyze* a book and to put your reaction to it into words.

Model: A Book Report

TITLE:	*Johnny Tremain*
AUTHOR:	Esther Forbes
KIND OF BOOK:	Historical fiction
CHARACTERS:	Johnny Tremain, Mr. and Mrs. Lapham, Dusty, Dove, Rab, Doctor Warren, Paul Revere, and other patriots of the Revolutionary period

An engraving by Paul Revere
illustrating the Boston Massacre

SUMMARY: *Johnny Tremain* is a story about a young boy living in Boston at the time of the American Revolution. The novel begins about 1773 when we meet Johnny living with the Lapham family. Mr. Lapham, at this time, was a silversmith who was teaching Johnny and two other apprentices, Dusty and Dove, the trade. Johnny was bright, gifted, and very capable of performing his duties, but sometimes he seemed to lord it over the other two boys. However, all this changed with a tragic accident. A container of molten silver broke and spilled over Johnny's right hand, making it useless.

Johnny was then forced to look for a new home and new work. During this period of his life, he became very discouraged and depressed.

Johnny met a young boy named Rab, who secured for him a home and work as a dispatch rider for the Committee of Public Safety. The work introduced him to Paul Revere, James Otis, John Hancock, John and Samuel Adams, and other important Boston patriots. These men found Johnny trustworthy and courageous, and permitted him to share in the events leading to the Boston Tea Party and the Battle of Lexington.

On the battlefield, Johnny learned from Doctor Warren that with treatment he would be able to use his hand again. His goal of becoming a great silversmith seemed possible, and the future looked bright.

REACTION: The novel *Johnny Tremain* held my interest from beginning to end. Reading about the exciting adventures of those early days in Boston, I saw a picture of the struggle for American liberty through the eyes of a clever, courageous, and patriotic boy of fourteen.

Activity A

Review the model book report and answer these questions.

1. Who is the author of *Johnny Tremain*?
2. Who is Johnny Tremain?
3. What is the problem, or conflict, in *Johnny Tremain*?
4. How is the problem resolved?
5. Why does the writer of the book report like *Johnny Tremain*?
6. Would you like to read *Johnny Tremain*? Why, or why not?

Activity B

Think of a book or short story that you particularly enjoyed and answer these questions about it.

1. What is the title?
2. Who is the author?
3. What kind of book or story is it?
4. Who are the important characters?
5. What is the problem or conflict?
6. What does the main character do to solve the problem?
7. What is the conclusion?
8. Why did you like this book or story?

Write Away!

The information you provided for activity B gives you the basic outline for a report on the book or story. Complete a report on that book or story in book report form. Remember to make the *summary* and *reaction* colorful and interesting. Draw a picture of one scene from the story and include it in your report.

Writing Corner 4

How and Why Tales

Have you ever wondered *how* things in nature came about? For example, *why* do animals have certain characteristics? A long time ago, people did not have science to explain nature. They made up reasons of their own for what happened. Usually they put these reasons in the form of a story or tale. They may have told a tale about

how the rainbow got its colors   why kangaroos hop
how the turtle got its shell   why the sun is hot

These have come to be called *how and why tales*. These kinds of tales often begin with phrases such as

When the world was very young...
Once, many thousands of years ago...

Characters are introduced, and a plot develops. Within the plot, a difficulty or complication often arises. The main character may have to overcome an obstacle, make a decision, or confront danger. Dialogue is often added to help make the characters seem real. On the next page is a tale about "How the Giraffe Became the Tallest Animal in the Forest."

Long ago, Giraffe was a very small creature. He was so small that he couldn't even see himself. One day he mentioned his complaint to Elephant. Elephant told him about a pool deep in the forest. This pool was so clear that Giraffe would surely be able to see himself. Giraffe was excited and Elephant promised to lead the way. When they arrived, Giraffe dashed to the edge of the pool, but being so short, he could not stretch over the water to see himself. Every time he tried, he fell into the pool.

"This will never do!" cried Giraffe.

"I have an idea," said Elephant. "If I hold your legs, you can stretch over the water and that way you can see yourself."

So Elephant held Giraffe's legs, and Giraffe stretched his head and neck over the water. He liked seeing himself so much that he stretched again and stretched again.

"Oh, I am beautiful!" exclaimed Giraffe, and he kept stretching and stretching until he stretched his neck right across the pool. Then when he could see himself no longer, Elephant pulled Giraffe straight up with his strong trunk. Now Giraffe stood taller than any other animal in the forest. To this day, no animal is as tall as the giraffe.

The ending of a *how and why tale* should answer the question the title raises. In this tale, Giraffe stretched so much to see himself that his neck became very long and he ended up being the tallest animal in the forest.

★ Brainstorm for other *how and why* titles to add to the list given. Then choose one and write an explanation with dialogue of *how* or *why* something happened. Be as imaginative and creative as you can. Illustrate your work if you like when you are finished. Then read your tale to the class.

Word Study 4

Homophones

Homophones are words that sound alike but that have different spellings and meanings.

Many writers are confused by words that sound alike but that have different spellings and meanings. These words are called homophones.

> Into the pitch black *night*, the *knight* rode on his white charger.

In this sentence, *night* and *knight* are homophones.

Be careful to use the correct spelling of words that are homophones. Always check the dictionary if you are unsure of a spelling.

Activity A

Give the definitions for each pair of homophones below. Use a dictionary if necessary.
1. bough—bow
2. coarse—course
3. knot—not
4. patience—patients
5. peace—piece
6. root—route
7. stationary—stationery
8. some—sum
9. threw—through
10. weather—whether

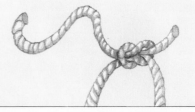

Activity B

Complete each sentence with the correct homophone. Use the list in activity A. Each word on the list should be used once.

1. A multicolored bird sat on the _____ of the tree and sang.
2. Vegetables, such as turnips, that grow underground are called _____ vegetables.
3. The submarine was far off _____.
4. Radar is an instrument used in _____ forecasting.
5. _____ seabirds travel more than 20,000 miles in their migrations.
6. Tricia fielded the ground ball and _____ it to first base.
7. The nomads wear loose garments made out of a _____ material that they weave themselves.
8. Gabriel could _____ decide _____ to study arithmetic or play volleyball.
9. After one week on the exhausting paper _____, Janine added up the _____ of her earnings.
10. Making a tiny model plane requires _____.
11. We drove _____ a long tunnel on our way into New York.
12. Afraid his arm was broken, Alex sat in the emergency room among the other _____.
13. Violet uses _____ with purple violets on it.
14. The sailor fastened the rowboat to the pier with an expertly tied _____.
15. The magician took a _____ and disappeared from the stage amid smoke and applause.
16. The important telephone number was on a tiny _____ of paper.
17. Now, desks in schools are movable; in the past, they were often _____.
18. The dove is a symbol of _____.

Chapter 5
Writing Letters

Lesson 1 The Parts of a Social Letter

A social letter is made up of a heading, salutation, body, complimentary close, and signature.

Do you have a close friend who lives in another city? A favorite relative who lives hundreds or even thousands of miles away? Unfortunately, the people you like best do not always live near you. Even though you cannot see them often, you can keep in touch with friends and relatives by writing *letters*.

What are some of the things you can share in a letter? When you are with a friend, you probably tell stories and jokes, and you talk about new experiences and future plans. You can share the same things when you write a friendly letter. Letters can be enjoyable to write and to receive.

You probably have already written some, or even many, social letters. Let's review the *parts* of a social letter, so that you will use the correct form. A social letter contains five parts: (1) the heading, (2) the salutation, (3) the body of the letter, (4) the complimentary close, and (5) the signature.

In this picture, many pieces of writing are being saved.
How valuable is a letter to you? Why?

Read the following letter, and take careful note of each part.

Heading
2690 Rowen Street
Denver, Colorado 80220
December 3, 19_

Dear Roberta, Salutation

I enjoyed getting your letter last week. It really made me homesick for all my old friends in Houston. I am getting to like Denver, though. I especially like the Colorado Heritage Center. It has items from the early cliff dwellers who once lived in this area. Body

Another thing I like about Denver is the snow. I've never seen so much snow! I'm taking skiing lessons, and my mom is going to buy me a complete ski outfit for Christmas (I hope!). So far, this city seems as if it will be great to live in.

Write soon and let me know what's going on with all my Houston friends.

Complimentary close Your good friend,
Signature Jenny

Here are some rules for each of the parts of a social letter.

1. Heading

The heading of a letter contains the address of the writer and the date. It is usually written on three lines. The address is written on the first line; the city, state, and zip code on the second line; and the date on the third line. The heading is written slightly to the right of the center of the paper, about an inch from the top of the sheet. If the letter is extremely short, the heading may be lowered. Ordinarily each line is written directly under the one above it. This is called *block form*.

Brief letters, or *social notes*, sometimes use only the date in the heading. Invitations, thank-you notes, and notes of acceptance or regret are examples of social notes.

2. Salutation

The salutation is the greeting at the beginning of a letter. It is only one line long and begins at the left-hand margin. The salutation varies, depending on the person to whom the letter is written. The first word and the person's name are always capitalized, and there is always a comma at the end of the salutation in a social letter.

These are examples of salutations:

> *Dear Denise,*
> *Dear Uncle Mac,*
> *My dear Aunt,*

3. Body

The body of the letter is the most important part because it contains the message. In this part, you carry on a conversation with the person to whom you are writing. In the next lesson, you will learn more about writing the body of some special kinds of social letters.

4. Complimentary Close

The complimentary close lets the reader know that the letter is ending. The first word begins with a capital letter and should line up with (be exactly under) the first word of the heading. The complimentary close is always followed by a comma. Make sure that the complimentary close is appropriate for the person to whom you are writing.

These are examples of complimentary closes:

Your friend,

Your classmate,

Your daughter,

5. Signature

The signature is the name of the person who is writing the letter. When you are writing to relatives and close friends, use your first name only. If the person to whom you are writing does not know you very well, use your full name. The name always begins with a capital letter, and there is no punctuation mark after the name. *Write* your signature neatly under the first word of the complimentary close.

Activity A

Arrange each of the following addresses and dates in the proper form for the heading of a letter. Use the current year for the date in your headings.

1. April 27, 19__, Anchorage, Alaska 99510, 123 Yukon Avenue
2. Chicago, Illinois 60613, June 29, 19__, 3843 North Greenview Avenue
3. 438 North Street, June 10, 19__, Norfolk, Virginia 23500
4. August 1, 19__, Pennsbury Hospital, Jonesboro, Arkansas 72401

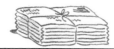

Activity B

Write the salutation for a letter written to each person listed below.

1. Your mother
2. A very close friend
3. Your cousin Teresa
4. Mrs. Gurek, a teacher in your school
5. Your Aunt Sally
6. A classmate
7. Mr. Santelli
8. Your brother

Activity C

Write the complimentary close for a letter written to each person listed below.

1. A classmate
2. Your uncle
3. Your brother
4. The captain of your soccer team
5. Your teacher
6. A friend
7. Your parents
8. Your cousin Alan

Write Away!

Think of three people you know who live too far away for you to visit very often. On a sheet of paper, write a heading, a salutation, and a complimentary close for a letter to each of them.

Lesson 2 Writing Social Letters

Types of social letters include the friendly letter, the invitation, and the thank-you letter.

The social letter is a form of writing that helps you keep in touch with people you know. The more you improve your writing skills, the more entertaining and informative your social letters will be.

Three types of social letters are the *friendly letter*, the *invitation*, and the *thank-you letter*. Remember the following points as you write each type of letter: (1) Talk about one topic only in each paragraph and finish that topic before introducing a new one. (2) Always write complete sentences. (3) Indent the first sentence of each paragraph about one inch.

In *friendly letters*, friends exchange news about each other (just as the writer of the letter in lesson 1 did). Read the friendly letter below in which a boy tells of his new hobby. Does the letter writer follow the rules of a good paragraph in describing his hobby? Does he write complete sentences? Is each paragraph indented?

Model: A Friendly Letter

105 Powder Boulevard
Dixon, Illinois 60329
December 17, 19__

Dear Jim,

    It was really great to hear from you. Your fitness class sounds like lots of fun. I'm glad to hear that you saved up enough money to buy a drum set. It seems as if you're keeping very busy.

    I've been quite occupied myself. You know that I was never the type to have hobbies, but in the past few months I've become a stamp collector. It started when my Uncle Ted sent me postcards as he traveled throughout Europe. I never realized before how many different stamps there were in the world. Now I look forward to the mail delivery and to each new collection that I have been able to order. Friends from all over have promised to watch carefully for any unusual stamps. Would you like to help me too?

    Say hello to your family, Jim. I'm glad you all like your new home.

Your friend,
Jason

An *invitation* should be as natural as a friendly letter. It should also state very clearly the kind of event, the day, the time, and the place. An invitation should be written so that the person who receives it will want to accept. Read this model invitation. Does it provide all the needed information? Does it make you want to attend the party?

<u>Model: An Invitation</u>

1666 Wall Street
Chattanooga, Tennessee 37400
December 5, 19—

Dear Anne,

    Are the first blasts of winter's cold getting you down? Does the early darkness make you feel like hibernating until April? If that's how you feel (or even if it isn't), please join us in cheering up the season with a tree-trimming party and dinner on December 17. My family would love to have you come to our house at two o'clock.

    Your friend,
    Becky

A *thank-you letter* shows your appreciation for a favor you have received. In your letter, you should try to make the person feel good about what he or she did. Read the following and decide if it is an effective thank-you letter.

Model: A Thank-you Letter

99 Hamp Street
Denver, Colorado 80220
January 5, 19__

Dear Aunt Gail,

    Thanks so much for giving me your old baseball card collection. It has many players that will make me the envy of all my friends who are collectors. Now I have cards of Roberto Clemente and Willie Mays!

    Thank you again. We are all looking forward to your visit at Easter.

               Your delighted niece,
               Jayne

Activity A

Choose one of the following topics and write a paragraph that you might include in a letter to your cousin in another city. Include a heading, salutation, complimentary close, and signature.

1. A good book you have read
2. A sport you have been playing
3. A visit to a museum
4. Your favorite television program
5. A day when everything went wrong
6. A movie you liked
7. Your favorite new record
8. (Choose your own)

Activity B

From the topics listed below, write one letter of invitation and one thank-you letter. Include a heading, salutation, complimentary close, and signature.

Invitations

1. An invitation to a Halloween party
2. An invitation to your grandparents to attend a school play in which you will appear
3. An invitation to an evening of VCR movies at your house

Thank-you Letters

1. A thank-you note to your aunt and uncle after you spent a week of your summer vacation on their farm
2. A thank-you note to your best friend for visiting you while you were in the hospital
3. A thank-you note to a friend for a birthday gift

Write Away!

Write a friendly letter to someone you would like to know: a book character, a movie or sports star, or a person from history. Tell this person why you are interested in him or her, ask questions, and comment on the things this person has done.

Revision: Time to Take Another Look

As you reread a social letter, ask yourself the following questions:

—Are there three lines in the heading?

    street address

    city, state, zip code

    month, day, year

—Do all the words in the heading fit without being squeezed?

—Does the salutation begin at the left-hand margin?

—Does each paragraph contain only one topic?

—Are the complimentary close and signature in line with the heading?

—Does the letter make sense?

If you need to work on anything from the above list, *do it now*. *Delete* or *add* words and *rearrange* ideas if necessary. After your revision, rewrite the social letter and go on to proofreading.

Proofreading: Time to Look at Capitalization, Punctuation, and Spelling

⅄	Add
ℐ	Omit
=	Capitalize
/	Lowercase
∿	Reverse
¶	New paragraph

Heading: Did I use a comma between city and state, day of the month, and year? Are all proper nouns capitalized?

Salutation: Is the first letter of each important word capitalized? (*Dear* is not capitalized unless it is the first word.) Did I put a comma at the end?

Body: Did I indent each paragraph? Is all the punctuation correct?

Complimentary close: Is the first word capitalized? Do the other words begin with a small letter? Is there a comma at the end?

Signature: Did I write my name clearly and legibly?

Start at the last word of the letter and check for spelling errors. If necessary, rewrite the letter in your best handwriting.

Lesson 3 The Parts of a Business Letter

A business letter is made up of a heading, inside address, salutation, body, complimentary close, and signature.

Sometimes you need to write to a business firm or an organization to request information, to order a product, or to complain about an unsatisfactory product. Such *business letters* have the same five parts as a social letter, as well as a part called the *inside address*. Read the following business letter and note the differences between business and social letters.

Heading
1111 Tenth Street
Moline, Illinois 61265
February 10, 19—

Carlson Book Shop
1425 Fifth Avenue
Moline, Illinois 61265

Dear Sir or Madam : Salutation

Please send me one package of five hundred stamps titled "World Collection" (#302 in your summer Body catalog). I am enclosing a money order for eight dollars ($8.00), which includes postage.

Complimentary close Very truly yours,
Signature Barbara Cox
Barbara Cox

Here are some rules for each of the parts of a business letter.

1. Heading

The form for the heading of a business letter is the same as for the heading of a social letter. It contains the writer's street address, city, state, and zip code, and the month, day, and year. The heading is written slightly to the right of the center of the paper, about an inch from the top.

2. Inside Address

The inside address should begin on the left-hand margin, below the heading. It consists of the full name and address of the business or organization to which the letter is being sent. The inside address follows the same form and punctuation as the heading except for one difference. If the letter is being written to a specific person, that person's name and title are included on the first line of the inside address. The name of the business or organization then appears on the second line. Make sure that the inside address is the same as the address on the envelope.

3. Salutation

The salutation of a business letter is followed by a colon (:) and is made up of a formal phrase such as the following:

Dear Ms. Spaulding:
Dear Sir or Madam:

The salutation is directly below the inside address.

4. Body

The body of a business letter follows the same form as that of a social letter. It is short and courteous, and contains only necessary information.

5. Complimentary Close

The complimentary close of a business letter is more formal than that of a social letter. Such phrases as the following are used:

Yours truly,   *Sincerely yours,*
Very truly yours,   *Respectfully yours,*

It is directly in line with the heading.

6. Signature

The signature of a business letter is also more formal. Directly below the complimentary close, write your full name. Below that, you should type or neatly print your name. This form is necessary for the signature of a business letter so that your name is readable.

Business letters are often typed since typed letters are easier to read. However, it is acceptable for you to send handwritten business letters.

Activity A

Arrange each of the following addresses in the proper order for an inside address. Write a salutation to go along with each inside address.

1. 229 West Forty-third Street, *New York Times*, New York, New York 10000
2. Agriculture Department, Ames, Iowa 50010, University of Iowa, Professor Leslie Brock
3. Marshall Field and Company, Chicago, Illinois 60602, 111 North State Street
4. 3441 North Ashland Avenue, Managing Editor, Chicago, Illinois 60657, Loyola University Press
5. New York, New York 10000, Program Director, National Broadcasting Company, 645 Third Avenue

Activity B

Copy this business letter on a sheet of paper and fill in the missing parts.

Marshall School
4358 Utica Avenue
Cheyenne, Wyoming 82001

_____

Business Manager

_____

2120 Market Street
Cheyenne, Wyoming 82001

_____

    A recent article in your newspaper indicated that you offer guided tours in which you show grade-school groups how the *Cheyenne News* is written and printed. The sixth-grade class that I teach would be quite interested in taking such a tour sometime in April.

_____

_____ We need to make our plans by March 15.

              _____

              _____

              Elizabeth Lopez
              Teacher, Room 301

Write Away!

Write a heading, inside address, salutation, complimentary close, and signature for a business letter to each of the following.
1. A local grocery store
2. A nearby department store
3. The mayor
4. The place of business of a family member
5. A business that you would like to visit

Lesson 4 Writing a Business Letter

A business letter should be short, courteous, and to the point.

A business letter is more formal than a social letter. A social letter helps people keep in touch and exchange various bits of news about each other. The purpose of a business letter is much more specific. The most common kinds of business letters do one of the following:

1. order a product
2. make a request
3. complain about a product or service
4. request that the writer be considered for a job

Since its goal is so specific, a business letter should be short and to the point. The letter writer must remember to be just as courteous in a business letter as in a social letter.

Letters Ordering a Product

One of the most common kinds of business letter is a letter in which the writer is ordering a product. It is important for the writer to give complete and precise information about what is being ordered. In addition, the writer should mention the method of payment.

Model: Placing an Order

110 George Street
Lynn, Massachusetts 01900
January 6, 19_

Inventors Supply Company
178 Tremont Street
Boston, Massachusetts 02180

Dear Sir or Madam :

Kindly send by parcel post as soon as possible one (1) Deluxe Young Inventor's Kit. Also, please include the complimentary Inventor's Notebook as advertised in your catalog.

I am enclosing a money order for ten dollars and twenty-five cents ($10.25), the price listed in your catalog. This includes postage and handling.

Very truly yours,
Carl Erley
Carl Erley

Notice that the letter is short and definite with no unnecessary words or information.

129

Letters of Request

You may wish to make a request of a business firm, such as asking for permission to visit a broadcasting studio or a manufacturing plant. When writing a letter of this type, include a stamped, self-addressed envelope for the reply. Be specific as to the number of persons and the date.

Model: A Letter of Request

Henry W. Longfellow School
Salem, Oregon 97300
April 6, 19—

Kleen Dairy Council
475 Baker Street
Salem, Oregon 97300

Dear Sir or Madam:

    Our class of twenty-five students is interested in the invitation you have extended to all schools to visit your dairy. We have been studying about the many products that a modern dairy supplies, and we welcome this opportunity to see a plant in operation.

    Please let us know the earliest date convenient to you.

        Very truly yours,
        Kathleen Schultz
        Kathleen Schultz (Secretary)

Letters Reporting Errors or Defects

There may be occasions when orders are not filled promptly and correctly, or when the articles received are damaged. When this happens, write a courteous letter to the company, calling attention to the error or defect and asking the firm to make the necessary adjustment.

Model: A Letter Reporting a Delay

401 Wisconsin Avenue
Mill Valley, Illinois 60135
December 15, 19—

Practical Fishing Products, Inc.
106 South Lake Road
Westminster, Maryland 21157

Dear Sir or Madam:

On April 29, I placed an order for the Friendly Fishing Pole and Reel set. On May 10, I received the set. Unfortunately, the reel arrived damaged. The handle had broken off from the body of the reel.

Since the product is guaranteed, I am returning the damaged part, along with a copy of my original order. Please send a new reel as soon as possible.

Very truly yours,
Terence Lunden
Terence Lunden

Activity A

You want to visit a museum in your area. On a sheet of paper, write the following.

1. *The heading*: Your address or your school's address.
2. *The inside address*: Use a real museum or make one up.
3. *The salutation*: Write one that is appropriate for this type of letter.
4. *The complimentary close*: Choose one that is appropriate.

Activity B

Now write a letter to the museum, requesting information about these points:
—a special exhibit that your class would like to see
—the days and times your class can visit
—the size of the group that can attend
—how to arrange a guided tour of the exhibit
Express your appreciation that the museum is available to student groups free of charge.

Write Away!

Recently you ordered two records from the following company:

> Golden Disc Music
> 1052 Record Avenue
> Miami, Florida 33136

When the records arrived, one was so warped that you could not play it. Write a letter telling the company what has happened. Explain that you would like the record replaced or your money returned. Remember to be brief, to the point, and courteous.

Revision: Time to Take Another Look

As you reread a business letter, ask yourself:
—Is the heading in the proper form?
—Is the inside address in the proper form? (Name of person, if known; name of company; street address; city, state, zip code)
—Is the salutation appropriate for the letter?
—Is the body of the letter brief, to the point, and courteous? Have I given all the necessary information?
—Is the complimentary close appropriate?

If you need to work on anything from the above list, *do it now*. *Delete* or *add* words and *rearrange* sentences as necessary. After you have revised the business letter, go on to proofreading.

Proofreading: Time to Look at Capitalization, Punctuation, and Spelling

⋏	Add
℘	Omit
≡	Capitalize
/	Lowercase
∿	Reverse
¶	New paragraph

Heading and Inside Address: Did I use a comma between city and state, day of the month, and year? Are all proper nouns capitalized? Is each of the parts in the proper place?
Salutation: Is the first letter of each important word capitalized? Is there a colon at the end? Does it begin at the left-hand margin?
Body: Did I indent the first line of the paragraph? Does every sentence end with correct punctuation?
Complimentary Close: Is the close in line with the heading? Is the first word capitalized? Does each of the other words begin with a small letter? Is there a comma at the end?
Signature: Is the signature in line with the heading? Did I write my first and last names neatly? Did I type or print my name under the written signature?

Start at the last word of the letter and check for spelling errors. If necessary, rewrite the letter in your best handwriting.

Lesson 5 Addressing the Envelope

The front of an envelope has the name and address of the person to whom the letter is being sent. It also has the return address of the sender.

You have probably addressed many envelopes. Let's review the rules to make sure that you have been addressing your envelopes correctly. Look at the following example.

Margaret Parker
Box 159
Arlington, VA 22200

Dr. Maria Sanchez
506 Long Street
Portland, OR 97200

Note that the envelope contains the full name and address of the person to whom the letter is being sent, including a title such as Dr., Mr., Miss, Mrs., or Ms. The form and the punctuation should follow the style of the inside address of a business letter. The person's name should begin just above the center of the envelope and slightly to the left. The street address goes below the name, and the third line gives the city, state, and zip code. Each line in the address is exactly under the line above it. This is called *block form*.

The name and address of the person who wrote the letter appears in the upper left-hand corner of the envelope. The name goes on the first line, the street address on the second line, and the city, state, and zip code on the third line. (It is not necessary to write a title, such as Mr. or Ms.) This part is known as the *return address*. If for some reason the post office cannot deliver the letter, the return address will ensure that the letter comes back to the person who sent it.

The only punctuation used on an envelope is the period after abbreviations of titles and the comma before the name of the state. Every state has a two-letter abbreviation, which you may choose to use instead of writing out the full name. A complete list of these abbreviations can be found in this book on page 429.

Folding the Letter

A letter should be folded neatly before it is put in the envelope. Some notepaper is small and can be folded in half. Put the folded edge into the envelope first.

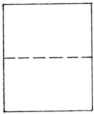 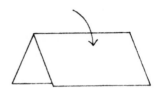

If you are using a large envelope and a large piece of paper, fold the bottom of the paper just a little past the center (a third of the way up). Fold the top part down about one-fourth inch from the crease. Then place the letter in the envelope with the last fold at the bottom.

 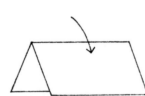 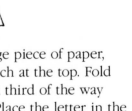

If you are using a small envelope and a large piece of paper, fold the paper in half, leaving one-fourth inch at the top. Fold the right side over a little past the center (a third of the way over), then do the same with the left side. Place the letter in the envelope with the last fold at the bottom.

 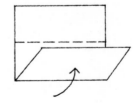 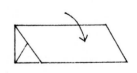

Activity A

Write the following names and addresses as they should be written on envelopes. Use your own return address and abbreviate the state. (Use page 429 to find the two-letter postal abbreviations.)

1. Juliet F. Jefferson, 724 Palm Street, Honolulu, Hawaii 96800
2. Dr. Chandra Singh, Saint Charles Hospital, 14 Front Street, Keokuk, Iowa 52632
3. Ms. Anne Gray, Rural Route 3, Big Bar, Idaho 83678
4. Mr. Roberto Flores, 5525 Penn Avenue, Pittsburgh, Pennsylvania 15200
5. Mrs. Howard L. Finkle, 123 Freeman Parkway, Providence, Rhode Island 02906
6. Thomas J. De Nero, 55 Flower Street, Santa Ana, California 92700
7. Ms. Carolyn Davis, 99 Hampshire Street, Denver, Colorado 80200
8. Mr. Paul Baird, University of Cincinnati, Cincinnati, Ohio 45200

Activity B

Bring in two envelopes from home. Using addresses from activity A or addresses of friends, complete each envelope. Remember to include your return address. If necessary, draw horizontal lines on the envelope to help keep your writing straight.

Write Away!

You have written social letters and business letters for this chapter. Once you are satisfied that one is ready to be "sent," address the envelope. Then fold the letter properly and put it into the envelope.

Lesson 6 Filling Out Forms

Filling out a form is an orderly way of providing essential information.

As you have learned, letters to businesses and organizations must be short and to the point, providing necessary information with the fewest possible words. In this chapter, you have already seen sample business letters that request information and order products. Each letter is very specific and to the point.

Many businesses and organizations want to make sure that you tell them exactly what they need to know. To help you do this, they provide *forms* for you to fill out. A form is a document that asks you questions and leaves blank spaces for you to answer.

You have probably already filled out many forms. A *coupon* that you use to send away for something is a kind of form. When you join a community center or a little league, you fill out a form that provides necessary information. If you have ever opened a bank account, you filled out forms for that, also. As you grow older, you will fill out more and more forms. These include forms that help you do such things as pay taxes, give information about a change in your address, obtain a charge card, and apply for a job.

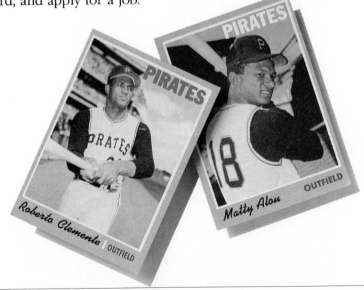

Activity A

Copy the coupon below on a sheet of paper, and fill it out to order the package of ten baseball cards called "All-Stars, 1970s and 1980s." Use your own name and address.

THE BASEBALL CARD SHOP
1010 East Main Street
Madison, WI 53703

Please send me the following ten-card package(s), which are SPECIAL OFFERS for this month (December, 19___) only.

CHECK CHOICES		PRICE
	Old-timers	$4.95
	Team pictures	$4.95
	All-Stars, 1970s and 1980s	$4.95
	Total	
	Postage	+ .50
	Total Enclosed	

SHIP TO:

Name _____

Address _____

City, State, Zip Code _____

Activity B

On a sheet of paper, complete the necessary information.

LAKESIDE PARK DAY CAMP

Application

Answer each question.

1. Name _____

2. Address _____

3. Phone number _____

4. Parents' names _____

5. Your age _____   6. Your birthday _____

7. Your height _____   8. Your weight _____

9. Your cap size _____   10. Your T-shirt size _____

Answer these questions by putting an *X* in the proper box.

11. I have attended summer day camp at Lakeside Park or at other parks for

    ☐ 0 years   ☐ 1 year

    ☐ 2 years   ☐ more than 2 years

12. I would be most interested in the following activities:

    ☐ baseball   ☐ singing

    ☐ volleyball   ☐ reading and storytelling

    ☐ soccer   ☐ hiking

    ☐ swimming   ☐ camping skills

    ☐ ceramics   ☐ others (please list below)

    ☐ woodworking

Camper's signature _____

Write Away!

Find a form to fill out. It can be from a magazine, newspaper, local store, community center, post office, or anywhere else. Complete the form and share it with the class.

Writing Answers

Many homework assignments and tests require that you answer questions in *clear* sentences and in *short* paragraphs. To do this, you need to

> *understand* exactly what the question is asking
> *focus* your answer on that point
> *select* the information that fits the question

Study the questions and answers that follow. Which of the two answers *focuses* better on what the question is asking?

Where is Washington, D.C.?

A. Washington, D.C., lies between Maryland and Virginia. Many people who work in Washington live in those two states.
B. Washington, D.C., is in the southeastern United States. It lies between Maryland and Virginia.

You are right if you noticed these points:

> Answer A includes the correct information, but the second sentence loses the focus on the question *where*.
>
> Answer B keeps the focus on *where* throughout, and it locates Washington first by region and then by state.

Describe the main characteristics of Washington, D.C.

A. Washington, D.C., is a beautiful city. It attracts visitors from all over the world. It has many fine buildings. In the spring, cherry blossoms are in bloom, adding to the beauty of the city. It is an interesting and educational city to visit. There are many museums to visit. More important, it is the capital of our nation. American citizens everywhere can take pride in the beauty of this city.

B. Washington, D.C., the capital of the United States, is noted for its fine buildings, its museums, and its natural beauty. The city has many government buildings—most impressive of all is the gleaming white Capitol with its imposing dome. There are many historical monuments, including the Lincoln Memorial with its colossal statue of the president. The Smithsonian Institution is the largest museum in the country, and its Air and Space Museum is the most visited. The city is also famous for its green areas and spring cherry blossoms.

You are right if you noticed these points:

> Answer A *discusses* many of Washington's characteristics rather than *describing* them.
>
> Answer B *describes* Washington's characteristics by giving specific *details*. It is a better answer.

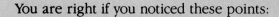

★ Choose one of the activities below, and answer the questions. Use books and travel brochures to help you answer. Try to focus on answering the question clearly and directly.

   A. 1. Where is Disneyland?
       2. Name some of the features of Disneyland that attract visitors.
       3. Describe the fun of a visit to Disneyland.
   B. 1. Who was Walt Disney?
       2. List the name of some of Walt Disney's productions.
       3. Select one of the characters Walt Disney created. Describe the character. Tell what the character looks like and how it acts.

Homographs

Homographs are words that are spelled the same but that have different meanings and are often pronounced differently.

Homographs can be confusing because they are words that are spelled alike. You can only identify a homograph by the way it is used. For example:

> From the rocky cliff, Manolo *dove* into the ocean.
> (*Past tense of* dive, *pronounced* dōv)

> As the sun broke through the clouds, a *dove* rested on the white picket fence in Jennie's yard.
> (*A kind of bird, pronounced* dəv)

Notice that the pronunciation of *dove* changes. There is a change in the *vowel sound*. The change in the vowel sound signals a difference in meaning. Look at the next two sentences:

> Akim takes pictures of any *object* that he finds interesting.
> (*A thing that can be seen or touched, pronounced* ŏb'jĭkt)

> Does anyone *object* to spending the dues on a dark room?
> (*Oppose, pronounced* əb jěkt')

Here the pronunciation of the word changes because there is a definite change, or shift, in the *accent*. The shift in the accent signals a difference in meaning.

Activity A

Read the list of homographs below and pronounce each word. Tell whether each pair of homographs has a different pronunciation because of a vowel change or a shift in accent. Then give the meaning of each word. Use a dictionary if necessary.

1. a. bow (bō)   b. bow (bau̇)
2. a. lead (lēd)   b. lead (lĕd)
3. a. live (līv)   b. live (lĭv)
4. a. present (prĕz′ nt) b. present (prĭ zĕnt′)
5. a. record (rĭ kôrd′)   b. record (rĕk′ ərd)

Activity B

Complete each sentence with the correct homograph from the list in activity A. Indicate whether the homograph you use is labeled *a* or *b* on the list.

1. I would like to _____ the new president of our class, Patty Layton.
2. The storm tossed the ship against a jagged rock, opening a massive hole in the _____.
3. During the 1800s, Galena, Illinois, was a center for the mining of _____.
4. Excitedly, Tisa tore the wrapping off the unexpected _____.
5. Charlie looked silly in that polka dot _____ tie.
6. Do any people _____ in Antarctica?
7. Jason's towering home run put his team in the _____.
8. Mary Lou will _____ today's important events in her diary.
9. Laura got tired of studying, so she put on a _____ and began to dance.
10. The cat's toy looked so real that for a moment I thought it was a _____ mouse.

Chapter 6

Speaking and Listening Skills

Lesson 1 Tools for Speaking Clearly and Correctly

Skilled speakers can use the tools of pitch, stress, and enunciation to speak more effectively and make their words come alive.

You have already learned a variety of ways to improve your writing. Although writing is an essential form of communication, it is not the only one—it is not even the most common. Days may pass when you do not write anything. Can you imagine a waking hour, however, when you do not express your thoughts and feelings through speech? Speech is such a common activity that you probably take it for granted. It includes a wide range of activities, such as casual conversation, reading aloud, introducing people to each other, debating, and making formal reports. The next few lessons will help you improve your skills of speaking and—just as important—listening.

Speaking requires many of the same skills as writing. A good speaker presents ideas in an organized and logical manner and makes these ideas more vivid by using language that "paints a picture." Speakers have another important tool—the voice. When you speak, you use the qualities of voice to make your words clearer and more vivid.

A tapestry is carefully designed and planned before it is woven. What kind of planning is needed to be an effective speaker?

Pitch

Pitch is the highness or the lowness of the speaker's voice. Variations in pitch can bring a spoken message alive. The speaker's voice becomes higher or lower in order to give the correct meaning to words.

Think about the following situation and listen to the pitch of your voice. Imagine that you have a role in a school play. The opening song is your cue that the play is about to begin. You hear the first notes of the song and say, "It's starting." You are stating a simple fact. The pitch of your voice is even. Now say the same sentence as a question, "It's starting?" The pitch of your voice is higher at the end. The meaning of the sentence is different. Through pitch, the listener understands that you are asking a question. Now say "It's starting!" with enthusiasm. The pitch of your voice starts high and then lowers. It shows your excitement.

Activity

Read the following sentences in at least two different ways by varying the pitch. Then tell what kind of feeling you are expressing with each change in pitch.

1. It snowed last night.
2. This pizza's delicious.
3. Stop it.
4. Let someone else do it.
5. This music is too loud.

Stress

Stress is the emphasis or degree of force you put on a word. The meaning of a sentence can change depending on what words are stressed. Read the following sentences aloud and listen to how different stress changes the meaning of the sentence. Put the emphasis on the italicized word.

Will *you* walk ten miles tomorrow? (This sentence emphasizes the person.)
Will you *walk* ten miles tomorrow? (This sentence emphasizes the action.)
Will you walk ten miles *tomorrow*? (This sentence emphasizes the time.)

Activity

Read the following sentences in at least two different ways by varying the stress. Tell what meaning you are expressing with each change in stress.

1. Anna and Carlos went to the zoo.
2. Did you like that old movie?
3. Paula won first prize.
4. We planted those tomatoes yesterday.
5. Will you practice with me now?

Enunciation

Enunciation, or exact pronunciation, conveys the spoken message clearly. When you *enunciate*, you say vowels and consonants clearly and fully. Your listener can easily understand what you are saying.

Activity A

Now try some *tuning-up* exercises to practice proper breathing and enunciation.

1. Inhale through your nose and hold your breath for ten counts. Then exhale with the sound of *ah*. This opens your throat and helps to relax the muscles so that you may breathe more easily as you speak.
2. Practice the long and short sounds of *a*.

māy	măt
māte	măn
sāy	păn

3. Practice these consonant sounds. Concentrate on enunciating each consonant clearly.

D	The double dip delighted Donna.
T	Tinkering Tom took ten toadstools.
S	The sight of the sea surprised the sailor.
Sh	Shall she shake the shawl?
Z	Zebras zoom through Zanzibar.
Zh	Azure sky measures pleasure.
J	Jeff and Jason jumped for joy.
Ch	The chattering chimps chuckled cheerily.
Th	Theodore thought his thumb had thawed.

Activity B

Now that you have had a chance to practice pitch, stress, and enunciation, recite these two poems aloud. Be sure to pronounce all of the words distinctly. Use pitch and stress to make the poems sound more interesting and to bring out the meaning of certain lines.

The Man in the Moon

The Man in the Moon as he sails the sky
Is a very remarkable skipper,
But he made a mistake when he tried to take
A drink of milk from the Dipper.
He dipped right out of the Milky Way,
And slowly and carefully filled it,
The Big Bear growled, and the Little Bear howled
And frightened him so that he spilled it!

Anonymous

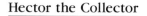

Hector the Collector

Hector the Collector
Collected bits of string,
Collected dolls with broken heads
And rusty bells that would not ring.
Pieces out of picture puzzles,
Bent-up nails and ice cream sticks,
Twists of wires, worn-out tires,
Paper bags and broken bricks.
Old chipped vases, half shoelaces,
Gatlin' guns that wouldn't shoot,
Leaky boats that wouldn't float
And stopped-up horns that wouldn't toot.
Butter knives that had no handles,
Copper keys that fit no locks,
Rings that were too small for fingers,
Dried-up leaves and patched-up socks.
Worn-out belts that had no buckles,
'Lectric trains that had no tracks,
Airplane models, broken bottles,
Three-legged chairs and cups with cracks.
Hector the Collector
Loved these things with all his soul—
Loved them more than shining diamonds,
Loved them more than glistenin' gold.
Hector called to all people,
"Come and share my treasure trunk!"
And all the silly sightless people
Came and looked . . . and called it junk.

Shel Silverstein

Lesson 2 Choral Speaking

Choral speaking is the art of speaking in a group.

Choral speaking is an enjoyable way to recite poetry. It is not a new discovery. The ancient Greeks were the first to use this manner of reciting poetry. In choral speaking, a chorus is a group of people who are divided into smaller groups according to the *pitch* of their voices. Do you think your voice is naturally high or low? If you have a low voice, the pitch of your voice is *deep*. If you have a high voice, the pitch of your voice is *light*. Many people fall in the middle and the pitch of their voice is *medium*. The natural pitch of one's voice is an essential element of choral speaking. Using the variety of voices of many students to recite a poem is fun to do and adds to the beauty and meaning of the poem.

In this lesson, you will find certain markings that aid in the phrasing and inflection (rising or falling of the voice) of the poems you recite together in chorus.

Use a falling inflection of the voice (\) for important or emphatic words:

> I see the soldiers \ dressed in gray.

Use a rising inflection of the voice (/) when asking a question:

> Are you ill? /

Pause (//) at the end of a sentence or where the thought demands a pause:

> Why, say "Sail on! / sail on! / and on!" //

In lesson 1 of this chapter, you did some *tuning-up* exercises. Here are a few more to try before you begin your choral speaking.

Tuning-up Exercises

Breathing

Inhale as if sipping. Hold your breath for ten counts, and exhale as if blowing a pinwheel. Imagine that you are making the wheel turn steadily and smoothly.

Enunciation

Practice the long and short sounds of *o* by saying the following words as they are arranged in columns. Then read across the page.

spōke	spŏt	hōpe	hŏp
lōaf	lŏt	mōde	mŏp
cōat	cŏt	rōde	rŏd

Consonant Exercise

Practice these consonant sounds. Say the sentences slowly the first few times, and then increase the speed.

Lena likes luscious long licorice lollipops.
Lilly lost her large yellow llama.
With radio and radium, we are really rich.
Rory returned the record to Roberta.

Activity A

Now you are ready to begin choral speaking. Each of the following poems has directions and inflection marks. Carefully follow the directions and the inflection marks in each of the following poems as you read in groups.

It Couldn't Be Done

LIGHT VOICES Somebody said \ that it couldn't be done, //
But he with a chuckle replied //

DEEP VOICES That "maybe it couldn't," \ but he would be one \
Who wouldn't say so \ till he'd tried. //

LIGHT VOICES So he buckled right in \ with the trace of a grin \
On his face. // If he worried \ he hid it. //

UNISON He started to sing \ as he tackled the thing \
That couldn't be done, // and he did it. //

LIGHT VOICES
SOLO Somebody scoffed: \
"Oh, you'll never do that; \
At least no one ever has done it"; //

DEEP VOICES But he took off his coat \ and he took off his hat, //
And the first thing we knew \ he'd begun it. //

LIGHT VOICES With a lift of his chin \ and a bit of a grin, //
Without any doubting or quiddit, //

UNISON He started to sing \ as he tackled the thing \
That couldn't be done, // and he did it. //

DEEP VOICES There are thousands to tell you \ it cannot be
done, //
There are thousands \ to prophesy failure; //

LIGHT VOICES There are thousands to point out to you, \ one by
one, //
The dangers that wait to assail you. //

DEEP VOICES But just buckle in \ with a bit of a grin, //
Just take off your coat \ and go to it; //

UNISON Just start to sing \ as you tackle the thing \
That "cannot be done," // and you'll do it. //

Edgar A. Guest

155

Velvet Shoes

UNISON   Let us walk in the white snow \
      In a soundless space; //
    With footsteps quiet \ and slow, \
      At a tranquil pace,\
      Under veils \ of white lace. //

LIGHT VOICES   I shall go shod in silk, \
      And you in wool, //
    White as a white cow's milk, \
      More beautiful
      Than the breast \ of a gull. //

DEEP VOICES   We shall walk \ through the still town \
      In a windless peace; //
    We shall step upon white down. /
      Upon silver fleece, \
      Upon softer \ than these. //

UNISON   We shall walk in velvet shoes: /
      Wherever we go //
    Silence \ will fall like dews \
      On white silence below. //
      We shall walk \ in the snow. //

Elinor Wylie

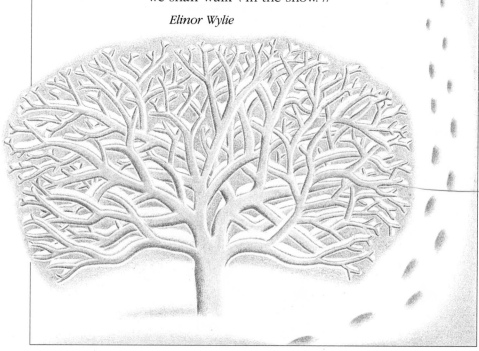

Mr. Nobody

GROUP 1: I know a funny \ little \ man, /
2:     As quiet as a mouse, /
3: Who does the mischief that is done /
4:     In everybody's house! //
5: There's no one \ ever \ sees his face, /
6:     And yet / we all agree /
7: That every plate we break \ was cracked /
UNISON   By Mr. Nobody! //

GROUP 1: 'Tis he / who always tears our books, /
2:     Who leaves the door ajar, //
3: He pulls the buttons \ from our shirts /
4:     And scatters pins afar; //
5: That squeaking door \ will always squeak /
6:     For, \ prithee, \ don't you see, /
7: We leave the oiling \ to be done /
UNISON   By Mr. Nobody. //

GROUP 1: He puts damp wood upon the fire, /
2:     That kettles cannot boil; //
3: His \ are the feet that bring in mud, /
4:     And all the carpet's soil. //
5: The papers always are mislaid, /
6:     Who had them last \ but he? //
7: There's no one \ tosses them about /
UNISON   But Mr. Nobody. //

GROUP 1: The finger-marks \ upon the door \
2:     By *none* of us / are made; //
3: We *never* \ leave the blinds unclosed, /
4:     To let the curtains fade. //
5: The ink we never spill, / the boots \
6:     That lying 'round you see /
7: Are *not our* boots; / they all belong /
UNISON   To Mr. Nobody.

    Anonymous

Stopping by Woods on a Snowy Evening

LIGHT VOICES
Whose woods these are / I think I know. //
His house is in the village though; /
He will not see me stopping here \
To watch his woods \ fill up with snow. //

MEDIUM
VOICES
My little horse must think it queer
To stop \ without a farmhouse near \
Between the woods and frozen lake \
The darkest evening of the year. //

DEEP VOICES
He gives his harness bells a shake
To ask \ if there is some mistake. //
The only other sound's \ the sweep
Of easy wind \ and downy flake. //

UNISON
The woods are lovely \ and dark \ and deep, //
But I have promises to keep. /
And miles to go \ before I sleep. //
And miles \ to go before I sleep. //

Robert Frost

Activity B

Decide as a class how you would like to read the next three poems, "The Camel's Complaint," "Raccoon," and "Wind Song." Choose which parts will be light, medium, and high voices and which will be in unison. Plan where your voices will rise and where they will fall. Finally, think about the *spirit* in which each poem should be read.

The Camel's Complaint

Canary-birds feed on sugar and seed,
　Parrots have crackers to crunch;
And, as for the poodles, they tell me the noodles
　Have chickens and cream for their lunch.
　　But there's never a question
　　About MY digestion—
　　　ANYTHING does for me!

Cats, you're aware, can repose in a chair,
　Chickens can roost upon rails;
Puppies are able to sleep in a stable,
　And oysters can slumber in pails.
　　But no one supposes
　　A poor Camel dozes—
　　　ANY PLACE does for me!

Lambs are enclosed where it's never exposed,
　Coops are constructed for hens;
Kittens are treated to houses well heated,
　And pigs are protected by pens.
　　But a Camel comes handy
　　Wherever it's sandy—
　　　ANYWHERE does for me!

People would laugh if you rode a giraffe,
　Or mounted the back of an ox;
It's nobody's habit to ride on a rabbit,
　Or try to bestraddle a fox.
　　But as for a Camel, he's
　　Ridden by families—
　　　ANY LOAD does for me!

A snake is as round as a hole in the ground,
　And weasels are wavy and sleek;
And no alligator could ever be straighter
　Than lizards that live in a creek.
　　But a Camel's all lumpy
　　And bumpy and humpy—
　　　ANY SHAPE does for me!

Charles Edward Carryl

Raccoon

One summer night a little Raccoon,
Above his left shoulder, looked at the new moon.
   He made a wish;
   He said: "I wish
   I were a Catfish,
   A Blowfish, a Squid,
   A Katydid,
   A Beetle, a Skink,
   An Ostrich, a pink
   Flamingo, a Gander,
   A Salamander,
   A Hippopotamus,
   A Duck-billed Platypus,
   A Gecko, a Slug,
   A Water Bug,
   A pug-nosed Beaver,
   Anything whatever
Except what I am, a little Raccoon!"

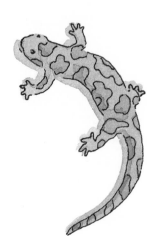

Above his left shoulder, the Evening Star
Listened and heard the little Raccoon
   Who wished on the moon;
   And she said: "Why wish
   You were a Catfish,
   A Blowfish, a Squid,
   A Katydid,
   A Beetle, a Skink,
   An Ostrich, a pink
   Flamingo, a Gander,
   A Salamander,
   A Hippopotamus,
   A Duck-billed Platypus,
   A Gecko, a Slug,
   A Water Bug,
   A pug-nosed Beaver,
   Anything whatever?
Why must you change?" said the Evening Star,
"When you are perfect as you are?
I know a boy who wished on the moon
That *he* might be a little Raccoon!"

William Jay Smith

Wind Song

When the wind blows
The quiet things speak.
Some whisper, some clang,
Some creak.

Grasses swish.
Treetops sigh.
Flags slap
and snap at the sky.
Wires on poles
whistle and hum.
Ashcans roll.
Windows drum.

When the wind goes—
suddenly
then,
the quiet things
are quiet again.

Lilian Moore

Lesson 3 Introductions

An introduction is a formal way of helping people become acquainted.

Throughout your life, you will introduce many people to each other. A skillful introduction is important. It arouses people's interest and helps get a conversation started. To introduce people properly, begin by mentioning each person's name clearly and distinctly (enunciate!). Include some interesting fact about each person, such as: *This is Ellen Jackson, the captain of our girls' basketball team*. When you are introducing a young person to an adult, first identify the young person, as in the model below.

Model: An Introduction

LINDA (*turning first to her father and then to her friend*): Dad, this is Marilyn McKenna, our class president. Marilyn, this is my father, Doctor Baker.

FATHER (*turning to Marilyn and putting out his right hand*): How do you do, Marilyn. I've heard Linda speak about you often. I'm glad to meet you.

MARILYN (*shaking hands with Doctor Baker*): Thank you, Doctor Baker. I'm glad to meet you, too.

Activity A

Form groups of three and practice these introductions. You may add interesting facts about the people.

1. Susan Mercer is a new student in your school who is interested in gymnastics. Introduce her to Miss Sheppard, the gymnastics coach.
2. You are going to an adventure movie with your friend, Billy Shaw. It is Billy's favorite movie, and he has seen it twice before. Introduce Billy to a classmate you meet in the lobby.
3. Introduce your uncle Ed Marino, a police detective, to your friend Chris Kellogg. Chris loves to read mystery stories.
4. At a charity dinner, you meet a famous hockey player. Introduce him to your best friend, who follows hockey very closely.
5. Your cousin Mary Lou Lansing is visiting from Florida. Introduce her to Jeff Kerr, who vacationed in Florida last winter.

Activity B

Form groups of three. Two students should make up new names and interesting characteristics and occupations for themselves and give this information to the third person. The third person should then introduce the two to each other. The two who are introduced should courteously acknowledge the introduction and start a brief conversation based on what they have just learned about each other.

Lesson 4 Listening to the Sounds around You

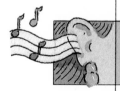

Listening is a skill that helps you become aware of what is going on all around you.

Sit still and listen carefully for a moment. What do you hear? Birds singing? Rain on the windows? Traffic in the street outside? The clock ticking? Other students whispering and giggling? Think about what these sounds tell you. What can you say about your surroundings after hearing these sounds?

Listening closely to sounds, not just *hearing* them, is an important skill. In chapter 3, you learned to use sensory impressions in your writing. *Sound* was one of those senses. The story of a camping trip can be brought to life, for example, with a description of crickets chirping, the campfire crackling, and perhaps even unexpected footsteps in the forest.

Listening carefully helps you in more than just writing. It can help you increase your awareness of what is going on around you. The sound of a car's horn as you cross the street warns you to be alert. The sound of a young child crying tells you to look and see what is wrong. You hear a siren go by. Everyone can hear the siren. However, people who listen more attentively and who think about what they hear are more likely to experience thoughts and emotions associated with the sound.

> Where is it?
> Where is it going?
> What should I do?
> I hope it's not serious.
> How frightening!
> My heart is really pounding.

These thoughts and emotions help you to understand, to act, to remember, and to describe.

Activity A

Imagine that you hear each of the following sounds. Describe each sound and tell what thoughts come to mind.

1. Someone practicing the piano late in the evening
2. A motorized sound in the sky
3. Someone coughing loudly
4. A group of people laughing heartily
5. Glass shattering
6. A screeching car
7. Someone yelling your name
8. A bell ringing unexpectedly in a crowded store
9. The splashing of a waterfall
10. The thud of a snowball against a tree

Activity B

Sit still for five minutes and listen to the sounds around you. List the different sounds you hear. When the five minutes are up, write the thoughts that each sound brings to your mind.

Lesson 5 Listening for Information

In listening for information, take notes to remember important details.

In most of your everyday conversations, the details you need to remember stay in your mind. You remember what is essential. Other times, however, you may want to write down the information to help you remember it accurately. For example, you may be taking a telephone message, listening to your teacher lecture about the Civil War, or interviewing someone for your school newspaper. In such instances you must take *notes*—written records of important details.

In chapter 4, you learned about note taking for a written report. There are many other reasons for taking notes, such as passing on messages, remembering information, and studying for a test. Some of the notes you take may be brief, while others must contain a number of details. Often your notes will have to be rewritten later in a more readable form. Look at the following examples of notes.

Model: A Telephone Message Received by the Answering Service of a Busy Executive

CALL FOR: Ms. Tracy
FROM: Mr. Goodman
            Goodman Limousine Service
            Dallas, Texas
DATE: Tuesday, April 4, 19____
TIME: 8:30 A.M.

Your limousine will be waiting at the Dallas Airport this evening. The driver will meet you at the baggage claim area at 7:30 P.M. If there is any change in your plans, call (214) 555-1200.

Model: A Telephone Message Received by Scott's Mother While Scott Was at the Doctor's Office

Message from Mike to Scott
—History quiz tomorrow, chapter on Roman Republic and Empire
—Math homework for tomorrow—Chapter 12, exercises 1–7
—Charity drive begins tomorrow. Bring your contribution.
—Trip to the Science Museum next Thursday, June 3. Be sure to pick up a permission slip.
—Practice for softball playoffs tomorrow at 3:00. Bring your "Roger Maris" bat.
—Hope you're feeling better. See you tomorrow.

Model: Classroom Notes

—Abraham Lincoln elected President in 1860.
—Many Southerners did not like Lincoln because of his stand against slavery.
—Soon after election, eleven states withdrew from Union and formed Confederate States of America.
—(and so on)

Activity A

Imagine that you have just answered the phone. The caller has asked for your mother, but she is not at home. Your teacher will pretend to be the caller and give you the message. Listen carefully and jot down notes. Then write out the message as accurately as you can.

Activity B

Make up a realistic-sounding telephone message that includes names, dates, and times. Read the message to another student, and have that student take notes. After the notes have been rewritten as a reminder, or *memo*, check to see that the information is clear and accurate. Then reverse roles. You take notes as your partner gives a message.

Writing Corner 6

Interviewing

Interviewing people is an interesting way for you to collect information for a report. In an interview, you would talk with someone and ask questions related to the report you were preparing. Study how Martin used an interview to prepare a report for his class.

Martin's class was working on a project called "Living History." The class realized that there were older people in their families and neighborhoods who were living history references. Each class member would *interview* one of these interesting people, write a report about the interview, and share it with the class.

Martin had heard his neighbor, Mrs. Haywood, talk about her childhood memories of the years when the United States was involved in World War II. He decided to interview Mrs. Haywood. These are the steps he followed.

Before the Interview

1. Martin called Mrs. Haywood *well in advance*. He explained the project and asked her for a short interview.
2. After she agreed, Martin asked her to suggest a *time* and *place* that would be convenient for her. He also asked her to *suggest* a few *ideas* she might like to talk about.
3. From her suggestions, and from an article he had read about United States civilians during World War II, Martin *prepared several thoughtful questions*. He wrote each question on the top of a separate card before the interview.

   What are your clearest memories about World War II?
   Do you recall anything about your experiences with food rationing, war bonds, or conserving scrap metal?
   Did your house have a small flag in the window with a star on it? Tell what you remember about this custom or any other special customs.

During the Interview

As Mrs. Haywood responded to the questions, Martin wrote a few words on each card. Most of the time, however, Martin did *not* write. He *listened* very carefully. If something wasn't clear, he asked about it. Then he listened again to Mrs. Haywood's response. At the end of the interview, Martin thanked her politely.

After the Interview

1. Right after the interview, Martin wrote the details he could remember from Mrs. Haywood's answers on the cards with the questions. He used these cards to write a report for the class.
2. He divided his report into paragraphs according to topic. For example, he wrote everything Mrs. Haywood remembered about food rationing in one paragraph.
3. Martin left out ideas that were repeated and selected the most interesting parts.
4. He wrote a paragraph at the beginning of his report about why he decided to interview Mrs. Haywood. At the end of the report, he said how he felt about what he had learned.

★ Interview a person who could answer the same questions that Martin prepared. Write your own report on this topic.
OR
Prepare questions for a person you know who could give you and your class interesting information about a different topic. Report on your interview.

Here are some topic ideas: how to run faster, how to care for houseplants, special activities in your community in which sixth-graders can participate.

Misused Words

Certain words that sound alike or that are similar in sound or spelling are often misused.

Pairs of similar words may cause confusion. One may be incorrectly used instead of the other. Some pairs are homophones, such as *passed* and *past*. Other pairs are words that are quite close in sound and in spelling, such as *were* and *where*. When you write, be careful to spell similar-sounding words correctly.

Activity A

The words in each set are often misused. Give the definition for the part of speech listed. Use the dictionary to complete the activity.

	Part of Speech	Definition
1. accept	verb	_____
except	preposition	_____
2. its	adjective	_____
it's	contraction	_____
3. loose	adjective	_____
lose	verb	_____
4. passed	verb	_____
past	preposition/adverb	_____
5. quiet	adjective	_____
quite	adverb	_____
6. than	conjunction	_____
then	adverb	_____
7. right	adjective	_____
write	verb	_____
8. were	verb	_____
where	adverb	_____

Activity B

Complete each sentence with the correct word from the list of misused words in activity A.

1. A famous quotation of the frontiersman Davy Crockett was "Be sure you're _____ and _____ go ahead."
2. Name one animal that is larger _____ an elephant.
3. _____ chilly outside today.
4. _____ _____ you when the electricity went out?
5. Mr. Pariser looked with horror at his new car and _____ dented fender.
6. When the bus was ready to leave, everyone was accounted for—_____ Amy.
7. The operator asked, "Will you _____ a collect call?"
8. In 1863, Jules Verne began to _____ his fascinating science fiction stories.
9. Walking through the snow on Christmas Eve, Miguel noticed how _____ the neighborhood was.
10. The seaplane _____ over the shore and landed smoothly on the lake.
11. Did anyone here _____ a black and white ski mitten?
12. The two sprinters streaked _____ the finish line at the same time.
13. The doorknob on the old house was _____, and it squeaked when I turned it.
14. Thomas Rockwell's book *How to Eat Fried Worms* is _____ popular with children.
15. Babies actually have more bones _____ adults.

Chapter 7

Library Skills

Lesson 1 The Organization of the Library

Knowing the arrangement of the library helps you to find information easily.

Where would you go to find a good story to read at the beach or to find information on the latest explorations into space? Where could you obtain the answers to questions such as these:

> What did Jim Thorpe accomplish?
> Who wrote *Mrs. Frisby and the Rats of NIMH?*
> How does a newspaper story develop?

You can find answers to these questions—and a wealth of other information as well—in your community or school library.

Sometimes, it is enjoyable just to browse through a library and see what is there. However, if you have an assignment or report to complete by a certain date, you will want to find materials and information as quickly as possible. Therefore, you need to know *what kinds* of books and information your library contains and *where* these materials can be found.

In the library, books are classified into two major groups: *fiction* and *nonfiction*. The nonfiction group contains a special group of books called *reference books*.

Exploring unfamiliar territory is a risk and an adventure. How does reading help you explore unfamiliar worlds?

Fiction Books

The group of fiction books, or fiction collection, is found in a special section of the library. These books, which are made-up stories, are arranged alphabetically, according to the author's last name. Most libraries identify fiction books with an *F* on the spine, or back edge. A shelf of fiction books, arranged in the correct order, would look like this:

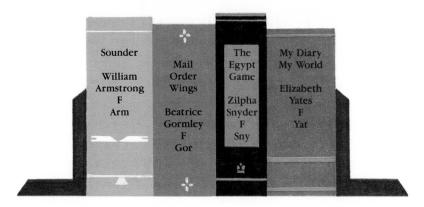

Activity

Visit the fiction section of your library. Copy the titles and authors of ten fiction books that look interesting to you. List them alphabetically, using the last names of the authors.

Nonfiction Books

The difference between fiction and nonfiction books is the difference between a story (something a writer has made up) and facts (things that actually happen or have happened). Nonfiction can be the record of a person's experiences, the historical record of a nation, or a book on one of the many sciences that explain the world of nature.

In most libraries, the collection of nonfiction is larger than the fiction collection. Nonfiction collections contain books from a vast number of subject areas. Because so many subjects are included in the nonfiction area, a system of classification is necessary for books to be located easily. In 1876, Melvil Dewey set up such a system. It is the most widely used library system in the world.

Dewey grouped all nonfiction books into ten major subject areas and assigned a group of numbers to each area. The system, which was named after him, is called the Dewey Decimal Classification System. The ten major areas and the range of their numbers are listed below. Subjects included in each of the areas are listed at the right.

000–099	General Reference	Encyclopedias, almanacs
100–199	Philosophy and Psychology	Beliefs, morals, personality
200–299	Religion	Bible, mythology
300–399	Social Sciences	Education, government, law
400–499	Languages	Foreign languages, dictionaries
500–599	Sciences	Astronomy, math, zoology
600–699	Useful Arts	Business, cooking, medicine, sewing, television
700–799	Fine Arts	Acting, music, painting, photography, sports
800–899	Literature	Novels, plays, poetry
900–999	History	Biography, geography, travel

This numbering system is not limited to the three-place numbers from 000 to 999. Numbers can be expanded by placing a decimal point after the three-digit numbers. This "decimal" system helps to create subdivisions for each category. For example, under Useful Arts (the 600–699 range of numbers), there are many subdivisions that have not been shown on the chart above. "Domestic animals" has the number 636. One subdivision is for Horses (636.1); another is for Dogs (636.7).

Activity

After studying the chart of the Dewey Decimal Classification on page 175, decide to which group of numbers you would go to find a book on each of the following topics.

1. Soccer
2. Spanish
3. Greek mythology
4. A biography of Bill Cosby
5. The sun and planets
6. A play to perform for Thanksgiving
7. The paintings of Mary Cassatt
8. Learning to sew
9. Modern philosophy
10. Schools in America

The Boating Party by Mary Cassatt

Lesson 2 The Card Catalog

The card catalog helps you to find books in your library quickly and easily.

Suppose your teacher assigns you a report on underwater exploration. In a conversation, your friend tells you that C. S. Lewis is a good author. Later, a classmate recommends the book *From the Mixed-up Files of Mrs. Basil E. Frankweiler*. Where can you find the information you need for your report, some books by C. S. Lewis, and *The Mixed-up Files of Mrs. Basil E. Frankweiler*? The place to begin is the library's card catalog.

The card catalog may be a computer terminal, or it may be a cabinet with small drawers containing 3″ x 5″ cards. In a cabinet, you will find material arranged alphabetically.

For fiction books, there are two listings: one lists the books by authors; the other, by titles. Each entry contains the same information about the book, but in a slightly different order.

If you know an author's name and want to find out the titles of his or her books, you should look up the *last* name of the author. Here are how the headings for two *author* cards for C. S. Lewis would look:

F
Lew   **Lewis, C. S.**
             The Lion, the Witch, and the Wardrobe

F
Lew   **Lewis, C. S.**
             Out of the Silent Planet

If you know only the title of a book, you have to consult the *title* card. The information is the same as on the author card except that the title is printed first. Title cards are arranged alphabetically according to the first word of the title. The words *a*, *an*, and *the* are not used for alphabetical arrangement. If you were looking for the title *The Lion, the Witch, and the Wardrobe*, you would look under the letter *L*, not *T*. A sample beginning of a title card is shown below.

> The Lion, the Witch, and the Wardrobe
>
> F
> Lew   Lewis, C. S.

The letters "F Lew" appear on both the author card and the title card. To find a book by C. S. Lewis, you would go to the shelves where the fiction books are located. You would look for the *L* section. There you would find the C. S. Lewis books that were available. Sometimes the book you want is not on the shelf, but you know from the card catalog that the library has a copy. You might request that the librarian put you on a waiting list for the book. You will then be notified when the book is available.

Nonfiction books have three kinds of cards: *author*, *title*, and *subject*. When you want to find information on a certain subject, such as underwater exploration, you need to refer to the *subject* card. There might be several subject cards for a particular subject, each listing a different book. After you checked all the cards on your subject, you would write down the titles and the identifying numbers of the books you wanted to use. At the top of the next page is a sample subject card for the subject "castles."

A castle in Spain

Castles

728.8
Sa5c   **Sancha, Sheila**
        The Castle Story. Crowell, 1983.
            224p   illus

        A reference that includes considerable information about
        types of castles.

        1 Castles   2 Buildings—Middle Ages   3 Architecture—
        History of
        I. Sancha, Sheila   II. Title

In the upper left-hand corner of each card is the call number. The first line is the Dewey decimal number assigned to the book. This is the number you would use to find the book on the shelf. Most libraries have maps posted showing you where each group of numbers (200s, 400s, 700s, and so on) is located. Once you find the correct shelf, you would then refer to the second line of the call number (*S* in the example) to find your book. The second line consists of the first letter or letters of the author's last name.

A helpful feature of most catalog cards consists of the cross references. Cross references are the numbered subject areas printed near the bottom of the card. These references suggest other topics for you to explore in order to obtain additional material.

If you looked up the subject "space flight," for example, you would probably find these cross references:
1. Aviation
2. Astronauts
3. Project Apollo

A castle in Germany

Activity A

Visit the library and use the card catalog to complete this assignment.

1. List two books by each author.
   a. Ursula Le Guin
   b. Madeleine L'Engle
   c. Scott O'Dell
   d. Robert Louis Stevenson
   e. Joseph Krumgold
2. Locate the title card for each of the following books and name the author.
   a. *Charlotte's Web*
   b. *The Secret of Crossbone Hill*
   c. *American Tall Tales*
   d. *The Witch of Blackbird Pond*
   e. *The Planet of Junior Brown*

Activity B

Use the card catalog in your library to answer the following items.

1. Who wrote the book *Little Women*?
2. Name a book by Elizabeth Speare.
3. Name a title and author from the subject area "transportation."
4. Who wrote *The Hobbit*?
5. Name two books written by Laura Ingalls Wilder.

Activity C

Visit your school or local library and look up the following subjects. List three cross references for each.

Pets
Sports
Hobbies
Music

Lesson 3 Dictionary Skills

A dictionary is a book of words arranged in alphabetical order. A dictionary provides the correct pronunciation, spelling, and definition of each word.

There are many different kinds of dictionaries. There are pocket dictionaries. There are dictionaries just for grammar school students, for high school students, and for college students. There are dictionaries that list the names of famous people. Each has a special purpose.

Dictionary writers, called lexicographers, work hard to include words that will fit the needs of the group for whom the dictionary is intended. A large dictionary may have more than one half million words. A dictionary for beginning readers may have only 30,000 words. For example, the word *funambulist* (tightrope walker) would appear in an advanced dictionary but not in a dictionary for beginning readers. It would be considered too difficult and not very common.

Alphabetical Order

Dictionary entries are arranged in alphabetical order. How well do you know your alphabet? The following exercise helps you check on how quickly you can alphabetize words.

Activity A

Alphabetize the words in each set as quickly and accurately as you can.

By First Letter	By Second Letter
honorable	persevere
suite	profile
windmill	pagoda
criticism	piccolo
venture	pyramid
refund	plague
luxury	physical
keystone	positive
goblet	pulse
journal	psychology

By Third Letter	By Fourth Letter
devotion	tricycle
decline	trillion
determine	triple
defraud	triumph
deposit	trial
destiny	trinket
derby	tribute

Activity B

Make up a list of eight to ten words beginning with *ar*. Each word should have a different third letter. Mix up the words and prepare an exercise to be given to another student to alphabetize. Do the same activity with words beginning with *do*, *mar*, and *sto*.

Guide Words

The two words printed at the top of every dictionary page are called *guide words*. They help you locate your word. The first word is the first entry on that particular page, and the second word is the last entry. Any word coming alphabetically between these two guide words will be located on that page. Here are two sample pages from a dictionary showing guide words.

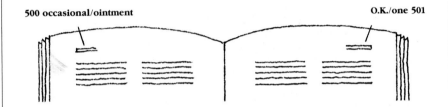

500 occasional/ointment

O.K./one 501

Off would be found on page 500 because *of* comes after *oc* and before *oi* in the alphabet. The word *old* would appear on page 501 since *ol* comes after *ok* and before *on*. The word *only* would come after page 501 because *onl* comes after *one*, and *one* is the last entry on page 501.

Activity A

Use the guide words in the introduction, and indicate whether each word below would be located *before* page 500, on page *500*, on page *501*, or *after* page 501.

1. occupy
2. onion
3. Oklahoma
4. ocean
5. octopus
6. occasion
7. Olympic
8. omit
9. obtain

Activity B

Set up *opossum* and *orchestra* as guide words. Write two words that would appear in your dictionary right before this page, four words that would appear on this page, and two words that would appear after this page. Do the same activity with *genealogy* and *gerbil* as guide words.

Reading a Dictionary Entry

Knowing all the parts included in a dictionary entry can help you discover important information about a word. The following sample shows you what is included in most entries.

A. division into syllables
B. pronunciation
C. accent
D. part of speech
E. definition
F. sample phrase or sentence

per mit (pər mĭt´ for 1, 2; pər´ mĭt or pər mĭt´ for 3) —v. 1 let; allow: *Her parents will not permit her to travel alone.* 2 give an opportunity: *If the weather permits, we'll head for the lake.* —n. 3 a license granted by one in authority: *Fishing permits are now available.*

Activity A

Refer to the sample dictionary entry to answer the following questions.

1. How many parts of speech are listed for *permit* in the entry?
2. How many meanings are listed for *permit* as a noun?
3. When *permit* is used as a verb, which syllable is accented?
4. Write the second definition of *permit* as a verb.
5. How many pronunciations are listed for *permit* as a noun?

Activity B

Tell whether *permit* is used as a *verb* or a *noun* in each sentence below. Then give the number of the definition that best shows how *permit* is used.

1. In a few days, Sally will receive her driving *permit*.
2. The guard *permitted* the reporters to enter the building.
3. If time *permits*, the guide will show us the Egyptian mummies.
4. *Permit* me to explain why I was late.
5. Do we need a *permit* to sell lemonade on the street?

Lesson 4 Thesaurus

A thesaurus is a special reference book that lists synonyms.

A thesaurus is a special kind of word book that lists synonyms. Synonyms are words that have the same or almost the same meaning.

Suppose you have written the following sentence:

> The carousel I rode in Santa Clara was *big*—it was ten stories high!

You decide that *big* is not a strong enough word to explain how big the carousel was. You look up the word *big* in a thesaurus, and you find the words *enormous, gigantic, huge,* and *large* as synonyms of *big*. You decide that *gigantic* is the best word to use to replace *big*.

In a thesaurus, words are generally arranged in alphabetical order, as in a dictionary. An entry might look like this:

bashful   shy, timid, modest   **bold**

The words *shy, timid*, and *modest* are synonyms for *bashful*. The word *bold* is an antonym for *bashful*. Often antonyms, or words opposite in meaning, are given in a thesaurus. Look up in a dictionary any words you do not understand. From the list of synonyms, you would choose the word that best fits the meaning of what you want to say.

185

In another kind of thesaurus, synonyms for a word would appear under a main entry. A sample entry would look like this:

BLOCK

As a verb, *block* means "to stop the movement of."

SYNONYMS

delay   To stop for a time
The teacher *delayed* the deadline for our reports.

hinder   To slow down the movement of something
The bad weather *hindered* the construction of the skyscraper.

prevent   To keep something from happening
Doctors try to *prevent* diseases from starting.

prohibit   To refuse to allow to be done
The city *prohibits* swimming at public beaches after 8 P.M.

This kind of thesaurus usually has an index. It is often best to look in the index first. Many times the word for which you need a synonym will not appear as a main entry, but will appear as a synonym *under* a main entry.

Why is a thesaurus a helpful tool? A thesaurus can help you
1. express yourself more exactly
2. build your vocabulary
3. improve your writing
4. avoid using the same word over and over in your writing

Activity A

1. Look up each word below in a thesaurus. Write three synonyms for each.

   awful   eat   funny   speak

2. Look up each word below in a thesaurus. Write two antonyms for each.

   make   quiet   rough

Activity B

Find the synonym for *block* that best completes each sentence. Use the sample entry on the left-hand page.

1. I tried to catch the vase, but I could not _____ it from falling and breaking.
2. Because of rain, it was necessary to _____ the start of the baseball game.
3. The government does _____ private citizens from printing money.
4. Messy handwriting will _____ reading.

Activity C

Each pair of sentences has the same italicized word. Look up the italicized word in a thesaurus, and rewrite each sentence using a more exact synonym.

1. The historical commission will *plan* the Fourth of July celebration.
   In a book by E. L. Konigsburg, Claudia and Jaime succeeded in their *plan* to spend a week in the Metropolitan Museum.
2. Fred was *sad* when his friend moved away.
   The Baker family was *sad* at the loss of their grandmother.
3. Pennsylvania was *started* by the Quakers.
   A general meeting and social *started* our year.
4. He *ended* the test as the bell rang.
   Our class *ended* the year with a party.
5. I have a strong *belief* that an education is important to success.
   The teacher's *belief* in Adam has helped him to win the poetry contest.

Lesson 5 Using Other Reference Tools

Reference materials are books designed to give information and facts on a wide variety of subjects.

Each kind of reference material has its special purpose. There are three kinds of reference materials that you will be studying: encyclopedias, almanacs, and atlases.

Become familiar with these reference materials and where they are located in your library so you can use these materials effectively and your time in the library efficiently.

Using the Encyclopedia

An encyclopedia is a set of books containing articles, pictures, and maps. It gives general information about people, places, things, and events. People with special knowledge in each area provide the information. Therefore, hundreds of people contribute their knowledge, talent, and research to produce an encyclopedia.

Encyclopedia articles are arranged in alphabetical order. Guide letters on the spine of each volume inform you that articles beginning with that letter can be found in that particular volume. For example, an article on "Rome" could be found in the *R* volume of the encyclopedia.

Just as there are guide words in a dictionary, there are guide words in an encyclopedia to help you find articles. However, in an encyclopedia, there is only one guide word at the top of each page. Articles that fit alphabetically between the two guide words will be found on either of the two pages. Look at the two guide words in the illustration on the top of the next page.

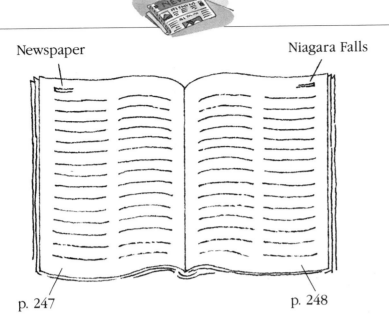

Newspaper   Niagara Falls

p. 247   p. 248

An article on "Newton, Sir Isaac" would be found on this set of pages since *Newt* comes after *news* and before *Ni*. An article on "Nicaragua" would come after page 248 since *Nic* comes after *Nia* in alphabetical order.

In order to find information in your encyclopedia, you might need to find the main idea of your topic. For example, if you were doing a report on "holiday customs in Japan," the main idea would be Japan. Articles that contain a great deal of information are usually divided into sections. For example, "Holiday and Customs" might be a subtitle under the general heading of "Japan." The most efficient way to use an encyclopedia is to find the general heading and then locate the specific subtitle.

Sir Isaac Newton

Another important feature of the encyclopedia is the cross-reference section at the end of the article. These titles suggest other articles to which you can refer if you need more information. For example, if you looked up "Nursery School," the cross references at the end of the article might be "Education," "History of Education," "Kindergarten," "Elementary School," and "Owen, Robert."

Activity A

Identify the main topic in an encyclopedia that would contain information on each of the following.

1. Name five aquariums in the United States.
2. How are photographs developed?
3. What are a few of the customs and ceremonies of Buddhism?
4. What is the capital, state bird, and state flower of Illinois?
5. Name some of the methods of food preservation.
6. Name the five basic emotions.

Activity B

Consult your encyclopedia for the following articles. Name two cross references that would give more information on the topic.

Entry	Cross References
Olympic Games	
Heart	
Bees	
Alphabet	
Blindness	
Grand Canyon	

Using the Almanac

An almanac is a reference book with current general information. It contains facts, general data, and current statistics on many subjects. An almanac is published every year so that all its information is kept up to date. As a result, a 1988 almanac would contain world information, government data, and population statistics from 1987.

A table of contents and an index are provided to help you find your information.

The most commonly used almanacs are

The World Almanac and Book of Facts
Information Please Almanac
Guinness Book of World Records

Activity A

Study this section from the general index of *The World Almanac and Book of Facts*. To which pages would you refer if you were trying to answer the following questions?

1. What are the current world pole vault records?
2. What are the words of the Pledge of Allegiance?
3. What are the changing patterns in the United States population?
4. Which playwrights received the Pulitzer Prizes last year?
5. What awards are given to poets?
6. What is the American Indian population of the United States?
7. Who discovered the North Pole?
8. If you looked up Pope John Paul II, to what entry in the index would you be referred?

A famous explorer at the North Pole

Activity B

Make up a quiz that requires the use of the almanac. Think of some main topics that an almanac would contain—for example, state capitals. Using the almanac, make a list of state capitals on a piece of paper. In a column across from this list, list the state for each capital, but mix up the order. Exchange papers with a partner. Use the almanac to match the pieces of information. (Other ideas are matching Olympic winners with the year or the field in which they won medals, or matching presidents with their birthplaces.)

Using the Atlas

An atlas is a reference book with maps. You can use an atlas to locate cities, towns, countries, continents, bodies of water, islands, or mountains and to find geographical information about such places. In addition, most atlases also give information on population, climate, and products. A table of contents in the front of an atlas or an index at the back will help you find the information you need.

Activity

Draw a map of your state. Label the major cities, bodies of water, boundaries, and the state capital.

Review of Library Materials

You now have a good overview on how to use the library efficiently and enjoyably. You have seen how each resource book helps you with a different kind of information. Try this review. For each statement or question below, tell which source you would use to find the information. For some items, more than one source would be correct.

A. a dictionary
B. a thesaurus
C. the card catalog
D. an encyclopedia
E. the almanac
F. an atlas

1. If you spent your vacation in Wyoming, what national parks could you visit?
2. Give two antonyms for the word *hurry*.
3. Is the book *Bridge to Teribithia* in your library?
4. What is a "queue," and how do you pronounce the word?
5. Give the definition of *marmoset*.
6. Does your library contain any *books* about knights in the Middle Ages?
7. What highway would you take from Atlanta, Georgia, to Montgomery, Alabama?
8. What are the different varieties of apples, and which are the leading apple-producing states?
9. What are the names of the present state governors?
10. Give a few more exact words for "walking."

Exploring Our Language

Part II

Grammar, Correct Usage, Mechanics

Chapter 1

Nouns

Lesson 1 Kinds of Nouns

A noun is a name word.

Read this paragraph. Each of the words printed in italics is a noun. Tell whether each names a person, place, or thing.

> The *sandwich*, which is easy to make and eat, is a common *food* in the *United States*. The *sandwich* is named after the *Earl of Sandwich*. This *aristocrat* lived in *England* two hundred *years* ago. The *earl* enjoyed *games* so much that he disliked stopping to eat. Then he had an *idea*. He had a *servant* put *meat* between two *slices* of *bread*, and he ate this while playing. Interestingly, the *earl* has another *connection* with *America*. An *explorer* named a *group* of *islands* after him. Those *Sandwich Islands* are now called by their original *name* of *Hawaii*.

The Earl never dreamed that today there would be different names for his sandwich. Can you name some? Submarine...

Proper Nouns and Common Nouns

There are two main kinds of nouns: *proper* and *common*.

> **A proper noun names a particular person, place, or thing.**
>
> **A common noun names one member of a class of persons, places, or things.**

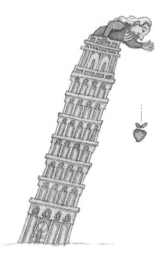

	PROPER NOUNS	COMMON NOUNS
PERSON	Galileo	scientist
PLACE	Seattle	city
THING	*Voyager 2*	satellite

Proper nouns may contain several words. The important words in proper nouns are capitalized.

the Great Wall of China   the Rock of Gibraltar

Exercise 1

Find the nouns in these sentences. Tell whether each noun is *proper* or *common*.

1. Rhode Island is the smallest state in the United States.
2. The attic of Greenwood Public Library is full of bats!
3. Christopher Columbus was always interested in ships.
4. Diana was a goddess of the Romans.
5. The boat sailed down the Mississippi River.
6. Ancient castles stand on the rugged hills of Belgium.
7. Beautiful lilacs bloom in our garden in May.
8. The teeth of a shark are as hard as steel.
9. The delicatessen bakes a giant cake each Fourth of July.
10. Buffalo Bill was a rider for the Pony Express.
11. Monica Carey lives in Chicago.
12. A storyteller from Africa told a legend of the spider.
13. The glassware sparkled on the table.
14. The visitors were fascinated by the Cascade Mountains.
15. The pyramids in Egypt are very old.

Exercise 2

Write a proper noun for each common noun.

Example: common noun, *state*
proper noun, *Wisconsin*

river	ocean	hero	explorer
island	street	museum	teacher
continent	building	holiday	author

Exercise 3

Write a common noun for each proper noun.

Example: proper noun, *Poland*
common noun, *country*

Kentucky	Dodgers	Paris	*Santa Maria*
Edison	Alps	Labor Day	Mediterranean
Mexico	Picasso	Amazon	Amy

Collective Nouns

> **A collective noun names a group of persons, animals, or things considered as a unit.**

Our *class* is large.

This sentence names all the students in a grade as one group. They make up the group known as our *class. Class* is, therefore, a collective noun. It is the name of a group of persons *considered as one*.

Here are some groups of persons or things that may be named by collective nouns.

GROUPS OF PERSONS OR THINGS	COLLECTIVE NOUNS
worshipers in church	congregation
ships of a navy	fleet
athletes who play together	team

Exercise 4

Find the collective nouns in these sentences.

1. Our committee uses a computer to plan the year's basketball schedules.
2. Today I saw a flock of geese flying south.
3. The storm took the crew of the sailboat by surprise.
4. The troop of scouts learned how to fold a tent.
5. The team of horses belonging to George Washington had a daily tooth cleaning.
6. The secretary of a club writes the minutes.
7. A bear on roller skates juggled eggs for the crowd.
8. Tom's family wanted an apartment near the city park.
9. The audience heard squeals instead of music when a mouse ran through the orchestra.
10. A colony of bees has workers, drones, and a queen.

Exercise 5

Make two columns on a paper. In the first, list all the collective nouns in these sentences. In the second, list the group of persons or things named by each collective noun.

Example: The fleet sailed at dawn.

COLLECTIVE NOUN	GROUP OF PERSONS OR THINGS
fleet	ships

1. The shepherd took special care of his flock.
2. Our organization is raising money to help save the whales.
3. Ray directed the cowhands who were trying to stop the stampeding herd.
4. Is the band rehearsing this afternoon?
5. As the audience applauded, the cast bowed.

Abstract Nouns

> An abstract noun expresses a quality or condition. It names something that cannot be seen or touched.

A marathon runner needs *strength* and *confidence* to finish a race.

Notice the abstract nouns in this sentence. They are *strength* and *confidence*. They name *qualities* a person can have.

Collective and *abstract* nouns are usually included among common nouns.

Exercise 6

Find the abstract nouns in these sentences.
1. Kim showed her flying ability as she landed the plane in a rocky field.
2. We admired the beauty of the handmade quilt.
3. If goldfish are left in darkness, they may turn white.
4. Can anyone ever have complete freedom?
5. Perseverance helped Shawn win the pie-eating contest.
6. It was Lloyd's idea to put the lobster in his mother's bathtub.
7. A cockroach will run to safety and clean itself if it touches a human being.
8. Joe spent most of his childhood on an Indian reservation.
9. George loses his patience when the bus is late.
10. Mrs. Cowell's knowledge of giraffes amazed the zookeepers.
11. A fear of water kept the puppy away from the flooded river.
12. The aviator Amelia Earhart possessed great courage.
13. The principal kept her promise—a free lunch for all.
14. Seth was in the garden when he noticed a strange smell.
15. Greta's ambition is to be the best soccer player in the city.

Exercise 7

Use these abstract nouns in sentences of your own.

charity	cleanliness	cheerfulness
sickness	enthusiasm	confidence
patriotism	pride	vitality
strength	happiness	pleasure
truth	humility	bravery

Exercise 8

Many abstract nouns may be formed from other words by adding the suffixes *-hood, -ion, -ity, -ment, -ness, -ship,* or *-ty.* Make abstract nouns from these words by adding the proper suffix. Then use each of the nouns in a sentence.

loyal	friend	swift
good	truthful	companion
enjoy	bright	protect
kind	knight	rapid
honest	celebrate	entertain
leader	major	detect

Exercise 9

Tell whether each noun is *abstract* or *collective.* Then use each one in a sentence of your own.

committee	hope	crew
carelessness	ambition	fleet
convoy	honesty	band
group	wisdom	gratitude

Concrete Nouns

> **A concrete noun names a thing we can see or touch.**
> **Most of the nouns we use are concrete nouns.**

Here are examples of concrete nouns.

bridge	violet
pilot	seal
Japan	Mount Everest

Exercise 10

Find the concrete nouns in these sentences.
1. Did you see the mischievous raccoon?
2. The dictionary was so big the librarian could barely lift it.
3. Huge waves washed the rocky cliffs.
4. Larry stood on the icy sidewalk with a shovel.
5. The Hawaiian Islands are actually the tops of volcanoes.
6. A strange dog dashed through our yard.
7. Early hunters in the Philippine Islands used the yo-yo as a weapon.
8. Who baked these delicious cookies?
9. The young boy needed a map to find the subway.
10. The students could see Mars clearly through the telescope.
11. The plumber took the pipe apart and found a ring inside.
12. A book of poems was selected.
13. Don't you wonder what is hidden in that old wooden trunk?
14. Some termites in Africa build mounds thirty feet tall!
15. Do you like jam on your bread?

A termite mound in Africa

Words Used as Nouns and Verbs

A noun is a name word. A verb expresses action or being. Many words can be used as either nouns or verbs.

We decided not to go to the *dance*. (*Noun*)
I *dance* to all kinds of music. (*Verb*)

Exercise 11

Tell whether each italicized word is a noun or a verb.

1. We left our blankets in the *shade* of the beach umbrella.
2. Elm trees *shade* Marina's prizewinning tulip beds.
3. Did Mark Twain really *pilot* a riverboat?
4. The *pilot* double-checked the map of small airports.
5. The Giorgio brothers still *work* in their Italian restaurant.
6. That *work* on the farm was harder than I expected.
7. We're planning a solar *experiment* for the first of May.
8. I *experiment* with color before I do a final design.
9. The top *step* was coated with ice.
10. Do not *step* on the mousetrap.
11. *Cover* the aquarium before you vacuum!
12. Kate drew a kangaroo on the *cover* of my notebook.
13. The *cut* required three stitches!
14. Paul Bunyan could *cut* a tree in half with one easy swing!
15. After pinning the pattern to the material, I *cut* the pieces for the dress.

Practice Power

Last night you met a very unusual person in a dream. Write a short paragraph about this interesting character. Include proper, collective, and abstract nouns.

204

Lesson 2 Qualities of Nouns

A noun has number, gender, and case. These are the *qualities* of a noun.

In this lesson, you will study *number* and *gender*. In the next lessons, you will learn about *case*.

Number

Number shows whether a noun refers to one person or thing (singular number) or more than one (plural number).

That *rose* is the most beautiful of all the *roses* in our garden.

Rose is singular; *roses* is plural. This change in the form of a noun to show whether the noun refers to one or more than one is called number.

Rules for Forming the Plural

Here are ten rules for forming the plural of nouns. If you want to use the plural of a noun that does not seem to be included in the rules, use the dictionary. You will find that a choice of plural forms is given for some words. In such cases, more than one form would be correct: for example, volcanos, volcanoes.

1. Most nouns form the plural by adding *s* to the singular.

SINGULAR	PLURAL		SINGULAR	PLURAL
home	homes		book	books
nurse	nurses		song	songs

2. Nouns ending in *s, x, z, ch,* and *sh* form the plural by adding *es* to the singular.

SINGULAR	PLURAL	SINGULAR	PLURAL
gas	gases	torch	torches
fox	foxes	sash	sashes
topaz	topazes	wish	wishes
dress	dresses	box	boxes

3. Nouns ending in *y*:
   a. Nouns ending in *y* preceded by a consonant form the plural by changing the *y* to *i* and adding *es*.

SINGULAR	PLURAL	SINGULAR	PLURAL
country	countries	baby	babies
melody	melodies	city	cities
duty	duties	fly	flies
colony	colonies	cry	cries

   b. Nouns ending in *y* preceded by a vowel form the plural by adding *s* to the singular.

SINGULAR	PLURAL	SINGULAR	PLURAL
day	days	pulley	pulleys
turkey	turkeys	play	plays
valley	valleys	chimney	chimneys
key	keys	attorney	attorneys

4. Nouns ending in *f* or *fe*:
   a. Most nouns ending in *f* or *fe* form the plural by adding *s* to the singular:

SINGULAR	PLURAL	SINGULAR	PLURAL
roof	roofs	safe	safes

   b. Some nouns ending in *f* or *fe* form the plural by changing the *f* or *fe* to *ves*:

SINGULAR	PLURAL	SINGULAR	PLURAL
scarf	scarves	loaf	loaves
half	halves	shelf	shelves
knife	knives	wolf	wolves
life	lives	thief	thieves

Use a dictionary if you are not sure of a spelling.

5. Nouns ending in *o*:

   a. All nouns ending in *o* preceded by a vowel form the plural by adding *s* to the singular.

SINGULAR	PLURAL	SINGULAR	PLURAL
radio	radios	bamboo	bamboos
cameo	cameos	studio	studios
trio	trios	portfolio	portfolios

   b. Nouns ending in *o* preceded by a consonant generally form the plural by adding *es* to the singular.

SINGULAR	PLURAL	SINGULAR	PLURAL
tomato	tomatoes	hero	heroes
potato	potatoes	echo	echoes
mosquito	mosquitoes	torpedo	torpedoes

   c. Some nouns ending in *o* preceded by a consonant form the plural by adding *s* to the singular.

SINGULAR	PLURAL	SINGULAR	PLURAL
piano	pianos	alto	altos
solo	solos	silo	silos

6. A few nouns form the plural by a change within the singular.

SINGULAR	PLURAL	SINGULAR	PLURAL
man	men	woman	women
tooth	teeth	goose	geese
mouse	mice	foot	feet

7. A few nouns form the plural by adding *en* or *ren*.

SINGULAR	PLURAL	SINGULAR	PLURAL
ox	oxen	child	children

8. A few nouns have the same form in the plural as in the singular.

SINGULAR	PLURAL	SINGULAR	PLURAL
deer	deer	corps	corps
trout	trout	salmon	salmon
sheep	sheep	Chinese	Chinese

9. Compound nouns usually form the plural by adding *s* to the principal word.

SINGULAR	PLURAL
brother-in-law	brothers-in-law
editor in chief	editors in chief
drive-in	drive-ins

10. Letters form the plural by adding *s* or *'s*. Lowercase letters and capital letters that would be confusing if *s* alone were added form the plural by adding *'s*.

SINGULAR	PLURAL
TV	TVs
a	*a*'s
I	*I*'s

The plural of numbers is formed by adding *s*.

SINGULAR	PLURAL
1980	1980s
3	3s

Exercise 1

Write the plural of each of the following words. Then go back to pages 205–207 to check your answers. Write the number of the rule that applies.

Example: fife   fifes   **4a**

dish	journey	candy
grape	piano	deer
cherry	loss	birdhouse
radio	dairy	wish
door	ox	sister-in-law
church	leaf	alley
sky	ostrich	gulf
alto	hero	goose
vessel	studio	family
daisy	fairy	child
monkey	i	Japanese
roof	1970	ax

208

Exercise 2

Make two columns on your paper. In the first, list all the singular nouns. In the second, list all the plural nouns. Then write the singular or plural form for each.

blackberry	colonies
sleigh	bookcases
cities	kisses
beet	man
surgeons	squash
six-year-olds	duty
baseball	studio
chief	chalkboard
butterflies	leaves
sheep	Vietnamese
ally	oxen
valley	sheriff

Exercise 3

Complete each sentence with the plural form of the noun in parentheses.

1. Falcons live on _____ (skyscraper) in _____ (city).
2. Paul always eats the _____ (i) in his alphabet soup first.
3. My _____ (sister-in-law) are also _____ (sister)!
4. Rivers make _____ (valley) as they flow through _____ (hill).
5. Are _____ (tomato) fruits or _____ (vegetable)?
6. In some states, sales _____ (tax) are put on food.
7. The shallow _____ (area) of sea around continents are called continental _____ (shelf).
8. After television was invented, _____ (radio) were used less.
9. I sat patiently and waited for the _____ (trout) to bite!
10. _____ (child) born in the _____ (1980) weigh more than those born in the _____ (1880).

Gender

Gender is that quality of a noun by which sex is distinguished. There are three genders: masculine, feminine, and neuter.

The masculine gender indicates males.

> The education of a *knight* began at the age of six or seven.

The feminine gender indicates females.

> The young page was placed under the guidance of the *lady* of the castle.

The neuter gender indicates objects.

> Every *castle* was a training school for knights.

Some nouns may be either masculine or feminine.

> Every *servant* had duties to perform in the castle.

Many nouns that include both genders are now in common use.

TRADITIONAL	ALTERNATE FORM (BOTH GENDERS)
fireman	firefighter
policeman	police officer
chairman	chairperson
councilman	councillor

A fifteenth century
book illumination
of the French countryside

How Gender Is Distinguished

Gender may be distinguished in three ways:

1. by using a different word

MASCULINE	FEMININE	MASCULINE	FEMININE
son	daughter	gander	goose
nephew	niece	ram	ewe
stallion	mare	bull	cow
drake	duck	husband	wife

2. by using a different ending

MASCULINE	FEMININE	MASCULINE	FEMININE
prince	princess	waiter	waitress
duke	duchess	emperor	empress

3. by changing part of the word

MASCULINE	FEMININE	MASCULINE	FEMININE
landlord	landlady	grandfather	grandmother
grandson	granddaughter	stepfather	stepmother

Exercise 4

Tell whether each noun is masculine, feminine, or neuter.
Remember, some nouns can include both masculine and
feminine genders.

doctor	nurse	heroine
waitress	mother	basketball
bicycle	writer	secretary
astronaut	lawyer	police officer
Alaska	actress	cook
computer	lad	hamburger
president	architect	husband

Exercise 4

Write the feminine form for each masculine noun.

husband   waiter   rooster
son   grandson   stepfather
hero   male   lion
brother   man   brother-in-law

Write the masculine form for each feminine noun.

cow   bride   mare
princess   actress   ewe
hostess   landlady   niece
widow   girl   grandmother

Practice Power

Find some newspapers and magazines. Look through headlines and titles, and cut out words that illustrate each spelling rule on pages 205–208. On a large piece of paper, make two columns, one headed *Singular* and the other *Plural*. Glue each word under the appropriate column.

Lesson 3 Nominative Case

The case of a noun shows its relation to some other word or words in the sentence.

Every noun in a sentence has a special use. Four of the common ways that nouns can be used are: as subjects, as subjective complements, as direct objects, and as objects of a preposition. *How a noun is used in a sentence* tells the case of the noun.

There are three cases of nouns: nominative, possessive, and objective. The first one you will study is the *nominative case*.

Subject

> **A noun used as the subject of a verb is in the nominative case.**

Marcos built a two-story tree house.
Lightning struck the tree during a big storm.

The person, the place, or the thing talked about is the subject of a sentence. It may be determined by placing *who* or *what* before the verb. Look at the sentences above. *Who* built? The answer is *Marcos*, the subject of *built*. *What* struck? The answer is *lightning*, the subject of *struck*.

A noun used as the subject is in the nominative case.

Exercise 1

Find the subject in each sentence.

1. Lily feeds her kittens tuna every other day.
2. The acrobats perform their act without a safety net!
3. Rembrandt was one of the great painters of Europe.
4. My birthday is in August.
5. Some colonies have over thirty million ants!
6. A silent crowd gathered in front of the mime.
7. Adventurers from Spain explored South America.
8. Oysters in the Persian Gulf produce fine pearls.
9. Willie's skateboard slid out from under her feet.
10. At midnight, the weary soldiers reached camp.
11. In 1927, movies with sound first appeared in theaters.
12. Antonyms are words with opposite meanings.
13. In a rented car, the visitors toured the ancient city.
14. In the very strong gust of wind, Julian's new umbrella flipped inside out.
15. Every morning Mr. Stolz sets his plants in the sun.
16. In May, the teacher takes her science class to the planetarium.
17. Two teams practice basketball in the gym on Fridays.
18. Without a sound, the babysitter tiptoed away from the crib.
19. By accident, Maria hit the softball directly through the principal's window.
20. The veterinarian nervously bandaged the grizzly bear's leg.

Exercise 2

Write ten sentences using the following nouns as subjects: vegetables, music, Margot, paper, tornado, summer, computer, bicycle, dentist, Jerry.

Subjective Complement

A noun used as a subjective complement is in the nominative case.

Beethoven was a famous *composer*.
Sally Ride was the first American *woman* in space.

A noun that refers to the same person or thing as the subject is a subjective complement. A subjective complement renames the subject.

SUBJECT		SUBJECTIVE COMPLEMENT
Beethoven	=	composer
Sally Ride	=	woman

A subjective complement follows a linking verb. The most common linking verb is *be* and its various forms: *am, is, are, was, were, being,* and *been.*

A subjective complement is in the nominative case because the subject is in the nominative case.

Exercise 3

Find the subjective complement in each sentence.
1. The Rhône is a large river in France.
2. A spelunker is an explorer of caves.
3. Fitzgerald was a lizard with a very long tail.
4. Bill's mother is a successful lawyer.
5. The twins were members of a rock-climbing club.
6. My guitar teacher is Professor Frank.
7. Drums and smoke signals were early forms of communication.
8. This album is the nicest gift!
9. Last year Tammy was the best swimmer on our team.
10. *Treasure Island* is a story of adventure.
11. Next Thursday will be a holiday.
12. Marmosets are small monkeys of South America.
13. My niece will be a guide for the hot-air balloon rides.
14. Even a small mosquito can be a big pest!
15. Neil Armstrong was the first astronaut on the moon.

Exercise 4

Make two columns on your paper. For each sentence, in the first column, write the subject. In the second column, write the subjective complement.

Example: Those two boys are best friends.

SUBJECT	SUBJECTIVE COMPLEMENT
boys	friends

1. The extinct dodo was a flightless bird.
2. A cheeseburger is Lou's favorite food.
3. This year the leader of our troop will be Mr. Duskin.
4. That dog is the noisiest animal in the shelter.
5. Bill was the only skier on the mountain.
6. Photography is an interesting hobby.
7. Nannie's voice was just a whisper.
8. Mules are often stubborn animals.
9. A sitar is a musical instrument.
10. Jessie was the winner of the weight-lifting contest.

Exercise 5

Complete each sentence by adding a subjective complement.
1. Michael is a _____ on the basketball team.
2. Someday Roberta will be a(n) _____.
3. The mysterious package was a(n) _____ for Liza.
4. Gary was a(n) _____ at the Halloween party.
5. The last piece of fruit in the bowl was a(n) _____.
6. Kareem's constant companion was his _____.
7. My usual lunch is a(n) _____.
8. Jennifer is the best _____ in the class.
9. The strange object in the picture was a(n) _____.
10. The most exciting performers in the circus are the _____.

Noun in Direct Address

A noun used in direct address is in the nominative case.

Carl, do you enjoy soccer?
Come with me to the pancake breakfast, *Sally*.

In each sentence, the noun printed in italics is not related to any of the other words in the sentence. Instead, it is used independently to show the person addressed. A noun used in such a way is called a noun in direct address.

A noun in direct address is in the nominative case. It is set off by a comma or commas.

Exercise 6

Find the noun in direct address in each of these sentences. Explain the use of the commas.
 1. Do you know what baklava is, Leo?
 2. Watson, I need you!
 3. Didn't you beat Reggie at the video game, Nina?
 4. Hurry, Nat, and catch that hairy spider!
 5. Connie, can you imagine living on a space station?
 6. Your sister just ate the last french fry, Kip.
 7. Thank you, Tony, for cleaning the computer area.
 8. Who left these fingerprints, Mr. Vermeer?
 9. Judy, a dance group will perform at school today.
10. Try to get all of us in the photograph, Jason, if you can.

Exercise 7

Copy the following sentences. Underline the noun in direct address in each, and put commas where they are needed.

1. Jim did you get grape jelly on my diary?
2. I saw a shooting star last night Brigette.
3. Forrest please leave the skis outside!
4. Bonnie does your aunt feel any better?
5. Your paper airplane Pete just flew out the door.
6. Did your brother join an aerobics class Lonnie?
7. Agnes the soup of the day is minestrone.
8. Hitch up the horses Susan and we'll go for a ride.
9. Did you make that papier-mâché sculpture Mrs. Campbell?
10. Make a wish Terry and blow out the candles.

Write five sentences using these words as nouns in direct address.

Jill   coach   boys and girls   Ray   Miss Jenkins

Appositive in the Nominative Case

> **A noun in apposition is in the same case as the noun it explains. An appositive that explains the subject is in the nominative case.**

A word or group of words that explains a noun is said to be in apposition with that noun. It is called an appositive.

> Jack Lane, the *wrestler*, weighs almost three hundred pounds.
> My older sister, *Cecilia*, built a mobile as an art project.

In the first sentence, *wrestler* explains the noun *Jack Lane*. It is an appositive. Since *Jack Lane* is the subject of the sentence and in the nominative case, *wrestler* is also in the nominative case. In the second sentence, *Cecilia* explains the noun *sister*. Since *sister* is the subject of the sentence and in the nominative case, *Cecilia* is also in the nominative case.

218

Here are some characteristics of appositives:
1. The appositive may be omitted from the sentence and a complete thought remains.
2. The appositive follows another noun.
3. The appositive has the same meaning or refers to the same person or thing as the noun it explains.
4. The appositive is frequently set off by commas.

Exercise 8

Copy these sentences. Draw two lines under each appositive and one line under the word it explains.
1. Clair, the lifeguard, rescued a toddler from the pool.
2. Leif Ericson, a bold Viking, visited North America.
3. Jai alai, a Spanish game, uses small wicker baskets.
4. Harry Houdini, a magician, would free himself from a locked box underwater.
5. The Cape Fear Cyclists, a new club, will have training rides every Sunday.
6. Wilma Rudolph, a famous American runner, won three gold medals in a single Olympics.
7. The pyramids, royal tombs, were built thousands of years ago in Egypt.
8. Mrs. Clarkton, the postal carrier, doesn't like loose dogs.
9. Pennsylvania, the Keystone State, produces much coal.
10. Theta Carson, a beekeeper, sells honey during the summer.
11. Washington, D.C., the nation's capital, was named for George Washington.
12. Mr. Wood, an ornithologist, photographs rare birds.
13. Steven, my brother, drew a purple dinosaur on the wall.
14. The flounder, a saltwater fish, can change its skin color to look like a checkerboard.
15. Benjamin Parkway, a busy street, will be closed for repairs.

Exercise 9

Copy these sentences. Put commas where they are needed to set off the appositives.

1. The South Pole,the coldest place on earth,has snow all year round.
2. The Eiffel Tower,a popular tourist attraction,is in Paris.
3. My second cousin,Barry,raises peacocks.
4. Chris Stevens,a textile worker,lost his job when the factory closed.
5. Gray Dove,Chief Lone Star's daughter,built her own tepee.
6. Mrs. Vance,the newspaper's proofreader,checks for errors.
7. Harriet Tubman,a former slave,helped many slaves escape to freedom before the Civil War.
8. Jason,a young inventor,is trying to think of a new use for paper clips.
9. Saturn,the second largest planet,takes almost thirty years to orbit the sun.
10. *A Wrinkle in Time*,a book by Madeleine L'Engle,tells of a girl traveling into another time dimension.

Exercise 10

Rewrite each sentence and put an appositive after the subject. Remember to use commas to set off the appositives. Choose from the appositives below.

Example: Roy asked his track coach to accept the trophy.
　　　　　Roy, the winner, asked his track coach to accept the trophy.

1. Tortoises have been known to live up to one hundred and fifty-two years.
2. Jack found an opossum asleep in the vegetable bin.
3. Pegasus is seen in the night sky of the Northern Hemisphere.
4. Arnold Lovitt draws cartoons for a children's magazine.
5. Grizelda cast a spell on the vain prince.

　　　our cook　　　the witch of Clearwell　　　the constellation
　　　the longest-living animals　　　an artist

Exercise 11   Review

Tell why the italicized nouns in these sentences are in the nominative case. The choices are *subject*, *subjective complement*, *noun in direct address*, or *appositive in the nominative case*.

1. Saint Bernard *dogs* are very strong *animals*.
2. *Bruce*, have you seen our candle-making project?
3. *Nadia*, my *grandmother*, wept when she visited the town where she was born.
4. Have you learned your part for the play, *Eileen*?
5. The very earliest *books* were *slabs* of stone.
6. *Nancy*, your *brother* was on the telephone all morning.
7. *Rome*, the *Eternal City*, is located on the Tiber River.
8. *Birds* have many different feeding habits.
9. The *currency* in Russia is the *ruble*.
10. *Thomas*, our *classmate*, carves wooden duck decoys.
11. *Leaves* floated lazily from the lower branches of the tree.
12. *Beverly Cleary* is a *writer* of children's books.
13. I promise you, *Olga*, that I'll return your book tomorrow.
14. *Hawks* are *birds* with excellent eyesight.
15. *Sasquatch*, a legendary *creature*, is also called Bigfoot.

Practice Power

A. To show your ability to use nouns in the nominative case, write two sentences using a noun as the subjective complement, two using a noun in direct address, and two using an appositive in the nominative case.

B. We often use appositives to add information to a sentence. This information helps explain a difficult or unusual idea. Add an appositive where indicated in each of the following sentences. Tell whether the appositive explains the subject or the subjective complement. Use a dictionary or an encyclopedia for the information you need.
1. Henry is a serious philatelist‸.
2. Claustrophobia‸is a common sensation to have in an elevator.
3. Our destination was the hacienda‸.
4. The water ouzel‸can run underwater.
5. Asteroids‸are photographed by satellites.

Lesson 4 Possessive Case

A noun that expresses possession or ownership is in the possessive case.

Bill's voice announced the winners.

The voice that announced the winners belonged to or was possessed by Bill. The word *Bill's*, therefore, is in the possessive case. The sign of the possessive case is the apostrophe (') and *s*.

Exercise 1

Find the nouns in the possessive case in these sentences. Then tell what is being owned or possessed.

1. We need Fran's notes for help on this math problem.
2. A ptarmigan's feathers change from white in the winter to brown in the summer.
3. The knight's armor gleamed in the sunlight.
4. Ellen's new red sneakers lay in the middle of the road.
5. The racers' cars were not damaged.
6. Shel Silverstein's humorous poems are popular with children and adults.
7. A person's eye blinks about ten million times a year!
8. Five of John's companions went with him to the dentist.
9. Our neighbors' cottages are covered with ivy.
10. Lizabel gave me the family's special recipe for perfect fudge.
11. On the calf's flank was the brand of the Rocking R Ranch.
12. Using Matt's compass, we managed to find our way back to the clearing.
13. The barks from the Harrisons' beagles warned us that someone was nearby.
14. Rising water slowly covered Annie McPhearson's cornfields.
15. Fred read all night to finish Ted's book.

Rules for Forming the Possessive Case of Nouns

1. The singular possessive is formed by adding 's to the singular form of the noun.

   > The *robin's* egg is blue.
   > Listen to the *comedian's* joke.

2. The plural possessive of plural nouns ending in s is formed by adding the apostrophe only.

   > The *robins'* eggs are blue.
   > Listen to the *comedians'* jokes.

   If the plural form of the noun does not end in s, add 's.

   > Ginny found the *children's tickets.*
   > Did you see the display of *women's* gloves?

3. Proper names ending in s usually form the possessive case by adding 's.

   > *James's* bicycle has just been repaired.
   > *Dickens's* novels are widely read.

4. In compound nouns the 's is added to the end of the word.

POSSESSIVE SINGULAR	POSSESSIVE PLURAL
My *brother-in-law's* car is new.	My *brothers-in-law's* cars are new.

Exercise 2

Write the singular possessive and the plural possessive forms for these nouns.

baby	trout	princess	child
sparrow	nurse	snake	witness
wife	artist	robot	dancer
coach	pharaoh	uncle	hedgehog
astronaut	reindeer	carpenter	owlet
classmate	woman	mouse	stepsister

Exercise 3

Write each group of words in another way to show possession.

Example: trick of the magician
the magician's trick

1. poems of Longfellow
2. wheelchair of Bobby
3. red nose of the clown
4. diary of the detective
5. hats of the cowboys
6. slipper of Cinderella
7. courage of the firefighters
8. daffodils of Mr. Beetle
9. colors of the chameleon
10. command of the sergeant
11. joy of the children
12. assignment of the reporter
13. pet shop of Uncle Louis
14. hiding place of the pirates
15. crown of the princess

Practice Power

Think of unusual or interesting presents for five people or groups of people you know. As you think of the people, use both singular and plural nouns. Plural nouns could be *parents, classmates, sisters*. Write two sentences about each gift.

Example: My neighbors' gift from me would be a pet alligator.
My neighbors' alligator could be walked on a leash.

Lesson 5 Objective Case

Direct Object

> **A noun used as the direct object of a verb is in the objective case.**

The championship team met the *governor*.
The school bought several *computers*.

The direct object of a verb may be determined by placing *whom* or *what* after the verb. The team met *whom*? The team met the *governor*. The school bought *what*? The school bought *computers*. The nouns *governor* and *computers* are, therefore, direct objects.

A noun used as a direct object is in the objective case.

Exercise 1

Find the direct object in each sentence.
1. In the parade, Theresa twirled a baton.
2. At the Chinese restaurant, we ate spicy soup.
3. Whitcomb Judson invented the zipper in 1893.
4. Kerry has moved the parsley from the windowsill.
5. I carry Mr. O'Connor's groceries upstairs to his room.
6. The Pueblos built their homes on the sides of cliffs.
7. Sergei slowly turned his flashlight toward the noise.
8. Did you see the double rainbow this morning?
9. A large dog patiently guarded the door.
10. Becky will weave these long strips into a basket.
11. A construction worker pushed an enormous wheelbarrow.
12. The male emperor penguin holds the female's egg on his feet!
13. Paul Revere once made a tiny collar out of silver for a customer's pet squirrel.
14. Lady Knotsworth sets a place at the table for the hound!
15. Columbus made four voyages to the Americas.

Exercise 2

Copy each sentence. Underline the verb and add a direct object.

1. Divers gather unusual _____ from the ocean floor.
2. Mr. Soon's art class made _____ for Fire Safety Week.
3. Kyle baked a(n) _____ for the first time.
4. The crowd anxiously watched the _____ in the darkening sky.
5. Nora lost her favorite _____ on her way to school.
6. Our class might visit a(n) _____ tomorrow.
7. A group of motorboats carry _____ to the island every month.
8. Earl read a(n) _____ to his blind friend.
9. I covered the _____ with a large, colorful quilt.
10. Evita wrote a(n) _____ about the dangers of smoking.
11. Roger dropped the squirming _____ into a huge bucket of water.
12. Sometimes you can find a(n) _____ in your own backyard.
13. Beth mails _____ to her pen pal in Denmark.
14. I cut the _____ in half with the rusty scissors.
15. Cary made a(n) _____ out of paper.

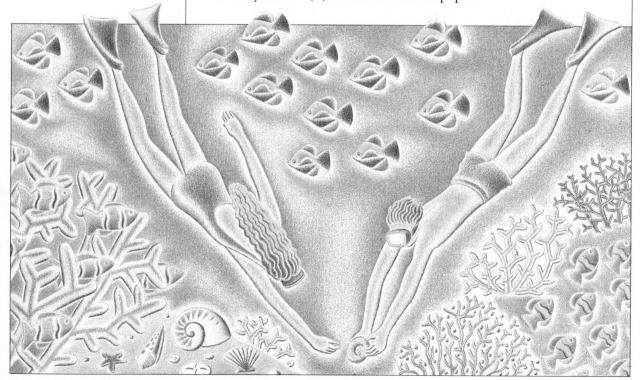

Object of a Preposition

A noun used as the object of a preposition is in the objective case.

Dr. Santilli lives and works in *Detroit*.
On *Thursday*, there will be a lunar eclipse.
During the *night*, rain washed away the snow.

In the first sentence, the noun *Detroit* is the object of the preposition *in*. In the second sentence, the noun *Thursday* is the object of the preposition *on*. In the third sentence, the noun *night* is the object of the preposition *during*. The nouns *Detroit*, *Thursday*, and *night* are in the objective case.

A noun used as the object of a preposition is in the objective case.

Exercise 3

For each sentence, find the noun that is the object of a preposition and name the preposition.
  1. The first Olympic Games were held in Greece.
  2. The Venus's-flytrap catches insects in its spiked leaves.
  3. We found the baseball mitt underneath the porch.
  4. We watched the rat escape into the junkyard.
  5. John's kite bobbed above our heads.
  6. A clay flowerpot crashed on the sidewalk.
  7. The longest day of the year is in June.
  8. We get oxygen from the air.
  9. Prairie dogs often dig tunnels ten feet under the surface of the ground.
 10. The division problems on the blackboard had mysteriously disappeared.
 11. Rodney's face lighted with surprise.
 12. Wes called to the engineer of the locomotive.
 13. Janet Guthrie drove in the Indianapolis 500.
 14. Dazzling fireworks exploded over the lake.
 15. Along the coastline, citizens prepared for Hurricane Kate.

Exercise 4

Complete each sentence with a preposition followed by an object.

1. Mrs. Wright took a trip _____.
2. _____, Sadie received a present.
3. Have you ever seen a collection _____?
4. The Arabian colts were _____.
5. Lennie found a large snake _____.
6. Some pigeons wobbled _____.
7. Most first-graders like books _____.
8. Not looking, Miguel ran _____.
9. Nonnie sang an Irish song _____.
10. _____, a herd of antelopes grazed.

Write sentences using each of the following.

11. over the rainbow
12. beside the flamingos
13. between the buildings
14. onto a horse
15. up the stairs

228

Indirect Object

> **A noun used as the indirect object of a verb is in the objective case.**

Some sentences contain two objects—the direct object or receiver of the action and another object that tells *to whom* or *for whom* the action is done. The object to whom or for whom something is done is called the *indirect object*.

> The librarian gave an *award*. (*Direct object*)
> The librarian gave *Amos* an award. (*Indirect object*)

The direct object of the verb *gave* is *award*. *Amos*, the indirect object, tells *to whom* the award was given.

The indirect object is ordinarily placed between the verb and the direct object. The preposition *to* or *for* can usually be placed before the indirect object without changing the meaning of the sentence.

> The librarian gave (to) Amos an award.

The following verbs may take indirect objects: *assign, bring, buy, deny, do, forbid, forgive, get, give, grant, hand, lend, offer, owe, pardon, pay, promise, read, refuse, remit, sell, send, show, sing, teach, tell, wish, write*.

Exercise 5

The direct objects in these sentences are italicized. Find the indirect objects. Put the word *to* or *for* in front of the indirect object to check your answer.

Example: Edna offered (to) her friend a *popsicle*.
Indirect object: friend

1. Leon sends my sister handmade *cards*.
2. The peasant woman sells tourists llama-hair *blankets*.
3. Frances wrote her father *directions* to the camp.
4. Mr. Key assigned the French class a three-page *report*.
5. I still owe my sister a *dollar* for Mother's present.
6. The mail carrier handed the clerk a large, oddly shaped *package*.
7. Show Maggie your new *calculator*.
8. You should give Jean some *advice* on the care of canaries.
9. Early bikes gave their riders a bumpy *trip*.
10. Ellen, tell the students the *story* of your kayak trip on the Haw River.
11. Mason handed the teacher the extra *copies* of the test.
12. Sandra gave her mother a microwave *cookbook*.
13. I'll read the class a *haiku* about snowflakes.
14. Jason lent his brother his *skates*.
15. Our father denied Marty *permission* to swim.

Exercise 6

Copy each sentence. Add an indirect object and underline the direct object.

1. Andrew writes _____ letters in code.
2. Give _____ the grasshopper before it escapes!
3. Donnie will buy _____ a newspaper at the corner.
4. A seismologist gave _____ an explanation of the Richter scale.
5. Who taught _____ that card trick?
6. Dorothy sent _____ an invitation to her birthday party.
7. Ms. McIver tells _____ unbelievable stories about the Loch Ness Monster!
8. I am happy to lend _____ my telescope.
9. First, read _____ the directions on the box.
10. In 1985, one Girl Scout sold _____ eleven thousand boxes of cookies!

Appositive in the Objective Case

A noun in apposition is in the same case as the noun it explains.

We cannot see oxygen, a colorless *gas*.
The players have confidence in Maria Ciardi, their *center*.

When you studied the nominative case you learned that an appositive explains a noun. The appositive is in the same case as the noun that it explains.

Appositives that explain nouns in the objective case are in the objective case. In the examples above, *gas* explains *oxygen*, the direct object. Therefore, *gas* is in the objective case. *Center* explains Maria Ciardi, the object of a preposition. Therefore, *center* is in the objective case.

An appositive is usually set off by commas.

Exercise 7

The appositives in these sentences are italicized. Name the word that each appositive explains. Give the case of the appositive and the reason it is in that case.

1. The adventurers crossed the Sahara, the largest *desert* in the world, in vehicles powered by the wind.
2. Bonnie did the Highland Fling, a lively Scottish *dance*.
3. The boy jumped onto the junk, a small wooden *sailboat*.
4. The visitors fed the noisy ducks, brightly colored *mallards*.
5. The stethoscope was invented in 1819 by René Laënnec, a French *doctor*.
6. A warm summer breeze drifted into the cottage, the families' vacation *house*.
7. The scientist spoke to Eliza, a talking *robot*.
8. I just met my new boxing coach, *Glenn Reilly*.
9. Yesterday we put our pottery bowls into the kiln, a special *oven*.
10. Miss Barrett eagerly opened the box, a *gift* from her sister in England.
11. A local lawyer saved Old Baldy, a hundred-year-old *lighthouse*.
12. We often buy flowers from Mr. Golgi, the street *vendor*.
13. King Arthur valued Excalibur, his magical *sword*.
14. A herd of deer appears every winter on Mr. Fenton's property, a Christmas tree *farm* near the state line.
15. Lynn played the part of Billie, the mysterious *stranger*.

Exercise 8

Copy these sentences. Set off the appositives by adding commas where they are needed.

1. The librarian showed the class a copy of *Odyssey* a magazine about outer space.
2. Have you met Annabelle Hart the lead singer?
3. I saw the runaway animal a Holstein calf.
4. Kim uses pork in *thit nuong cha* Vietnamese meatballs.
5. The setting of *The Incredible Journey* a classic children's novel is the Canadian wilderness.
6. George Washington was inaugurated in New York City the nation's first capital.
7. Agatha gives Wiggin her parakeet speaking lessons daily.
8. Brett bought his mother a gift an ink pen a week ago.
9. Winnie works at the Bookshelf a shop on Lang Street.
10. Allen met my older sister Dana at the airport.

Exercise 9   Review

Tell why the italicized nouns in these sentences are in the objective case. The choices are *direct object*, *object of a preposition*, *indirect object*, or *appositive in the objective case*.

1. In ballet class, we learned a new *step*.
2. With a smile, the camper watched the *antics* of the *raccoon*.
3. Flowering bushes grow on both *sides* of the Victorian *house*.
4. The customer gave the *clerk* two dollars in change.
5. My family visited *New York*, the *Big Apple*.
6. Very young early American boys and girls all wore *dresses*.
7. Danny asks his *brother questions* constantly.
8. Radio waves were first sent through the air by *Marconi*, an Italian *inventor*.
9. Jacqueline Smith set a parachute-jumping *record* in 1978.
10. The Ringling Brothers and Barnum & Bailey Circus conducts the only *college* for clowns in the *world*.
11. Tony promised *Rose* a *reflector* for her bike.
12. We will build a giant *sandwich* with plenty of *onions*.
13. Yuri plays Russian songs on his *balalaika*, a stringed *instrument*.
14. Gina snapped a *photograph* of the brightly colored *rainbow*.
15. Plants use the *energy* of sunlight through *photosynthesis*.

Practice Power

Give the number, gender, and case of each italicized noun.
1. My *sister* will start a new job on *Monday*.
2. *Moonquakes* are *tremors* on the moon similar to earthquakes.
3. *Martha's* straight black hair brushes her *shoulders*.
4. The street artist quickly finished the *drawing*, a young girl's *portrait*.
5. Several *children's games* can be adapted for sign language.
6. *Mr. Santiago* gave the *students* some information on how to obtain a library card.
7. Badminton, a *game* from India, was first played in *England* in the 1870s.
8. Ben Franklin's suggestion for the national *bird* was the *turkey*.
9. Did you find this antique *train* in the toy store, *Grandfather*?
10. The *crew's* dog ran down to the *galley*, the *kitchen* of the ship.
11. Officer Kelly brought his *partner* news from the *station*.
12. *Cammie*, put your wet *towels* from the beach into the drier.
13. The *babies' spoons* sailed across the kitchen.
14. The *hummingbird* is the only *bird* that can fly backwards!
15. I haven't signed your *cast* yet, *Kate*.

A hummingbird

234

Chapter Challenge

Read this paragraph carefully and answer the questions.

¹Would you rather watch a television program or listen to the radio? ²To some people, news on the radio is dull. ³They prefer to see a television reporter's tape. ⁴To many people, plays on television are more interesting since the audience can see as well as hear. ⁵Some people, however, say that listening to a play on the radio allows them to use their imagination. ⁶Both television and radio have advantages and disadvantages. ⁷Television presents pictures to its audience. ⁸Radio, the earlier invention, gives its listeners only sound. ⁹Radio, however, is more portable. ¹⁰You can be doing chores or traveling and still listen to the radio.

1. Why is *radio* in sentence 1 in the objective case?
2. Why is *news* in sentence 2 in the nominative case?
3. Name two nouns in the objective case in sentence 2.
4. What is the gender of *reporter's* in sentence 3?
5. What is the case of *reporter's* in sentence 3?
6. Name two plural nouns in sentence 4.
7. Name an abstract noun in sentence 5.
8. Name a collective noun in sentence 7.
9. What is the direct object in sentence 7?
10. What is the object of the preposition in sentence 7?
11. What is the indirect object in sentence 8?
12. Name the appositive in sentence 8.
13. In sentence 9, *radio* is in what case?
14. In sentence 10, *radio* is in what case?
15. Write the plural of the noun *radio*.

Creative Space 1

A peacock's fantasy of color
Spreads a rainbow fan
Giving a view
Of feathered
Eyes

Exploring the Poem...

Have you ever seen a peacock? A peacock's tail has a very interesting and colorful design. Do you know what unusual marks appear on its tail?

In this poem, what do you think the peacock's "fantasy of color" means? What is its "rainbow fan"? Do you get a clear picture of the peacock's tail from these images? Where on the peacock can you find "feathered eyes"?

This kind of poem is called a *cinquain* (pronounced "sĭng kān´"). *Cinquain* comes from the French word *cinq*, which means "five." The poem has five lines.

A pattern is a specific form to follow. It is a model that you can use to make another just like it. For example, look at each line of this poem. Count the number of words in each line and discover the pattern. You can see that the first line has five words, the second line has four words, the third line has three words, and so on. The pattern is 5-4-3-2-1. The five lines make up one complete sentence.

★ A cinquain contains just one idea. Think of some ideas for your own cinquain. You will want to be specific because you only have *one* sentence to describe your subject. Instead of "sports" you will want to think of just one sport. Try writing a colorful, descriptive sentence about your idea. Then work with the words. Put them into cinquain form. Add or take out words until your poem fits the pattern.

Practice putting this sentence into a cinquain before you write your own.

A roller coaster ride takes you up and down over hills and valleys until your stomach drops!

Chapter 2

Pronouns

Lesson 1 Personal Pronouns

A pronoun takes the place of a noun.

Read the following paragraph.

> [1]Chester Greenwood was a boy with a problem. [2]Chester suffered from cold ears. [3]To make matters worse, Chester lived in Maine, where winter can be very cold. [4]Then an idea occurred to Chester. [5]The idea made Chester the inventor of earmuffs. [6]Chester asked his grandmother to sew fur and velvet on metal loops that would fit against his ears.

The noun *Chester* is used six times in the above paragraph. The noun *idea* is used twice. Now read this paragraph.

> [1]Chester Greenwood was a boy with a problem. [2]He suffered from cold ears. [3]To make matters worse, he lived in Maine, where winter can be very cold. [4]Then an idea occurred to him. [5]It made him the inventor of earmuffs. [6]He asked his grandmother to sew fur and velvet on metal loops that would fit against his ears.

In the second paragraph, pronouns take the place of many of the nouns. As a result, the second paragraph sounds smoother than the first. In the second paragraph, the pronouns *he* and *him* take the place of the noun *Chester*. The pronoun *it* is used in place of the noun *idea*.

Traveling by train is popular. What advantages does a train trip have over a plane trip?

The word to which a pronoun refers is its *antecedent*.

Sara shook the package but did not open *it*.

In the sentence above, the antecedent of *it* is the noun *package*.

Since pronouns take the place of nouns, they have the same qualities as nouns: gender, number, and case. You will study more about the qualities of pronouns in this chapter.

Person

A personal pronoun shows by its form
  the speaker (first person)
  the person spoken to (second person)
  and the person or thing spoken about (third person)

I saw the famous painting at the museum. (*Speaker*)
Sheila called when *you* were out. (*Person spoken to*)
They enjoyed the barbecue. (*Persons spoken about*)

Pronouns that indicate the speaker are not the same as pronouns that indicate the person spoken to or the person spoken about. Since the forms of pronouns change in this way, personal pronouns are said to show *person*.

The personal pronouns of the first person (speaker) are *I, me, we, us.*

The personal pronoun of the second person (person spoken to) is *you*.

The personal pronouns of the third person (person or thing spoken about) are *he, she, it, him, her, they, them.*

Exercise 1

Find the personal pronouns in these sentences. Give the number of each: *first, second,* or *third.*

1. Didn't you see them crawling up the wall?
2. One of them stuck all over him like glue.
3. We watched it slowly dissolve into a puddle.
4. He ordered me to mop it up with a rag.
5. You should chase them outside.
6. It watched me like a hawk.
7. I clapped my hands, and they scattered.
8. Did you help her push them into the box?
9. It might try to escape from us when the opportunity arises.
10. She covered them before they could bite her.

Complete each sentence with personal pronouns. Give the person of each. Be sure to vary your choice of pronouns.

11. _____ ended when _____ rang the cowbell.
12. _____ were happy to sneak away from _____.
13. _____ jumped up and down beside _____.
14. _____ saw three of _____ on the ceiling.
15. _____ pushed _____ toward _____.

241

Number

> **A singular pronoun takes the place of a singular noun.**
>
> **A plural pronoun takes the place of a plural noun.**

The singular personal pronouns are *I, me, you, he, she, it, him, her.* These pronouns refer to one person or thing.

The plural personal pronouns are *we, us, you, they, them.* These pronouns refer to more than one person or thing.

Exercise 2

Find the personal pronouns in these sentences and tell whether each is *singular* or *plural*.

1. Don't blame me if the power goes off!
2. He sent us a burlap bag full of oysters.
3. They yelled at him from across the crowded sidewalk.
4. The race began when he set off the cannon.
5. We will hang bunches of mistletoe from the rafters.
6. She fell asleep in the grass as bagpipes droned in the distance.
7. They strung together the turquoise beads for her.
8. Maria, you have been chosen by them to head the cleanup committee.
9. I plan to take it to obedience school.
10. They left a message on the electronic bulletin board for us.

Gender

A pronoun that refers to males is masculine gender.

A pronoun that refers to females is feminine gender.

A pronoun that refers to an object is neuter gender.

Only pronouns in the third person singular change form to show gender. The masculine pronouns are *he* and *him*. The feminine pronouns are *she* and *her*. The neuter pronoun is *it*. In the plural, the pronouns *they* and *them* are used for all three genders.

Exercise 3

Give a pronoun that will take the place of each of the following nouns. For some nouns, more than one pronoun can replace the noun.

Rick	brothers	travelers
campfire	Maggie	gossip
carpenter	stereo	mother
aunt	men	necklace
arcade	nephew	joke
hairbrushes	pasta	keyboard
refrigerator	giraffe	actor
pilots	apartment	clerk
screams	newspaper	clown

Compound Personal Pronouns

Compound personal pronouns end in *self* or *selves*.

Forms of the Compound Personal Pronouns

	SINGULAR	PLURAL
FIRST PERSON	myself	ourselves
SECOND PERSON	yourself	yourselves
THIRD PERSON	himself, herself, itself	themselves

Andrea *herself* met us at the airport.
Muhammad Ali called *himself* "The Greatest."
Cats groom *themselves* diligently.

Exercise 4

Find the compound personal pronouns in these sentences.
1. You should give yourselves extra time for this math quiz.
2. We made the antismoking posters ourselves.
3. Freddie will have to do the dishes by himself.
4. Mickey Mouse himself greeted us at Disney World.
5. Sally wrote the award-winning play herself.
6. Did you hurt yourself in the sledding accident?
7. I myself will play the drum and trumpet at the same time.
8. Please relax and make yourselves comfortable.
9. The cat itself opened the cabinet door!
10. Sea urchins move themselves by using the spines on their bodies.

Complete each sentence with the correct compound personal pronoun.
11. Mr. Mackie _____ saw the Loch Ness monster.
12. The children _____ pulled the heavy crate up from the basement.
13. Couldn't you keep _____ from opening the present before your birthday?
14. Nancy _____ kept the fire burning through the night.
15. We decided to dig up the treasure _____.

Practice Power

Choose any ten nouns from exercise 3 in this lesson. Write sentences using both the noun and the pronoun in two related sentences.

Example: The *pasta* was difficult to eat. *It* kept wiggling off my fork.

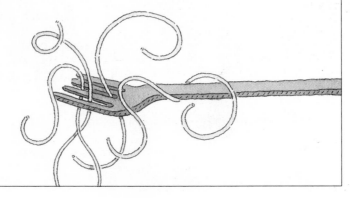

Lesson 2 The Case of Personal Pronouns

Nominative Case

Subject of a Verb

> A pronoun used as the subject of a verb must be in the nominative case.

Grace and (I, me) joined the spring cleanup committee.

Here is the correct form: Grace and *I* joined the spring cleanup committee.

The pronoun *I* is in the nominative case because it is the subject of the verb *joined* together with the noun *Grace*.

The nominative case personal pronouns are

	SINGULAR	PLURAL
FIRST PERSON	I	we
SECOND PERSON	you	you
THIRD PERSON	he, she, it	they

Exercise 1

Choose the correct form of the personal pronoun for each sentence.

1. The McLeans and (we, us) went white-water rafting on the Snake River.
2. Justin and (me, I) tried on the worker's hard hat.
3. Chip and (he, him) are watching the sailboat race.
4. Tommy and (her, she) climbed up on the Indian elephant.
5. The boys and (us, we) tried panning for gold.
6. (They, Them) will try to ride their bikes up the high hill.
7. My sister and (I, me) are good friends.
8. Tyler and (him, he) learned to play square ball.
9. Lauren and (she, her) pitched a tent in our backyard.
10. Did (them, they) catch the bus to the mall?

Complete each sentence with the correct form of a personal pronoun. Be sure to vary your choice of pronouns.

11. Marian and _____ will be here early.
12. You and _____ need to cut Mr. Collie's grass.
13. Did Elizabeth and _____ go to the table tennis match?
14. He and _____ will feed the puppies for you.
15. Jean and _____ want to see your four-foot-tall cactus.
16. The twins and _____ washed Ms. Kelso's Saint Bernard.
17. Carl and _____ raced home today.
18. Tonya and _____ will wait until two o'clock.
19. Will Julio and _____ watch the television special tonight?
20. Myron and _____ bought a program at the circus.

Subjective Complement

> **A pronoun used as a subjective complement is in the nominative case.**

The acrobat on top of the pyramid is (she, her).

Here is the correct form: The acrobat on top of the pyramid is *she*.

She is in the nominative case because it is the subjective complement. *She* follows the linking verb *is* and refers to the same person as the subject, *acrobat*.

Exercise 2

Choose the correct form of the personal pronoun for each sentence. Notice that the subject and the subjective complement can often be switched.

Example: The winner was *he*.
　　　　　He was the winner.

1. The farmhand who swept the barn floor was (she, her).
2. That is (him, he) without the sunglasses.
3. Is that (he, him) at the kitchen door?
4. The slow car washers were (they, them).
5. Was it (her, she) on the phone?
6. The first ones to get tickets were (us, we)!
7. The person in the lion mask is (she, her).
8. The champion skaters were (they, them).
9. Was it (him, he) in the cab?
10. Those boys on the baseball field are (they, them).

Complete each sentence with the correct form of a personal pronoun. Be sure to vary your choice of pronouns.
11. The man in the sweat suit must be _____.
12. Was that _____ in the wrinkled photograph?
13. The most impressive hula dancers were _____.
14. Which one of you made this mess? It was _____!
15. That was _____ with the stack of books.

Exercise 3

Choose the correct form of the personal pronoun for each
sentence. Tell whether the personal pronoun is the *subject* or
the *subjective complement*.

1. My friend and (me, I) built a robot for our science project.
2. Aren't those pilots on the runway (they, them)?
3. Ennis and (him, he) bought a long-haired guinea pig.
4. Is that (she, her) in front of the fire station?
5. Margie and (me, I) made the whole wheat bread.
6. That was (we, us) on the news last night.
7. Was it (he, him)? No, it was (me, I)!
8. Either Fay or (I, me) will rinse the alfalfa sprouts.
9. Has (her, she) sent her story to the newspaper?
10. (Them, They) gave us the wrong directions to the miniature
    golf course.
11. Eddie and (he, him) created a comic book.
12. It is (him, he) banging at the door.
13. This is (her, she) speaking.
14. That is (they, them) on the Ferris wheel.
15. Helen and (him, he) will grill hamburgers tonight.

Objective Case

Object of a Verb

> **A pronoun used as the direct object of a verb is in the objective case.**

Dorothy invited (I, me) to the rock concert.

Here is the correct form: Dorothy invited *me* to the rock concert.

Me is the direct object of the verb *invited*.

The objective case pronouns are

	SINGULAR	PLURAL
FIRST PERSON	me	us
SECOND PERSON	you	you
THIRD PERSON	him, her, it	them

Exercise 4

Choose the correct form of the personal pronoun for each sentence.

1. Maxie will have to call (he, him) about our lunch order.
2. They sent Armand and (me, I) to the citywide math contest.
3. The white laboratory mice fear (them, they).
4. I know (she, her) from somewhere, I'm sure!
5. A carpenter helped (we, us) with the doghouse blueprints.
6. Jenna admires Pat and (him, he) for their knowledge of antique toys.
7. The smell of smoke in the room alarmed (we, us)!
8. Did the talent scout choose (her, she)?
9. Flora blamed Meryl and (I, me) for that mix-up!
10. Jonathan wants (they, them) on his soccer team.

Complete each sentence with the correct form of a personal pronoun. Be sure to vary your choice of pronouns.

11. The class election results surprised the principal and

    _____.
12. Did the snake handler impress _____?
13. Of all of the science fiction writers, I like _____ best.
14. The baby lions amused Ramona and _____ with their attempts at ferociousness.
15. The roller coaster car slowly carried Sally and _____ to the top.

Object of a Preposition

> **A pronoun used as the object of a preposition is in the objective case.**

Directions for feeding the hamsters came with (they, them).

Here is the correct form: Directions for feeding the hamsters came with *them*.

The pronoun *them* is the object of the preposition *with*.

Exercise 5

Choose the correct form of the personal pronoun for each sentence.
1. Can she show the shortcut to (we, us)?
2. That is a secret between my mom and (I, me).
3. Did you leave the leftovers in the microwave for (they, them)?
4. The new pitcher threw a fast ball to (she, her).
5. On the stairs, I could hear heavy footsteps above (me, I).
6. A slow-footed donkey trailed behind Frank and (him, he).
7. Is this bunch of mail from Alicia and (her, she)?
8. The house was painted last summer by (they, them).
9. I hope the skywriter will speak to Ted and (we, us).
10. Please save the leftover plum pudding for Marsha and (I, me).

Complete each sentence with the correct form of a personal pronoun. Be sure to vary your choice of pronouns.
11. The restless crocodile gnashed its teeth at _____.
12. Cheryl offered to toast pumpkin seeds for Brigid and

_____.
13. The ice-cream vendor stopped near _____.
14. The hall monitor grabbed the jump rope from Curtis and

_____.
15. We'll learn to play the lute with _____.

Exercise 6

Choose the correct form of the personal pronoun for each sentence. Tell whether the personal pronoun is the *direct object* or the *object of a preposition*.
1. The librarian asked the children to sit beside (she, her).
2. Dominique rolled the baby carriage toward (them, they).
3. Tony's grandfather will help (I, me) with repairing the rocking chair.
4. Won't you take (we, us) to the horror movie?
5. That cornhusk doll was made by (him, he).
6. Coach Simmons hurled the basketball down the court to (she, her).
7. Did you see Roland and (they, them) up on the roof?
8. Kyle practiced his bird calls for (us, we).
9. We found (they, them) in the garden beside the scarecrow.
10. Don't touch that diary! It belongs to (me, I)!

Complete each sentence with the correct form of a personal pronoun. Be sure to vary your choice of pronouns. Tell whether the pronoun is the *direct object* or the *object of a preposition*.
11. Emilie brought _____ to Mr. Fred's Fudge Factory.
12. Joan knit a heavy sweater for _____ last winter.
13. I quilted a simple pattern on the pillow top for _____.
14. Mom sent _____ to the store for cayenne pepper.
15. A tall man sat in front of _____ just as the movie began.

Exercise 7   Review

Find the word to which each italicized pronoun refers (antecedent). Then give the case of the pronoun.
1. Rhoda's favorite books have many illustrations in *them*.
2. The ballerina who lost a shoe was *she*.
3. Did Jason take all twenty pints of blueberries with *him*?
4. Buddie, how did *you* fix the bicycle gears?
5. The owner of this unusual drawing is *he*.
6. The boys dragged the bag of newspapers behind *them*.
7. Tessie unfolded the map and studied *it*.
8. The two sisters playing marbles are *they*.
9. Ruby's canary landed on top of *her*.
10. The fish with white spots is *it*.

Exercise 8   Review

Find the personal pronoun in each sentence. Then give the case of each pronoun and tell how it is used: *subject, subjective complement, direct object,* or *object of a preposition*.

1. He ate every chocolate chip in the cookie dough.
2. They read the newspaper from front page to back.
3. That child without a scarf is she.
4. The blue envelope was addressed to her.
5. We deserve the tug-of-war prize!
6. The lion tamer warned them to stay away from the animals.
7. Marilyn did not recognize him in a coat and tie.
8. The Frisbee spun straight toward me!
9. I looked around the firelit igloo.
10. Paula rowed the boat through the marsh for us.

Exercise 9   Review

Choose the correct form of the personal pronoun to complete each of these sentences. Give the reason for your choice.

1. Fanny and (her, she) are paper carriers.
2. The pilot spoke to Karen and (him, he).
3. The tent will shelter my brother and (I, me).
4. Allan and (I, me) offered to work backstage for the play.
5. Ted and (she, her) will work together to solve the clues for the crossword puzzle.
6. I bought the book on genealogy for (they, them).
7. Richard and (they, them) forgot their gym clothes.
8. Alice and (he, him) saw a bear across the lake.
9. The woman asked (us, we) about the way to the beach.
10. The person flipping the pancakes was (she, her).

Complete each sentence with the correct form of a personal pronoun. Be sure to vary your choice of pronouns.

11. Una and _____ spent two hours watching the workers put up the building.
12. The acrobats' stunts really amazed _____.
13. Was it _____ who left the burned popcorn in the sink?
14. Ryan and _____ are about to leave for the game.
15. Grace, give the paintbrush to _____.

Practice Power

Complete each sentence with a personal pronoun. The person, number, and gender to use for each pronoun are given in parentheses. Be sure to use the correct case.

Example: Greta blew the balloon so much that __it__ burst.
(*third, singular, neuter*)

1. Where are ____?
   (*third, plural, masculine/feminine*)
2. The librarian told ____ about the new riddle books.
   (*first, plural, masculine/feminine*)
3. ____ was large, dark, and loud.
   (*third, singular, neuter*)
4. ____ saw lovebirds in the open-air market.
   (*third, singular, masculine*)
5. Garrison brought a copy of the contest rules for ____.
   (*third, singular, feminine*)
6. ____ explained that the koala is really not a bear.
   (*third, plural, masculine/feminine*)
7. ____ baked a batch of soft pretzels for the yard sale.
   (*first, singular, masculine/feminine*)
8. The robot mouse rolled into ____.
   (*third, singular, masculine*)
9. The baby-sitter called ____ about ten o'clock.
   (*third, plural, masculine/feminine*)
10. ____ plans to grow petunias in the window box.
    (*third, singular, feminine*)

Lesson 3 Possessive Pronouns and Contractions

Possessive Pronouns

> Possessive pronouns are used to show *possession* or *ownership* by the speaker, the person spoken to, or the person or thing spoken about.

The yellow tennis balls are *mine*, and the white ones are *yours*.

The possessive pronouns are

	SINGULAR	PLURAL
FIRST PERSON	mine	ours
SECOND PERSON	yours	yours
THIRD PERSON	his, hers, its	theirs

Exercise 1

Find the possessive pronouns in these sentences.
1. Stephen found an aardvark. Has anyone lost theirs?
2. I put mine in the closet last week.
3. His is playing the piano.
4. We got ours from a traveling circus.
5. Yours is hiding underneath the bed.
6. I just saw theirs in the refrigerator.
7. Hers just called on the phone.
8. This one can't be mine!
9. David has his on a leash.
10. Those must be its!
11. Mine will not eat split pea soup.
12. The Rutherfords took theirs to Alaska.
13. The one climbing out of the washer must be yours.
14. Hers is purple with orange stripes.
15. Ours was wearing Joannie's new backpack.

Exercise 2

Complete each sentence with an appropriate possessive pronoun. Be sure to vary your choice of pronouns.

1. This is _____, but not _____.
2. The flying saucer is _____.
3. _____ has already been to outer space.
4. Keep a lookout for _____.
5. All this strange equipment must be _____.
6. If _____ is fixed, then please fix _____.
7. Collect _____ and store the rest in the barn.
8. Let's make a new one and pretend it's _____.
9. It has to be better than _____.
10. Everyone will be impressed by _____.

Contractions Containing Pronouns

> The personal pronouns are used with verbs to form contractions. The apostrophe (') is used to show where a letter or letters have been left out.

Study the spelling and meaning of these contractions.

CONTRACTION	MEANING	CONTRACTION	MEANING
I'll	I will	it's	it is
they're	they are	they'll	they will
I've	I have	they've	they have
we're	we are	you'll	you will
I'm	I am	he'll	he will
you're	you are	she'll	she will

257

Exercise 3

Find the contraction in each sentence and tell what pronoun and verb have been used to form it.
1. I'll stir this bubbling pot of spaghetti sauce.
2. You're going to walk into a huge sticky spider web!
3. It's time for the leaves to start changing colors.
4. Boyd said that he'll finish the soap carving tomorrow.
5. We're learning origami, Japanese paper folding.
6. They'll be happier if they can run through the sprinkler.
7. I'm looking for a suspenseful mystery story.
8. You'll be late if you watch one more television program.
9. Edna, you're holding the marshmallows too close to the fire!
10. They're on their way to a surprise party.

Exercise 4

Complete each sentence with an appropriate contraction.
1. _____ planning a trip to Timbuktu!
2. Did you know that _____ be in a three-legged bag race?
3. _____ try to answer your questions.
4. The builders report that _____ found a hole in the roof.
5. _____ already put two coats of paint on the motorcycle.
6. I believe that _____ the first person to discover this.
7. _____ going to be guests of the governor!
8. _____ happy to see the crocuses bloom.
9. The weather reporter promised that _____ not going to rain.
10. Carron Haddad hopes that _____ buy a subscription to the newspaper.

Correct Use of Possessives and Contractions

> Possessives are often confused with contractions because they sound alike. Possessives express ownership or possession. They *do not use* apostrophes.

Its leg is hurt. (*Possessive*)

> A contraction is one word made from two words. The apostrophe is used in a contraction to show where a letter or letters have been left out.

It's time for school. (*Contraction*—It is)

Study these possessives and contractions and learn the difference between them.

POSSESSIVES	CONTRACTIONS
its collar	it's (it is) sleeping
your friend	you're (you are) late
their house	they're (they are) not here

Exercise 5

Tell whether each italicized word is a *possessive* or a *contraction*.
1. *Their* basketballs are in the equipment room.
2. *It's* the biggest bullfrog that is the loudest croaker!
3. A sunflower will turn *its* head to follow the sun.
4. What would you trade for *your* latest baseball card?
5. Children used to do *their* handwriting with quill pens.
6. Helena, *you're* not going to believe this!
7. *Your* sister is digging earthworms for her fishing trip.
8. *They're* going to learn a new song in music class today.
9. *It's* a huge bowl of steaming chili.
10. André says that *it's* too stormy to fly a kite.

Exercise 6

Choose the correct word for each sentence.
1. (You're, Your) painting must be dry before you frame it.
2. Pandas try to limit (their, they're) diet to bamboo shoots.
3. (You're, Your) wearing my new sneakers again.
4. (They're, Their) ready to start the backgammon game.
5. An oil-covered bird cannot clean (its, it's) own feathers.
6. (You're, Your) next in line, Elijah.
7. Some people believe they can remove (they're, their) freckles with lemon juice.
8. (Its, It's) a good time to try that new brownie recipe.
9. The men left (their, they're) work boots at the front door.
10. How is (you're, your) headache?
11. (They're, Their) the biggest apples I've ever seen!
12. Large acorns fell from (it's, its) gnarled branches.
13. I would like to know if (your, you're) finished with the Monopoly game.
14. The turtles climbed out of (their, they're) box.
15. We heard that (its, it's) going to snow all day!

Practice Power

You and your friend(s) are dressed alike for Halloween, but there are some differences in your costumes and makeup. Write five sentences comparing *theirs* (*his* or *hers*) with *yours*. Make sure you use possessive pronouns.

Lesson 4 Interrogative Pronouns

An interrogative pronoun is used in asking a question.

The interrogative pronouns are *who, whom, which, what,* and *whose.* Study the following examples.

Who is used in speaking of persons.

> *Who* opened the door?

Who is the subject of *opened.*

Whom is used in speaking of persons.

> *Whom* did they elect?

Whom is the direct object of *elect.*

Which is used in speaking of persons or things.

> *Which* is your favorite writer?
> *Which* of the ingredients did you forget?

In the first sentence, *which* is the subject of *is.* In the second sentence, *which* is the object of *did forget.*

What is used in speaking of things and in asking for information.

> *What* will you do?

What is the object of *will do.*

Whose is used in speaking of persons.

> *Whose* is the pink-striped umbrella?

Whose shows possession.

Exercise 1

Find the interrogative pronouns in these sentences. Tell whether they refer to persons or to things.

1. Which of the Wright brothers was the older?
2. What does a yak eat?
3. For whom was the Taj Mahal built?
4. Which would you choose to put in a time capsule—a photograph or a diary?
5. Who brought an early version of the hamburger to America?
6. What would a podiatrist check?
7. Which of these writers created Frankenstein?
8. What should a first-aid kit contain?
9. Whose were the words "All the world's a stage"?
10. What does the Richter scale measure?

Exercise 2

Complete each sentence with an interrogative pronoun, *who, which,* or *what*. Use *who* for persons, *which* for persons or things, and *what* for things or general information.

1. _____ invented the safety match?
2. _____ is the duty of a forest ranger?
3. _____ of the deserts is largest?
4. _____ are the three primary colors?
5. _____ wrote *Alice in Wonderland*?
6. _____ was Duke Ellington's full name?
7. _____ of the mountains has the highest peak, Mount McKinley or Mount Everest?
8. _____ of the jewels is the most valuable?
9. _____ is Anne Frank?
10. For _____ is the Red Sea named?
11. _____ is a synonym for *zephyr*?
12. _____ did Jack Sprat not eat?
13. _____ of the Indian chiefs wrote an alphabet for his people?
14. _____ would you measure with a craniometer?
15. _____ is the name of our galaxy?

The Use of *Who* and *Whom*

> The interrogative pronoun *who* is used when the sentence requires a pronoun in the nominative case.
>
> The interrogative pronoun *whom* is used when the sentence requires a pronoun in the objective case.

Who may be used as a subject. *Whom* may be the direct object of a verb or the object of a preposition.

> *Who* were present at the meeting? (*Who* is the subject.)
> *Whom* did the class elect? (*Whom* is the direct object.)
> To *whom* was the trophy awarded? (*Whom* is the object of the preposition.)

Exercise 3

Complete each sentence with *who* or *whom*.

1. _____ was that man in the stovepipe hat?
2. _____ is the guitarist in that group?
3. For _____ did the dance troupe perform?
4. By _____ was the self-defense class taught?
5. Lem, _____ invited the ants to our picnic?
6. To _____ was the stamp catalog sent?
7. _____ is the stargazer in your family?
8. By _____ was the pantomime performed?
9. _____ wants to photograph wolves in the wilderness?
10. To _____ did you tell my secret?
11. _____ did you invite?
12. _____ landed this paper airplane on my desk?
13. Marty, _____ should we ask for permission?
14. For _____ are you writing that note?
15. _____ is the person wearing the bicycle helmet?

Practice Power

Write four sentences with the interrogative pronouns *who, whom, which,* or *what.* Use social studies, science, or math topics for your questions.

Lesson 5 Distributive and Indefinite Pronouns

Distributive Pronouns

> **A distributive pronoun refers to each person, place, or thing separately.**

Each has to give a short talk before the election.
Neither likes butter on popcorn.

The distributive pronouns are *each, either,* and *neither.* They are singular in number.

Exercise 1

Find the distributive pronouns in these sentences.
1. Each will wear an arm band and carry a banner.
2. Neither could remember the address of the pet shop.
3. Do you like either of these modern paintings?
4. Neither of your brothers has red hair like you.
5. You should feed each a can of food a day.
6. We concluded that neither would win the frog-jumping contest of Calaveras County.
7. Have you read either of the assigned stories yet?
8. Each of the jockeys wore bright colors.
9. I think that neither of the clocks is correct.
10. If we divide the cherries evenly, each of us will get seven and a half of them.

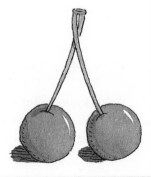

Indefinite Pronouns

> **An indefinite pronoun refers to no specific person, place, or thing.**

Everyone wonders who the new president will be.
Many plan to attend the open house at the school.

Some singular indefinite pronouns are

anybody	everybody	nobody	somebody
anyone	everyone	no one	someone
anything	everything	nothing	something

Some indefinite pronouns that are usually plural are

both	many
few	several

Some indefinite pronouns that may be singular or plural are

all	some

Exercise 2

Find the indefinite pronouns in these sentences.
1. Somebody keeps sounding a car horn.
2. Everyone has signed Felicia's leg cast.
3. Would someone take this computer back to the lab?
4. This hot curry is ordered by very few.
5. Many complain about the weather, but no one can do anything about it.
6. Everyone must complete a map showing the state's products by Friday.
7. Does anyone that you know have an unusual hobby?
8. All of the red balloons were sold before we arrived.
9. Crosswords and hangman are popular word games, and I like doing both.
10. We went to the zoo to see gorillas, and we saw several in the monkey house.

The Correct Use of Indefinite Pronouns with Negatives

> When a sentence contains a negative such as *not* or *never*, use *anything* or *anyone* to express negation.

There wasn't (nobody, anyone) at the beach on the chilly spring day.

Here is the correct form: There wasn't *anyone* at the beach on the chilly spring day.

The sentence contains one negative word: *n't,* which is the contraction of *not.* To choose another negative word, *nobody,* would be incorrect. The use of double negatives is incorrect.

Exercise 3

Choose the correct indefinite pronoun to complete each sentence.
1. There was (nothing, anything) left in the white elephant booth by the end of the day.
2. The kangaroo doesn't have (nothing, anything) in its pouch.
3. I have never seen (anything, nothing) so homely as the wildebeest.
4. The camp counselor told us not to bring (nothing, anything) except our lunches.
5. I have never met (anyone, nobody) who could swallow a goldfish.
6. Since (nobody, anybody) had bowled before, we all threw many gutter balls.
7. I promise not to tell (nobody, anybody) your secret.
8. (Nothing, Anything) makes me scratch more than a mosquito bite!
9. (Nobody, Anybody) in our class knew that the first Olympic Games were held in 776 B.C.
10. Didn't (nobody, anyone) bring pickles for the picnic?

Practice Power

There has been a lively class discussion about choosing the name for the new playground in your school. Write a paragraph in which you report on the discussion. Include at least three of these distributive and indefinite pronouns in your paragraph: *everybody, nobody, somebody, neither, either, anything.*

Chapter Challenge

Read this paragraph carefully and answer the questions.

¹Helen Keller was less than two years old when she was afflicted by a serious disease. ²It left her blind and deaf. ³For the next five years, she wasn't able to speak. ⁴She was a frightened and bewildered child who couldn't understand the strange silence around her. ⁵Helen's life began to change when Anne Sullivan, from the Perkins Institute for the Blind, became her teacher. ⁶Helen learned to understand the names of objects spelled into her hand. ⁷A whole new world opened up for her. ⁸She proved that every struggle could end in victory. ⁹Few have had to overcome the enormous obstacles she faced. ¹⁰Helen herself enjoyed a brilliant career helping the deaf and the blind.

1. Find the personal pronouns in sentences 1 and 2.
2. Give the case of each of the pronouns in sentences 1 and 2.
3. What is the antecedent of the pronoun *It* in sentence 2?
4. What pronoun is the subject of sentence 3?
5. How is the pronoun *She* in sentence 4 used?
6. In which case is the pronoun *her* in sentence 4? Why?
7. In which case is the pronoun in sentence 7? Why?
8. Name the person, number, and gender of the pronoun in sentence 8.
9. Name the compound personal pronoun in the paragraph.
10. Name the indefinite or distributive pronoun in the paragraph.

Helen Keller and Anne Sullivan

Creative Space 2

City

In the morning the city
Spreads its wings
Making a song
In stone that sings.

In the evening the city
Goes to bed
Hanging lights
About its head.

Langston Hughes

Exploring the Poem...

We usually think of a city as a big, busy place with many people, cars, and buildings. In this poem, the poet Langston Hughes has a fresh, new vision of the city.

The poet uses a metaphor to help you "see" the city differently. *A metaphor is a comparison of two unlike objects or things.*

In the first stanza, to what does the poet compare the city in the morning? (The word *wings* is a clue.) What are some city noises you might hear?

Name the sets of words that rhyme in the poem. How would you describe the way the poem rhymes (for example, each pair of lines, every other line)?

★ You can build a poem around a clear metaphor. First try to think of two things that are *unlike* in the way they look, but *alike* in what they do. Here are some ideas:

> The *airplane* was an *arrow* shooting across the sky...
> The *moon* is a floating *ship* in the night...
> The *ice* was a polished *mirror*...
> *Lucy*, a spinning *top*, twirled across the stage...

Now work with your own metaphor and write one stanza of a poem. You can add rhyme if you want to. Here are two example poems.

The moon floats	In winter the ice
Like a ship	Is a polished mirror
Across the dark sky	And the silver sound of skates
On its night trip.	Is all you can hear.

269

Chapter 3

Adjectives

Lesson 1 Descriptive Adjectives

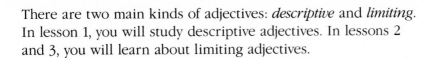

An adjective describes or limits a noun or a pronoun.

There are two main kinds of adjectives: *descriptive* and *limiting*. In lesson 1, you will study descriptive adjectives. In lessons 2 and 3, you will learn about limiting adjectives.

> **A descriptive adjective describes a noun or a pronoun.**

Read these sentences.

> The dolphins jumped through the ring.
> The sleek, playful dolphins jumped through the red ring.

In the second sentence, notice how the words *sleek* and *playful* describe the noun *dolphins*. The word *red* describes the noun *ring*. These words are descriptive adjectives. A descriptive adjective modifies a noun or pronoun. It usually tells *what kind* about the noun or pronoun it modifies.

You can hear the sound of this wave. What words would you use to describe this sound?

There are two classes of descriptive adjectives: *proper adjectives* and *common adjectives*.

A proper adjective is formed from a proper noun.
A common adjective is any adjective not formed from a proper noun.

PROPER ADJECTIVES

Persian rug
Hawaiian pineapple
French perfume

COMMON ADJECTIVES

valuable rug
delicious pineapple
fragrant perfume

Exercise 1

Find the descriptive adjectives in these sentences. Tell whether they are *common* or *proper*.

1. In the trunk, we found a red Spanish scarf.
2. The uniforms were decorated with bright buttons.
3. Beautiful grounds surround the old mansion.
4. Skillful Belgian needleworkers make fine lace.
5. *Hans Brinker* is a heartwarming story.
6. Have you ever seen a double rainbow in a stormy sky?
7. Toads move in short, clumsy hops.
8. A silver moonbeam fell on the narrow path.
9. Brazilian coffee is imported by the United States.
10. The ancient Peruvian city bustled with curious tourists.

Complete each sentence with a common or proper adjective according to what is indicated in parentheses.

11. The (*common*) seagulls swooped down onto the (*common*) beach.
12. It is hard to find real (*proper*) spaghetti sauce.
13. The (*common*) cookie jar fell from the kitchen shelf.
14. A (*proper*) ship cruised up the Mississippi River.
15. A (*common or proper*) guide showed us the sights of the (*common*) city.

Exercise 2

Form adjectives from each of these proper nouns. Use a dictionary to check your spelling.

Example: proper noun, *China*; proper adjective, *Chinese*

Spain	Italy	Alaska
Arabia	France	Ireland
Greece	Europe	Peru
Japan	America	Egypt
Africa	Denmark	Switzerland

Exercise 3

Form adjectives from each of these common nouns. Use a dictionary if you need help.

Example: common noun, *winter*; common adjective, *wintry*

wind	gold	truth
wood	mischief	hero
silk	luck	mountain
athlete	storm	skill
courage	cloud	courtesy

Exercise 4

Write one synonym for each of these adjectives.

comical	clever
faithful	amiable
ignorant	sincere
dangerous	famous
expensive	ancient
angry	clumsy
confident	beautiful
peaceful	odd
huge	lively

Greek ruins

273

Exercise 5

Write one antonym for each of these adjectives.

ugly	clean	beneficial
enormous	early	tame
awkward	distant	plentiful
strong	incorrect	dark
sweet	idle	brave
proud	silent	flimsy
dull	rich	high
swift	coarse	friendly
kind	careless	shallow

Position of Adjectives

The usual position of the adjective is *before* the noun.

The *agile* acrobats amazed the audience.

In this sentence, *agile* comes right before *acrobats*, the noun it describes.

Some adjectives follow and complete a linking verb. Such adjectives are called subjective complements.

The pretzels are *chewy*.
That gorilla looks *intelligent*.

The first sentence describes *chewy* pretzels, and the second sentence describes an *intelligent* gorilla. In both of these sentences, the adjective does not come before the noun. Instead, it follows a linking verb. The most common linking verb is *be*. An adjective that completes a linking verb modifies the subject. It is called a subjective complement.

Exercise 6

Find the adjective used as the subjective complement in each sentence and tell which noun it modifies.

1. The chairs for dollhouses are tiny.
2. This jar of peanut butter was full yesterday.
3. The plan for a bake sale might be workable.
4. This velveteen seems smooth.
5. Suddenly the wind was silent.
6. A trip into the haunted house could be dangerous.
7. Frances Hodgson Burnett's novels remain popular with children and adults.
8. The lemonade tasted bitter.
9. The noses of the presidents on Mount Rushmore are really gigantic!
10. The basket of laundry is heavy.

Complete each sentence with an adjective used as a subjective complement.

11. Buck's saddlebags are _____.
12. This morning the chimes from the cathedral were

    _____.
13. Those mugs are _____.
14. Mr. Graham's antique sleigh looks _____.
15. The mountains ahead of us appear _____.

Exercise 7

Tell whether each italicized adjective comes before a noun or is a subjective complement.

1. Can you name the *smallest* ocean?
2. The *natural* beauty of Switzerland is described in this book.
3. Becky is planning a *big* party for her cat.
4. The results of Arno Sierra's experiment were *remarkable*.
5. These streets are *narrow* and *steep*.
6. She heard a *weird* sound.
7. We gazed upon *endless* miles of *dusty* desert.
8. Abebe Bikila was *barefoot* when he won the Olympic marathon in 1960.
9. The *ordinary* incident was described in an *exaggerated* manner by Rodney.
10. The Taj Mahal in India is an *exquisite* building made of *white* marble.
11. Sean will travel through *Italian* vineyards.
12. The Assyrians were *firm* rulers.
13. Mr. and Mrs. Seton have been *generous* neighbors.
14. *Twenty* guards have already surrounded the *open* vault.
15. The *large* praying mantis on the vine was *motionless*.

A hilltop in Italy

Words Used as Nouns and Adjectives

> **The use of a word in the sentence determines its part of speech. Some words can be used as nouns or adjectives.**

It frequently happens that the same word may be used as different parts of speech. Notice the use of the word *light* in the following sentences:

Ron extinguished the *light*. (*Noun*)
I couldn't find the *light* switch in the dark. (*Adjective*)

A noun is a name word. An adjective describes or limits a noun.

Exercise 8

Tell whether each word in italics is a noun or an adjective.
1. Her fingers flew over the *ivory* keys on the piano.
2. Elephant and walrus tusks are made of *ivory*.
3. Marbles are sometimes made by melting scraps of *glass*.
4. The old books are protected in a *glass* case.
5. Early trains were often called "*iron* horses."
6. The *iron* left a brown spot on my shirt.
7. The swimming pool should reopen in *May*.
8. Because of the harsh winter, I don't think there will be many *May* blossoms.
9. In some parts of France, there are *cave* homes.
10. By the entrance to the magical *cave* was a small dragon.
11. I can't write my report if I don't have any *paper*.
12. Some potato chips are packaged in *paper* cans.
13. This *country* road will lead you through fields of cantaloupes.
14. Can you name the smallest *country* in the world?
15. My uncle has a *country* house where he spends the summer.

Practice Power

A. Rewrite the following paragraph and add descriptive adjectives. Try to add at least five descriptive adjectives.

   The sun shines through the water near the shore. Here the floor of the sea is a garden. Stones and shells and coral rest on the bottom. Schools of fish flitter past. Seaweed moves with the waves. In places, a can or an object shows the presence of people on the beach nearby.

B. Write five descriptive sentences about the picture on this page. Some of these sentences should use descriptive adjectives before the noun, and some should use descriptive adjectives following the verb.

Lesson 2 Limiting Adjectives

A limiting adjective either points out an object or indicates number.

The band marched down the street. (*Points out an object*)
There are *twenty* jellybeans in the jar. (*Indicates number*)
This gift arrived from South America. (*Points out an object*)

You will learn about the most important kinds of limiting adjectives in this lesson and in lesson 3.

Articles

The articles are *the, a,* and *an*.

***The* is the definite article. *A* and *an* are indefinite.**

The rodeo last week drew thousands of people. (*Definite*: refers to a *specific* rodeo)
A rodeo is exciting. (*Indefinite*: refers to *any* rodeo)

The following rules apply to articles:
1. The definite article *the* may be used with either singular or plural nouns: *the* ship, *the* brushes.
2. The indefinite articles *a* and *an* may be used only with singular nouns: *a* clock, *an* ostrich.
3. The article *an* is used before a vowel sound: *an* apple.
4. The article *a* is used before a consonant sound: *a* feather.

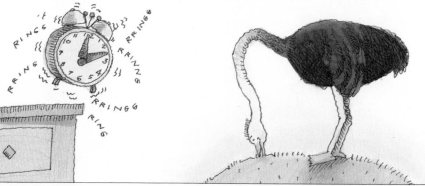

Exercise 1

Use an indefinite article before each of these nouns.

festival	hammer	relative	engineer
eggshell	curb	opening	football
pueblo	actor	villager	Icelander
umbrella	apron	antler	oboe
hour	eagle	kingdom	bonfire

Exercise 2

Complete these sentences by adding definite or indefinite articles.

1. _____ apple _____ day keeps _____ doctor away.
2. _____ unusual sight greeted us when we opened the door.
3. With bursts of speed up to thirty miles _____ hour, dragonflies are _____ fastest flying insects!
4. _____ Mississippi River is _____ longest river in North America.
5. _____ dog walked slowly along _____ railroad tracks.
6. _____ designs inside _____ kaleidoscope are formed from _____ reflections of plastic chips in small mirrors.
7. _____ crocodile slipped into _____ shallow water.
8. I felt _____ huge, hairy arm wrap around my shoulders!
9. We did not have _____ answer to _____ riddle.
10. _____ skinny dog followed Ms. Lopez into _____ butcher shop.

Numeral Adjectives

A numeral adjective indicates exact number.

I have *one* sandwich and *two* cookies in my lunch bag.
The *first* day of the week is Sunday.

Numeral adjectives may refer to the number of things or to the arrangement of things in numerical order. *One* and *two* tell how many. *First* gives the numerical position or rank of the day.

Exercise 3

Find the numeral adjectives in these sentences. Tell which noun each adjective modifies.

1. We celebrated my sister's fifth birthday by baking a peppermint cake.
2. After the first wolf howls, the rest of a pack often joins in.
3. We saw seven small kayaks going down the river.
4. You need the fourth edition of this thesaurus.
5. Twelve Americans have walked on the moon.
6. Four airplanes from the Blue Angels performed maneuvers.
7. All forty-one men on the ship signed the Mayflower Compact.
8. On their twentieth anniversary, our parents bought their second car.
9. Name the five contestants remaining in the spelling bee.
10. Aren't there eleven days left in this month?
11. Alfredo sat in the second row of the empty auditorium and sang aloud.
12. If the thirteenth day of a month is on Friday, some people actually believe they'll have bad luck.
13. One American flag waved in the breeze.
14. Two cars limped from the racetrack toward the pit.
15. The third little pig was smart to build its house out of brick.

Demonstrative Adjectives

> A demonstrative adjective points out a definite person, place, or thing.

The demonstrative adjectives are *this* and *that*. The plural of *this* is *these* and the plural of *that* is *those*. *This* and *these* refer to persons or things that are near at hand. *That* and *those* refer to persons or things that are farther away.

> *This* puzzle is impossible to solve. (*Near at hand*)
> *That* park has many bicycle trails. (*Farther away*)
> *These* machines will be very useful. (*Near at hand*)
> *Those* spectators will be late. (*Farther away*)

Each of the italicized adjectives points out a definite person, place, or thing.

A demonstrative adjective agrees in number with the noun it modifies. This is usually the noun closest to it.

Exercise 4

Put the correct demonstrative adjectives before the names of the following objects, which are *near at hand*.

_____ sandwiches   _____ kinds of problems
_____ doughnuts   _____ style of car
_____ street   _____ sort of thing
_____ dollar   _____ color of ink
_____ size of shoe   _____ styles of hair

Exercise 5

Put the correct demonstrative adjectives before the names of the following objects, which are *far away*.

_____ game   _____ pineapple
_____ magazines   _____ blueprints
_____ saxophones   _____ type of work
_____ kind of trap   _____ brands of butter
_____ sorts of pencils   _____ kinds of sports

Exercise 6

Find the demonstrative adjectives in these sentences. Tell whether each is *singular* or *plural*.

1. That stage is beautifully decorated with flowers.
2. We won the game because our shortstop fielded that last grounder.
3. This shield made of feathers belonged to an Aztec king centuries ago.
4. Amanda took these pictures of her relatives in Venice.
5. What were those strange sounds?
6. Kenneth brought this crystal radio to show the class.
7. Cotton will not grow in that hard soil.
8. The Beebes planted those kinds of vegetables last spring.
9. These colors are our school colors.
10. The scientist explained what this symbol on the chart meant.
11. That tongue twister is a tough one.
12. I didn't order this kind of soft drink.
13. These people are the hardest workers on the assembly line.
14. My mother uses this brand of flour for biscuits.
15. Are those model trains on sale?

Those and *Them*

Those is used to point out something. *Those* may be an adjective or a pronoun. *Them* is always a pronoun. It can never be used as an adjective.

Don't pick *those* flowers. (*Adjective*)
She likes these, but I prefer *those*. (*Pronoun*)
Do you like *them*? (*Pronoun*)

Exercise 7

Choose the correct word to complete each sentence.

1. I watched (those, them) sky divers jump from the plane.
2. Who knows how to handle (them, those) snapping crabs?
3. We plan to invite (them, those) to a jazz concert in the park.
4. Mr. Ziegler is going to move (those, them) bales of hay with a tractor.
5. Where did you buy (them, those) hockey sticks?
6. Dietra bought a pet mongoose from (those, them) yesterday.
7. The yard was bright with the flickering of (those, them) fireflies.
8. (Them, Those) toy cars have windup spring motors.
9. Whitney presses (those, them) flowers in a book.
10. Ms. McKay met (them, those) on a streetcar in San Francisco.

Complete each sentence with the correct word, *those* or *them*.

11. _____ boiled ears of corn are dripping with butter.
12. Did you meet _____ after their concert?
13. Scuba divers removed _____ pieces of red coral from the ocean floor.
14. Henry found _____ old photographs in a shoe box.
15. Who will carry _____ bags of cement to my car?

Practice Power

Find the words that describe or limit nouns in these sentences.

1. These trees are sturdy and strong.
2. A black spaniel jumped from the car!
3. These modern highways actually follow old Indian trails.
4. Those small white boats will try to dock at the busy harbor.
5. We believe the Babylonians made wise laws.
6. Those villagers have a Dutch tulip festival in the spring.
7. That hungry squirrel thought the small toy was an acorn.
8. Three players have already fouled out.
9. Brown bears climbed over the wooden fence.
10. An oasis is a fertile spot in a desert.

Lesson 3 More Limiting Adjectives

Possessive Adjectives

> A possessive adjective indicates ownership.

My dress is green.
The change is in *her* pocket.
Its wing is broken.

Our car is in the garage.
I met *your* uncle.
Their house is new.

Because the italicized words in these sentences modify nouns, they are adjectives. Since they show possession, they are called *possessive adjectives*.

The possessive adjectives are

	SINGULAR	PLURAL
FIRST PERSON	my	our
SECOND PERSON	your	your
THIRD PERSON	his, her, its	their

Exercise 1

Find the possessive adjectives in these sentences. Tell what noun each adjective modifies.

1. Why is our dog under the bench?
2. Young people all over the world read her book.
3. I want May Nguyen to sample my rice with saffron.
4. Carolyn painted her boat a soft shade of gray.
5. An oystercatcher slides its beak into the shell of an oyster, and then it cuts the muscle and pulls the meat out.
6. Did your brother bring his mitt to the ballpark?
7. Graham crackers got their name from Sylvester Graham, an early nutrition expert.
8. My friends are arriving from Australia next month.
9. This is our chance to see the world!
10. Ella stretched her long trunk to reach the marshmallow.

Complete each sentence with an appropriate possessive adjective. Be sure to vary your choices.

11. _____ new coat is made of wool.
12. Helen is named after _____ aunt.
13. Little Gordon Schuster likes to wear _____ cowboy outfit.
14. Grandfather and I enjoy sitting on _____ back porch while the sun sets.
15. Mr. Wilson is _____ candidate for president of the Senior Citizens' Craft Guild.
16. _____ son became a wise and powerful emperor.
17. The sparrow hawk missed _____ prey as it swooped down.
18. The woman felt that _____ voice was a musical one.
19. Have you seen _____ new stereo?
20. We should spend more of _____ time baby-sitting for Katrina.

Interrogative Adjectives

An interrogative adjective is used in asking a question.

Which and *what* are interrogative adjectives when they modify nouns and ask questions.

> *Which* road takes us to the stadium?
> *What* color is your new backpack?

Exercise 2

Find the interrogative adjectives in these sentences. Tell the noun that each modifies.
1. On what surface would you schuss?
2. What tree grows to be the tallest?
3. Which country is the most densely populated?
4. What sound does a kookaburra make?
5. Which color does ocher resemble?
6. In what country did the tulip originate?
7. From which direction does a zephyr blow?
8. What name did President Franklin Roosevelt give his dog?
9. Which leaves do silkworms eat?
10. Of what fruit is guacamole made?

Complete each sentence with an interrogative adjective.
11. _____ picture was on the first American postage stamp?
12. _____ animal is called a leviathan?
13. _____ purpose does a cranium serve?
14. _____ number of surfaces are on a dodecahedron?
15. On _____ part of your body would you wear a chapeau?

Practice Power

Do you like quiz questions? How many answers do you know to the questions in exercise 2? If you don't know the answer, where do you think you can find the information? Think of three quiz questions to ask your classmates. Use interrogative adjectives and in at least one of your sentences use a possessive adjective. Use the encyclopedia or other research books if you need to!

Lesson 4 Comparison of Adjectives

Comparison is the change that adjectives undergo to express different degrees of quality, quantity, or value.

Most adjectives have three degrees of comparison: the positive degree, the comparative degree, and the superlative degree.

The positive degree shows a quality.

That horse is *slow*.

The comparative degree shows a quality in a greater or a less degree.

Of the two, it is the *slower* horse.

The superlative degree shows a quality in the greatest or the least degree.

There goes the *slowest* horse of all.

The comparative degree is used when speaking of two persons or things. The superlative degree is used when three or more persons or things are compared.

How Adjectives Are Compared

1. Most adjectives of one syllable and some adjectives of two syllables form the comparative degree by adding *er* to the positive. They form the superlative degree by adding *est* to the positive.

POSITIVE	COMPARATIVE	SUPERLATIVE
tall	taller	tallest
rich	richer	richest
dark	darker	darkest
clear	clearer	clearest
quick	quicker	quickest
bright	brighter	brightest
soft	softer	softest
narrow	narrower	narrowest

a. If the positive degree of the adjective ends in *e*, the comparative degree is formed by adding *r*. The superlative degree is formed by adding *st* to the positive form.

POSITIVE	COMPARATIVE	SUPERLATIVE
safe	safer	safest
wise	wiser	wisest
brave	braver	bravest
ripe	riper	ripest
pure	purer	purest
large	larger	largest
tame	tamer	tamest

b. If the positive degree of an adjective of one syllable ends in a single consonant preceded by a single vowel, the consonant is doubled before adding *er* and *est*.

POSITIVE	COMPARATIVE	SUPERLATIVE
slim	slimmer	slimmest
hot	hotter	hottest
sad	sadder	saddest
big	bigger	biggest

c. If the positive degree of the adjective ends in *y*, preceded by a consonant, the *y* is changed to *i* before adding *er* and *est*.

POSITIVE	COMPARATIVE	SUPERLATIVE
noisy	noisier	noisiest
lazy	lazier	laziest
funny	funnier	funniest
friendly	friendlier	friendliest
happy	happier	happiest
pretty	prettier	prettiest
wealthy	wealthier	wealthiest
easy	easier	easiest

2. Adjectives of three or more syllables, and some of two syllables, form the comparative degree and the superlative degree by adding *more* and *most* or *less* and *least* before the positive form of the adjective.

POSITIVE	COMPARATIVE	SUPERLATIVE
courteous	more courteous	most courteous
generous	more generous	most generous
difficult	less difficult	least difficult
famous	less famous	least famous

3. Some adjectives may be compared by both methods: *worthy, worthier, worthiest; worthy, more worthy, most worthy.*

4. Certain adjectives are compared irregularly.

POSITIVE	COMPARATIVE	SUPERLATIVE
little	less	least
bad	worse	worst
good	better	best
many, much	more	most
late	later, latter	latest, last
far	farther	farthest
old	older, elder	oldest, eldest
near	nearer	nearest, next

5. Some adjectives cannot be compared; for example, *dead, perpendicular, eternal, circular, four, fifth, round, golden, this, that, square, every, all, triangular, whole, several.*

Exercise 1

Give the comparative and the superlative degrees of each of these adjectives by using *er* and *est*.

young	tough
brave	thick
mild	gentle
hazy	rude
glad	wet
lucky	shady
glossy	dim
cheap	poor
dreary	juicy
handy	strange

Exercise 2

Compare each of these adjectives by using *more* and *most* or *less* and *least*.

beautiful	common	industrious	numerous
thoughtless	successful	generous	helpful
gracious	fruitful	charitable	sensitive
reliable	dependable	comfortable	interesting
brilliant	familiar	valuable	fortunate

Exercise 3

Find the adjectives that can be compared and tell the degree of comparison of each.

1. Sir Galahad was a brave knight.
2. I prefer the smaller pumpkins for jack-o'-lanterns.
3. You gave a good description of the ghost town, Pete.
4. Courageous firefighters entered the burning building.
5. Did you see the rugged mountains in the distance?
6. Tyrannosaurus Rex was the fiercest dinosaur.
7. Let's walk down the sunnier side of the street.
8. The ripest blueberries will make the best pies.
9. These rocks are more difficult to climb over than the ones we just climbed.
10. It's a common mistake in multiplication.
11. The element mercury is the most sensitive to heat.
12. A python is longer than a boa constrictor.
13. According to the latest report, we can expect snow.
14. Is Sadie's car reliable?
15. The most valuable book in the world is a copy of the Bible printed in 1455.
16. Bicycle shops are busier in the summer than in the winter.
17. Clovers with four leaves are less numerous than those that have three.
18. We found interesting designs on the Easter eggs.
19. The deepest cave extends down 48,360 feet into the earth.
20. Much fruit is grown in California.

Correct Use of the Comparative and Superlative Degrees

Use the comparative degree when two persons or things are compared. Use the superlative degree when more than two are compared.

Miles is the *better* swimmer of the two. (*Two compared*)
Miles is the *best* swimmer on the team. (*More than two compared*)

HINT: The comparative degree is used with the word *than*.

Oranges are generally *larger than* limes.

For the comparative form, do not use *er* and the word *more* (or *less*) at the same time.

INCORRECT: more noisier

For the superlative form, do not use *est* and the word *most* (or *least*) at the same time.

INCORRECT: most noisiest

Exercise 4

Choose the correct word(s) to complete each sentence.

1. Which is (older, oldest)—the telegraph or the radio?
2. Lincoln was the (taller, tallest) president.
3. It is (colder, coldest) in Antarctica than it is here.
4. Of the triplets, Kip is the (less mischievous, least mischievous).
5. Which is (thinner, thinnest), a needle or a pin?
6. Jeanette is the (better, best) driver in her family.
7. The triangle is the (simpler, simplest) instrument in an orchestra.
8. China has the (greater, greatest) population in the world.
9. The San Diego Zoo has the (larger, largest) number of animals of any zoo in the world.
10. Which subject is (less difficult, least difficult), math or science?

Riding camels in Mongolia

295

Exercise 5

Complete each sentence with the correct form of the adjective in parentheses. Give a reason for your answer.

1. The Amazon River is the (long) river in South America.
2. This problem is (difficult) than the other one.
3. Researchers believe that gliding opossums of Australia are the (small) of all gliding animals.
4. The saguaro is the (tall) cactus in North America.
5. This book is the (good) one that Andy has read.
6. Moles spend (much) time underground than any other place.
7. Rhode Island is (small) than Delaware.
8. Wyatt raised the (big) pumpkin of all.
9. The diamond is the (hard) of all stones and will even cut glass.
10. Was J. P. Morgan (wealthy) than John D. Rockefeller?

Write a sentence showing the correct use of these adjectives.

11. more cheerful
12. worst
13. warmest
14. better
15. most delicate

Practice Power

Write two sentences comparing two sports teams, two sentences comparing two styles of clothes, and two sentences comparing three television personalities. Each sentence should contain the comparative or the superlative degree of an adjective.

Chapter Challenge

Read this paragraph carefully and answer the questions.

¹The harbor is alive with ships from around the world. ²Several freighters rock on the tide, graceful liners glide up to the piers, and tugs wander in and out of the harbor. ³The tugs, which are smaller than the other vessels, look tiny compared to the black hulls of the freighters. ⁴Two pleasure boats cruise up the river. ⁵Strains of cheerful music from their orchestras float toward shore. ⁶What a busy picture of life on American waters this port shows!

1. Name an adjective used as a subjective complement in sentence 1.
2. What noun does this subjective complement modify?
3. Name a limiting adjective in sentence 1.
4. Name an adjective in the comparative degree in sentence 3. Write the two other degrees of this adjective.
5. Name the three descriptive adjectives in sentence 3.
6. Find a numeral adjective in the paragraph.
7. What noun does the numeral adjective modify?
8. Is the word *pleasure* used as a noun or an adjective in sentence 4?
9. Is *cheerful* in sentence 5 a descriptive or limiting adjective?
10. Find a proper adjective in the paragraph.
11. Name an indefinite article in sentence 6.
12. Find a demonstrative adjective in sentence 6.
13. Does the demonstrative adjective modify a singular or plural noun?
14. Write the comparative and the superlative forms of *cheerful* in sentence 5.
15. Does the paragraph contain any adjectives in the superlative degree?

Creative Space 3

Buffalo Dusk

The buffaloes are gone.
And those who saw the buffaloes are gone.
Those who saw the buffaloes by thousands and how they
　　pawed the prairie sod into dust with their great hoofs,
　　their great heads down pawing on in a great pageant
　　of dusk,
Those who saw the buffaloes are gone.
And the buffaloes are gone.

　Carl Sandburg

Exploring the Poem...

Carl Sandburg was one of the first American poets to experiment with *free verse*. Free verse does not use rhyme. The poem in Creative Space 2, "City," uses rhyme to help express the meaning of the poem. In this poem, Sandburg uses *repetition* instead of rhyme to provide clear, powerful images.

Repetition comes from the word *repeat*. What sentences are repeated in this poem? Why do you think they are repeated? In the middle section of the poem, Sandburg describes the buffalo. What words does he repeat? Does the repetition help you to see the buffalo clearly?

★ With your classmates, think about some things that have changed from the past to today. Choose an idea and put it into a sentence, like the first sentence of Sandburg's poem. Your idea can be serious, like Sandburg's, or more lighthearted.

Here are some possible first sentences.

The summer is gone.	The Model T car is gone.
The dinosaurs are gone.	The Pilgrims are gone.
My pet mouse is gone.	My favorite old sneakers are gone.

Try writing your own poem. Follow the same form as Sandburg does. Here is an example.

My pet mouse is gone.
And the cat that ate my pet mouse is gone.
The cat that eyed my pet mouse for days and dreamed
    of tasty mouse desserts in its cat sleep for nights,
    and watched my mouse with its shining cat eyes
    until today,
My pet mouse is gone.
And the cat that ate my pet mouse is gone.

Chapter 4

Verbs

Lesson 1 Working with Verbs

A verb is a word used to express action or being.

In her seventies, Grandma Moses *started* a new hobby. She *sewed* pictures with yarns. Then the rheumatism in her hands *worsened*. Needlework *was* now difficult for her. At her sister's suggestion, she *switched* to painting as a pastime. Some of her paintings on display in a drugstore window *attracted* the attention of an art collector. Several years later, there *was* an exhibit of her paintings in New York City, and Grandma Moses *gained* fame by the age of eighty-five. Grandma's paintings *remain* popular. People *admire* them for their simplicity and charm. Her paintings *show* the countryside of America in all its bright colors and throughout its changing seasons. Grandma once *wrote* that her choice of a hobby *was* chicken raising until she *began* painting. Many people *are* happy that she *began* her new hobby.

Look at the italicized words in the paragraph. Some express action. They are the verbs *started, sewed, worsened, switched, attracted, gained, admire, show, wrote,* and *began*. Some express being. They are the verbs *was, remain,* and *are*.

Without a verb, there can be no sentence.

Find a cool, shady spot for our picnic. (*A sentence—with the verb* Find)
In the shade of the elm tree. (*Not a sentence—no verb*)

There is much activity on this farm before Thanksgiving. Can you give action verbs that tell what the people and animals are doing?

Exercise 1

Make a sentence from each group of words by adding an action verb or verb of being.

1. My little brother _____ only the green jellybeans.
2. Those German music boxes _____ several tunes.
3. The airplane _____ over the Grand Canyon.
4. Grandpa Walsh _____ an expert fiddle player.
5. A hungry tabby cat _____ in our yard.
6. White _____ a good color to wear in hot weather.
7. The average child in the United States _____ about thirty-three quarts of popcorn a year.
8. Yesterday the crowd in Carter Stadium _____ through the gates.
9. Aunt Elise's story about the disastrous camping trip _____ everyone.
10. These photographs _____ of the first bathing suits.
11. The instructor at the YMCA _____ the basic pool safety rules.
12. The Scottish word for a lake _____ *loch*.
13. Leonardo da Vinci _____ some of the world's most beautiful art.
14. The puzzle _____ five thousand pieces.
15. Hermit crabs _____ along the rocks in the tide pools.

Exercise 2

Some of these groups of words are sentences. Others are not because they do not have a verb. For those that are sentences, name the verb.

1. Thousands of buffalo roamed the open prairie.
2. The graceful skaters circled the ice rink.
3. Here nearly three hundred years ago.
4. Without a shadow of a doubt!
5. Adam typed forty-five words in one minute.
6. Straight black hair, blue eyes, and high cheekbones.
7. A maroon and yellow hot-air balloon drifted overhead.
8. At the first eerie sound, the tired camper crawled quickly out of her tent.
9. On the top of the huge mountain.
10. The beagle chased the squirrel under the towels on Mrs. Pettigill's clothesline.
11. The mess on the table and in the sink.
12. Larry shoved the canoe into the muddy currents.
13. We slid across the lake on the slippery ice.
14. Marian tiptoed through the vegetable garden.
15. Down the street and around the corner.
16. My uncle handed me a foreign coin as a souvenir from his trip overseas.
17. A parade of children marched off the roller coaster.
18. Because of all their creative, exciting ideas.
19. After takeoff, Mikhail relaxed.
20. The first weavers, shoemakers, and other such craft workers.

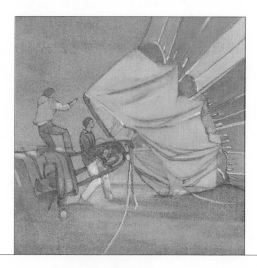

Verb Phrases

> **A verb phrase is a group of words that does the work of a single verb.**

The verb in some sentences consists of only one word. In many sentences, however, the verb is made up of two or more words, as in these examples:

The baby *was named* Leo.
The glasses *were resting* on Grandfather's stomach.
Marsha *has received* a certificate for free ice cream.

The words in italics are all verb phrases, since they do the work of single verbs.

The words that make up a verb phrase are usually written together. In some sentences, however, particularly in interrogative and negative sentences, the parts of the verb phrase may be separated.

Have you *read* about the adventures of Tom Sawyer?
When *did* you *live* in Italy and Japan?
My name *was* not *called* by the leader.

Have read, did live, and *was called* are verb phrases. The principal verbs in these sentences are *read, live*, and *called*. The other words, *have, did*, and *was*, are auxiliary verbs.

> **Any verb used with the principal verb is called an auxiliary verb.**

The common auxiliary verbs are

am	was	did	had	may	could
is	were	have	shall	can	should
are	do	has	will	might	would

Exercise 3

Find the verb phrases in these sentences. Tell which verb is the *principal verb* and which one is the *auxiliary verb*.

1. You might enjoy the pyrotechnics display.
2. A thousand weeds are growing in our garden—and only one flower!
3. Two tourists had lost their way among the winding streets.
4. Ellen will explain the dance steps.
5. Tom has tried several cleaners on this chocolate stain.
6. Have you ever watched dolphins in the ocean?
7. These topics were arranged in alphabetical order.
8. Frankly, I could eat four more hot dogs!
9. The African baobab tree can store more than twenty thousand gallons of water.
10. After that tumble, I am seeing stars.
11. How do people get those model ships into bottles?
12. Our track coach has developed special exercises for us.
13. You will always find money in a dictionary.
14. Tall Gothic cathedrals were built during the Middle Ages.
15. We shall help with the muscular dystrophy carnival.
16. Hans was secretly hoping for a postponement of his dental appointment.
17. Do you know the second verse of "Jingle Bells"?
18. Should you call a taxidermist for a rented tuxedo?
19. Coral reefs have changed the geography of the world.
20. Can you tell me the difference between a fruit and a vegetable?

Notre Dame Cathedral in Paris

Practice Power

Choose any nine auxiliary verbs from the list on page 304. Write nine sentences using these auxiliary verbs with the principal verbs listed below. Include at least two sentences that are interrogative as well as two with adverbs that divide the verb phrase.

excavate	launch	scamper
giggle	surprise	gaze
pretend	interrupt	juggle

Lesson 2 Principal Parts of Verbs

The principal parts of the verb are the present, the past, and the past participle.

These three parts are so important that they are called the *principal parts*. If you know the principal parts, you can use any form of the verb correctly.

The *past* never takes an auxiliary or helping verb. The *past participle* is always used with an auxiliary or helping verb.

> They *flipped* a coin for the last brownie. (*Past tense*)
> My cousins *have lived* in Australia for three years. (*Past participle with auxiliary verb*)

Regular and Irregular Verbs

A regular verb forms its past and its past participle by adding *d* or *ed* to the present.

PRESENT	PAST	PAST PARTICIPLE
bake	baked	baked
call	called	called
like	liked	liked
offer	offered	offered
play	played	played

These verbs and many others add *d* or *ed* to the present to form the past and the past participle. They are *regular verbs*.

> An irregular verb does not form its past and its past participle by adding *d* or *ed* to the present.

PRESENT	PAST	PAST PARTICIPLE
buy	bought	bought
sit	sat	sat
wear	wore	worn
write	wrote	written

The principal parts of irregular verbs are formed in various ways, generally by a change in the word itself. That is why they are called irregular verbs. There is no general rule for forming the principal parts of such verbs. It will be necessary for you to learn the principal parts in order to use the different forms of the verbs correctly.

The past and the past participle of irregular verbs are often confused. Remember the *past* never takes an auxiliary or helping verb. The *past participle* is always used with an auxiliary or helping verb.

A koala bear

Australian scenery

Here are the principal parts of the more common irregular verbs. They should be carefully studied.

PRESENT	PAST	PAST PARTICIPLE
	(These stand alone.)	(These require a *helper*, such as *have*.)
am (is, be)	was	been
beat	beat	beat, beaten
begin	began	begun
bend	bent	bent
bet	bet	bet
bind	bound	bound
bite	bit	bitten
blow	blew	blown
break	broke	broken
bring	brought	brought
build	built	built
burst	burst	burst
buy	bought	bought
catch	caught	caught
choose	chose	chosen
come	came	come
do	did	done
draw	drew	drawn
drink	drank	drunk
eat	ate	eaten
fall	fell	fallen
fight	fought	fought
find	found	found
flee	fled	fled
fly	flew	flown
forget	forgot	forgotten
freeze	froze	frozen
give	gave	given
go	went	gone
grow	grew	grown
have	had	had
hear	heard	heard
hide	hid	hidden
hurt	hurt	hurt

PRESENT	PAST	PAST PARTICIPLE
keep	kept	kept
know	knew	known
lay	laid	laid
leave	left	left
lend	lent	lent
let	let	let
lie (recline)	lay	lain
lose	lost	lost
make	made	made
meet	met	met
ride	rode	ridden
ring	rang	rung
rise	rose	risen
run	ran	run
see	saw	seen
send	sent	sent
set	set	set
shake	shook	shaken
sing	sang	sung
sink	sank	sunk
sit	sat	sat
speak	spoke	spoken
spend	spent	spent
stand	stood	stood
stick	stuck	stuck
swim	swam	swum
swing	swung	swung
take	took	taken
teach	taught	taught
tear	tore	torn
tell	told	told
think	thought	thought
throw	threw	thrown
wear	wore	worn
win	won	won
write	wrote	written

Exercise 1

Complete each of the following sentences with the past tense or the past participle of the irregular verb at the left. If an auxiliary verb is given, the past participle is to be used.

see
1. Yes, I _____ him perform in a concert.

burst
2. After the party, Teddy _____ every blue balloon.

eat
3. I _____ caviar for the first and last time yesterday.

come
4. A thundercloud _____ across the valley at thirty miles an hour.

wear
5. People _____ beautifully decorated masks for the Mardi Gras festival.

send
6. The magazine _____ over a thousand valentines to subscribers.

make
7. Toby had _____ three different cakes for the baking contest.

ride
8. Have you ever _____ on the back of a yak?

freeze
9. It's so cold that the water in the birdbath has _____.

ring
10. Has the fire alarm _____ yet?

grow
11. The banana plant has _____ a foot every year.

lose
12. The tourists have _____ their map and their guidebook.

write
13. Al _____ about the customs of the early Greeks.

hide
14. Where have they _____ the colored eggs?

go
15. Who has _____ to look for Ed?

tear
16. The bird _____ the paper into strips for its nest.

throw
17. I have _____ those dirty sneakers into the washer.

shake
18. After climbing from the pond, the retriever _____ water on everybody.

fall
19. Six feet of snow had _____ while we slept.

begin
20. Commercial television _____ in 1941.

sing
21. The court jester _____ a riddle for the king.

take
22. We have _____ this rocky path as a shortcut.

find
23. Archaeologists have _____ many human fossils in Tanzania.

break	24. Walt has _____ his big toe while kicking the football with his bare foot.
draw	25. Ron _____ cartoons for the class newspaper.
ride	26. The Lone Ranger always _____ a white horse.
give	27. This bag of peanuts has _____ me a burst of energy.
see	28. Have you _____ a falling star?
run	29. The sprinter _____ to the end of the track.
teach	30. No one _____ me how to fix my bicycle chain.
do	31. What have you _____ with the photographs of me?
know	32. I have _____ Fenster, the handyman, for years.
win	33. Who _____ the new sports car?
drink	34. Pearl's dog _____ the whole quart of lemonade!
hear	35. We have _____ the warning siren for several minutes now.
stand	36. The giraffes _____ around the acacia trees.
buy	37. I _____ a musical birthday card for my piano teacher.
choose	38. Bonita has _____ to study aikido, a martial art.
hear	39. The fire department had already _____ the tornado reports.
build	40. The ancient British _____ Stonehenge, a mysterious group of large stones.
sit	41. The cowardly lion _____ down behind the knight.
grow	42. The Chinese have _____ oranges for over four thousand years.
forget	43. Homer has _____ where he left his bicycle key.
bend	44. The blacksmith slowly _____ the iron into a horseshoe.
hurt	45. Ms. Graystone _____ her back pulling weeds.
fly	46. The birds have _____ north for the summer.
sink	47. My feet _____ into the sand.
lose	48. Who _____ the presidential election in 1984?
think	49. Sally _____ of a new use for her computer.
stand	50. On the top of the hill _____ the observatory.

Stonehenge in England

Troublesome Verbs

Lie and *Lay*

> The verb *lie* means to *rest* or *recline*. The principal parts are *lie, lay, lain*.
>
> The verb *lay* means to *put* or *place* in position. The principal parts are *lay, laid, laid. Lay* is usually followed by a direct object.

The soccer ball *lay* in the field. (=*rested*)
The veterinarian *laid* the sea gull on the table. (=*put*)

Study the chart below.

	REST OR RECLINE	PUT OR PLACE
PRESENT	lie	lay
PAST	lay	laid
PAST PARTICIPLE	(have) lain	(have) laid

Exercise 2

Choose the correct verb form to complete each sentence.
 1. Amelia (lies, lays) down for a nap every afternoon.
 2. Now (lie, lay) your hands on your head and run in place.
 3. Three yellow rosebuds (lay, laid) in the wicker basket.
 4. Where have you (lain, laid) Aunt Aggie's cowboy hat?
 5. Corinne (lain, laid) a towel over the kneaded dough.
 6. Your skates have (lain, laid) there for a week!
 7. Who will (lie, lay) the foundation of this house?
 8. The leopard (lies, lays) behind the bushes.
 9. Where should I (lay, lie) in the tent?
10. Julianna likes to (lie, lay) in the sun and listen to the radio.
11. Do you think the mail carrier (lay, laid) this package here?
12. Thomas, (lie, lay) on this cot and rest.
13. The carpenter (lay, laid) a hammer on the edge of the table.
14. How long has it (lain, laid) there?
15. A huge tree, chopped by beavers, (laid, lay) across the pond.

Sit and Set

> The verb *sit* means to *have* or *keep* a seat. The principal parts are *sit, sat, sat*.
>
> The verb *set* means to *place* or *fix* in position. The principal parts are *set, set, set. Set* usually has a direct object.

The monkey *sits* on a swing. (=*has a seat*)
Tom *set* the Christmas tree in a stand. (=*placed*)

Exercise 3

Choose the correct verb form to complete each sentence.
1. Louie and Huey (sat, set) in the sandbox this morning.
2. Please (sit, set) the pancakes in front of me.
3. Bonnie (sat, set) on the porch and looked at the stars.
4. (Sit, Set) those light bulbs down carefully.
5. Let's (sit, set) where we can see the stage.
6. The old hen (sits, sets) on any nest except her own.
7. (Sit, Set) the groceries in the back of the car.
8. Who (sat, set) this piece of bubble gum on his plate?
9. Our cat (sets, sits) in the window and stares at the birds.
10. (Sit, Set) here until you give your speech.
11. She made the child (set, sit) under the beach umbrella.
12. We (sat, set) on a log at the edge of the forest.
13. Dwayne (sit, set) his terrarium in the kitchen.
14. The hikers (sat, set) under the stone bridge.
15. (Sit, Set) the alarm for six o'clock.

Rise and Raise

The verb *rise* (*rise, rose, risen*) means to *ascend*.

The verb *raise* (*raise, raised, raised*) means to *lift*. *Raise* usually has a direct object.

The smoke *rose* from the chimneys. (= *ascended*)
Patti *raised* her hand to answer the question. (= *lifted*)

Exercise 4

Choose the correct verb form to complete each sentence.
 1. The speaker (rose, raised) to address the cheering crowd.
 2. Helena slowly (rose, raised) her hand.
 3. The camels (raised, rose) from their knees.
 4. Caleb's hang glider had (risen, raised) above the treetops!
 5. The captain of the boat (rose, raised) the flag.
 6. Jeff (rises, raises) before five o'clock.
 7. The Chinese kite (rose, raised) rapidly.
 8. She (rose, raised) her eyebrows at the question.
 9. A plume of smoke (rose, raised) from the campfire.
10. Cane Creek was (raising, rising) because of heavy rain.
11. (Rise, Raise) the freezer lid so we can get the meat out.
12. The temperature has (risen, raised).
13. The startled crows (rose, raised) from the cornfield.
14. Yoshi (rose, raised) the magnifying glass from the table.
15. Many people (raise, rise) earlier in the summer.

Let and Leave

> The verb *let* (*let, let, let*) means to *permit* or *allow*.
>
> The verb *leave* (*leave, left, left*) means to *abandon* or *depart*.

Let Monica play her violin. (=*permit* or *allow*)
We *left* for the parade early to get a good view. (=*departed*)

Exercise 5

Choose the correct verb form to complete each sentence.
1. Sy, (let, leave) the song end before you turn the radio off.
2. The express bus (lets, leaves) at three o'clock.
3. (Let, Leave) those pennies in the fountain!
4. Diego (let, left) his backpack behind the old shed.
5. (Leave, Let) me go with you on the nature walk!
6. He (let, left) all the dinosaur bones undisturbed.
7. Why has Deirdre (let, left) the room?
8. Ross (let, left) me help paint the St. Patrick's Day mural.
9. The plane does not (let, leave) until noon.
10. Has he (let, left) his new address with you?
11. We shall (let, leave) the children name the new park.
12. (Leave, Let) Mikey try it first!
13. I promise that I'll (let, leave) you use my mitt.
14. The puppy (let, left) a trail of cookie crumbs.
15. Don't (leave, let) anyone eat my french fries!

Teach and *Learn*

The verb *teach* (*teach, taught, taught*) means to *give* instruction.

The verb *learn* (*learn, learned, learned*) means to *receive* instruction.

I *taught* them how to yodel. (= *gave instruction*)
I've already *learned* how to yodel. (= *received instruction*)

Exercise 6

Choose the correct verb form to complete each sentence.
 1. The coach (taught, learned) me how to spin a basketball on my finger.
 2. Our dog, Sauerkraut, (taught, learned) to beg for German food.
 3. I (teach, learn) about the world economy by reading the newspaper.
 4. Abe Lincoln (taught, learned) himself by reading borrowed books.
 5. Baby woodpeckers watch their parents and (teach, learn) how to find worms.
 6. Linda, (teach, learn) me how to play bocce.
 7. Did the scouts (teach, learn) you how to tie a half hitch?
 8. Each student (teaches, learns) a first-aid procedure to a younger partner.
 9. Will you (teach, learn) your lines in the play by tonight?
 10. Please (teach, learn) me how to adjust the gears on my bike.

Practice Power

Write a short paragraph about wrapping a gift. You wanted to make the outside of the gift as special as the inside. Explain what you did. Use at least five irregular verbs from the list on pages 308 to 309.

Lesson 3 Transitive and Intransitive Verbs

Transitive Verbs

A transitive verb expresses an action that passes from a doer to a receiver.

DOER	ACTION	RECEIVER
Mary	read	the book.

In this sentence, the action (*read*) passes from the doer (*Mary*) to the receiver (*book*). The verb *read* is, therefore, a transitive verb.

To determine the receiver of the action, ask the question *whom* or *what* after the verb. Mary read *what*? The word that answers the question is the receiver of the action. It is called the direct object of the verb. The direct object of the verb *read* in this sentence is *book*.

The verbs in the sentences below are transitive.

Charlie *caught* a firefly. (*The word* firefly *is the direct object.*)
Stella *delivers* the newspaper. (*The word* newspaper *is the direct object.*)

317

Exercise 1

The verb in each sentence is transitive. Identify the verb. Then name the doer and the receiver of the action.

1. With a steady hand, Mamie carefully lit the candle.
2. Simon wears a heavy cape at his magic lessons.
3. We baked the brownies just a little too long.
4. In 1891, Dr. James Naismith invented basketball.
5. The chickadees ate all the seeds in the feeder.
6. You tore a valuable piece of paper.
7. The tourists stalked the lions with their cameras.
8. The tailor made clothes for everyone but himself.
9. The Great Wall of China protected that country for centuries.
10. My dog makes spectacular catches of my Frisbee.
11. Galileo studied the moon with a telescope.
12. The winner broke the record for the school.
13. My friend wrote this letter in our secret code.
14. The class celebrated all the birthdays on one day.
15. Carolyn learned violin through the Suzuki method.

The Great Wall of China

Intransitive Verbs

> **An intransitive verb has no receiver of its action.**

Franklin *lived* on the seventy-fifth floor.

The action of this verb, *lived*, begins and ends with the doer. There are no answers to the questions "Franklin lived *whom?*" or "Franklin lived *what?*"

An intransitive verb may be followed by a prepositional phrase or an adverb. The phrase or adverb does not receive the action.

The scouts hiked *in the wilderness*. (*Prepositional phrase*)
The ice melted *quickly*. (*Adverb*)

Exercise 2

The verb in each sentence below is intransitive because there is no *receiver* of the action. Find the verb. Then name the doer in each sentence.

1. Skiers raced recklessly down the icy slope.
2. An excited fan leaned forward.
3. Christmas Island lies in the Indian Ocean.
4. Those astronauts spoke about their next space flight.
5. Finally beside a warm fire, Gabby whistled happily.
6. A moose suddenly appeared at the edge of the lake.
7. The snowy ground glistens in the early morning sun.
8. The bells on Karin's costume jingled softly.
9. A Moroccan flag floated in the warm breeze.
10. The starlings nest in these trees every night.
11. James went to countless Little League baseball practices.
12. Houseflies walk upside down or right side up.
13. Uranus travels around the sun every eighty-four Earth years.
14. The president resides in Washington, D.C.
15. The entire group of seals plunged beneath the waves.

Verbs That Are Transitive or Intransitive

> Some verbs may be either transitive or intransitive, according to their use in the sentence.

TRANSITIVE	INTRANSITIVE
Orlando *counted* the pennies.	Orlando *counted* carefully.
Jean *painted* stars on the ceiling.	Jean *painted* all day.
The rock *broke* the window.	The glass *broke*.

Exercise 3

The verbs in these sentences can be used as transitive or intransitive verbs. Find the verb in each sentence, and tell whether it is *transitive* or *intransitive*.

1. My aunt grows prize-winning tomatoes.
2. The alfalfa sprouts grew in a glass jar on the windowsill.
3. Chewy entered a bubble-gum-blowing contest.
4. We entered quietly through the back door.
5. I actually flew in a helicopter.
6. My uncle flew an antique plane in the air show.
7. For our class project, we wrote a complicated program on the computer.
8. George always writes with a number-two pencil.
9. Carita lost the tennis match to her best friend.
10. Joe and Carlos seldom lose in Scrabble competitions.

Exercise 4

Find the verb in each sentence. Name the doer of the action.
Name the receiver if there is one. Tell if each verb is *transitive*
or *intransitive*.

1. The cold winds howl fiercely through the cracks in the wall.
2. Sir Spencer answered the wizard's question correctly.
3. The hot-air balloonist postponed his flight until a sunny day.
4. Cut daisies wilt quickly.
5. The fast train runs between Paris and Lyons.
6. Our dog likes chocolate, bananas, and peanut butter!
7. That factory recycles old newspapers.
8. The marching band plays during halftime.
9. Fresh sawdust completely covered the floor of the workshop.
10. Joey Weitzman hurried into the noisy henhouse.
11. We saw the old ship on display in the harbor.
12. Mitchell's cousin came from New Zealand.
13. During the day, hippopotamuses spend their time in water.
14. The excited puppy bounded after the red car.
15. Vacationers see active volcanoes in Hawaii.

Practice Power

Write sentences using these four verbs as transitive verbs:

 carry, dip, explore, paint

Write sentences using these four verbs as intransitive verbs:

 bounce, relax, fly, travel

Lesson 4 Linking Verbs

A linking verb links the subject with a noun, pronoun, or an adjective. The word that follows a linking verb is called a *subjective complement.*

SUBJECT	LINKING VERB	SUBJECTIVE COMPLEMENT
Those girls	are	club *members*. (*Noun*)
That boy	is	*he*. (*Pronoun*)
Ted	was	*enthusiastic*. (*Adjective*)

Each of the verbs in these sentences needs a *complement* to *complete* its meaning. The verb links this complement with the subject. The verb *are* links the complement *members* with the subject *girls*. The verb *is* links the complement *he* with the subject *boy*. The verb *was* links the complement *enthusiastic* with the subject *Ted*.

The noun, pronoun, or adjective that completes the meaning of these verbs is called a subjective complement.

The verb *be* is the most common linking verb. Its various forms are

am	is	was	being
be	are	were	been

The following verbs also can be used as linking verbs.

appear	feel	remain	sound
become	grow	seem	taste
continue	look	smell	

When these verbs are used as linking verbs, a form of the verb *be* can be substituted for the original verb.

John *looked* healthy.	John *was* healthy.
The whistles *sounded* shrill.	The whistles *were* shrill.
The day *grew* hot.	The day *was* hot.

Exercise 1

Find the linking verb in each sentence. Tell whether the italicized complement is a *noun*, a *pronoun*, or an *adjective*.

1. The beach was *sunny* all morning.
2. The girl in the chemistry class is *she*.
3. These handwoven Navaho blankets are very *warm*.
4. The duck-billed platypus is an egg-laying *mammal*.
5. Trojans were *enemies* of the ancient Greeks.
6. The trip through Mavis Hargrove's old mansion was *scary*.
7. The lumberjack in the red plaid jacket was *he*.
8. Prizes at rodeos were often *buckles* for the cowboys' belts.
9. The poppy seed bagels are still *warm*.
10. A bookmobile is a *library* on wheels.

Exercise 2

Find the linking verb and complement in each sentence. Then substitute a form of the verb *be* for the original verb.

1. The cornstalks in Kansas grow very tall.
2. This grapefruit ice cream tastes unique.
3. Marilee, the librarian, seems knowledgeable about cats.
4. The Red Sea appears reddish—but only at certain times.
5. Five blocks away, the siren still sounds clear.
6. The sky looks cloudy today.
7. Uncle Jack's fried crawfish smell appetizing.
8. We feel happy about the election results.
9. Irene Ross became our class president.
10. Somehow, Ramona remained calm throughout the Olympic competition.

Exercise 3 Review

Find the verbs in these sentences. Tell whether each is *transitive*, *intransitive*, or a *linking verb*.

1. Louis was friendly to the new boy down the street.
2. The ferocious tiger and the friendly cat are members of the same family.
3. The runaway toboggan slid down the hill.
4. Mr. Waldorf saw the Coast Guard cutter in the harbor.
5. Beavers build new dams across Lumbee Creek every year.
6. A balloon pops in a tiny fraction of a second.
7. A computer chip is actually a tiny piece of sand.
8. Wild red foxes never grow completely tame in captivity.
9. Harriet trudged to the farmhouse.
10. A brightly uniformed band leads the parade.
11. We heard the screech of a blue heron from the marsh.
12. More than twenty million people live in the Himalayas.
13. Many Spaniards danced in the streets of Pamplona.
14. An usher in a tuxedo conducted us to our seats.
15. Sir Arthur Conan Doyle, a doctor, wrote many famous detective stories.
16. The kite rose above the pine trees.
17. Louisa became an excellent gymnast.
18. The photographer waited patiently for a zebra.
19. I eagerly pulled the bundle of letters from the mailbox.
20. President Ulysses S. Grant was one of Mark Twain's friends.

Practice Power

You have just walked into the world-famous shop the Sweet Tooth. What kind of food do you think this shop sells? Describe the shop. Write sentences using some form of these six linking verbs:

taste, look, feel, smell, appear, seem

Lesson 5 Simple Tenses

The tense of a verb shows the time of the action or being.

You *walk* the dog today.
Calvin *walked* the dog yesterday.
Myra *will walk* the dog tomorrow.

Today is present time, *yesterday* is past time, and *tomorrow* is future time. Notice how the verb *walk* changes in form when used to show these various times. This quality of a verb is called *tense*. The word *tense* means "time."

> **The *present tense* shows action or being in present time.**

He *sings* in the musical today.
We *are* members of the drama club.

If the subject is a singular noun or a pronoun in the third person singular, the verb form ends in *s* in the present tense.

Josie *acts* in all the school plays.

> **The *past tense* shows action or being in past time.**

He *sang* last night.
We *were* members of the drama club last year.

> **The *future tense* shows action or being in future time.**

He *will sing* tomorrow.
They *will be* members of the drama club next year.

The auxiliary verb *shall* or *will* is used to form the future tense.

Exercise 1

Find the verb in each sentence and give its tense.

1. Big Paul Bunyan combed his curly hair with a saw!
2. Felix found his key on the dusty shelf.
3. A flea jumps two hundred times the length of its own body.
4. When will your sister return from her watercolor workshop?
5. The first surfers were the Polynesians of the South Pacific.
6. I play classical music for my plants every morning.
7. Paige will perform a solo on the grand piano.
8. Our mail carrier delivers the mail at ten o'clock every day.
9. Juan lives in a one-bedroom apartment in Dallas.
10. The pipe organ is the largest musical instrument.
11. The dancer twirled close to the edge of the stage.
12. We froze two trays of ice cubes for our lemonade stand.
13. Will you watch the last golfers tee off?
14. My cousins catch king mackerels from the pier at night.
15. Chan painted the fence with short, quick strokes.
16. Some redwood trees live more than one thousand years.
17. Will there be a holiday tomorrow?
18. The soapy water bubbled merrily over the sides of the washing machine.
19. Frankie will write a complaint to the president of the soft drink company.
20. In 1889, the reporter Nellie Bly traveled around the world in seventy-two days.

Exercise 2

Complete these sentences by supplying the tense indicated in parentheses for the verbs listed.

Talk

1. The club members _____ about their favorite books. (*Present*)
2. You _____ on the telephone for over an hour! (*Past*)
3. James _____ about nothing but his new motorcycle for a week. (*Past*)
4. The fire chief _____ to our class next week. (*Future*)
5. Mrs. Takada _____ quickly when she is excited. (*Present*)

Bring

6. My sister _____ my lunch to school when I forget it. (*Present*)
7. I _____ my bicycle inside whenever it looks like rain. (*Present*)
8. They _____ your guitar books back tomorrow. (*Future*)
9. The Spanish _____ the horse to the New World. (*Past*)
10. The museum director _____ some dinosaur bones for us to examine. (*Future*)

Burst

11. Bill grabbed the balloon and _____ it. (*Past*)
12. The dirt-covered detectives _____ through the door. (*Past*)
13. When I dropped it on the floor, the fat tomato _____ open. (*Past*)
14. The cherry trees _____ into bloom all around Washington. (*Future*)
15. My zebra finches _____ into song whenever a light is turned on. (*Present*)

Eat

16. They _____ a box of doughnuts in the bus station. (*Past*)
17. The construction workers _____ their lunch in the truck. (*Future*)
18. We _____ Italian dressing on our tossed salad. (*Present*)
19. An elephant _____ up to five hundred pounds of leaves, grass, and bark daily! (*Future*)
20. My friend has an allergic reaction if she _____ chocolate. (*Present*)

Choose

21. Magpies usually _____ thorny bushes for their nests. (*Present*)
22. The hikers _____ a spot under a sprawling oak tree for the picnic. (*Past*)
23. Oliver Smith _____ a plaid tie as his favorite. (*Past*)
24. The club _____ its slogan with a secret vote. (*Future*)
25. Lola _____ these flowers for the hall table. (*Present*)

Wear

26. The players _____ their uniforms for the first time. (*Past*)
27. Alice always _____ the ring her parents gave her. (*Present*)
28. He _____ a penguin outfit to the costume party. (*Future*)
29. The men _____ their hair short and their beards long. (*Present*)
30. I _____ an orange obi with my flowered kimono. (*Present*)

Practice Power

You probably have seen many exciting adventures in movies and on television. Pretend you are marooned on a deserted island. Write a paragraph explaining the situation you are in, how you got on the island, and what you will do to survive. Try to use verbs in the present, past, and future tenses in your paragraph.

Lesson 6 Compound Tenses

The compound tenses are the present perfect tense, the past perfect tense, and the future perfect tense.

> **The *present perfect tense* shows action completed in present time.**

He already *has sung* today.
We *have studied* geometry today.

The present perfect tense is formed by the auxiliary *have* or *has* plus the past participle of the verb.

> **The *past perfect tense* shows action completed before some definite time in the past.**

He *had sung* before we arrived at the recital.
We *had studied* algebra before we studied geometry.

The past perfect tense is formed by the auxiliary *had* plus the past participle of the verb.

> **The *future perfect tense* shows action that will be completed before some specified time in the future.**

He *will have sung* the song before you return.
We *shall have studied* geometry before evening.

The future perfect tense is formed by the auxiliaries *shall have* or *will have* plus the past participle of the verb.

Exercise 1

Find the verb phrase in each sentence, and give its tense.
1. My brother has driven his car about one thousand miles.
2. The prince and the pauper had switched places.
3. By dawn, my father will have reached his secret fishing spot.
4. Have you heard any good jokes lately?
5. I have done my best with the snake-charming act.
6. Had the zookeepers decided on a name for the baby panda?
7. Josey has spilled perfume all over her dresser.
8. They will have finished their African masks by noon.
9. Where have the cowhands taken that noisy herd of longhorns?
10. The slick tires had made a strange noise on the pavement.
11. Mr. Andretti and his wife have fed the pigeons the last bread crumbs.
12. Thomas had never made apple cider before.
13. By tomorrow, they will have completed decorations for the Christmas tree.
14. The carpenter has hit his thumb with the hammer.
15. The fox had wanted the grapes.

Exercise 2

Complete each sentence by supplying the tense indicated in parentheses for the verbs listed.

Talk

1. Carl _____ about the monster movie all day. (*Present perfect*)
2. The bus driver already _____ to us about wearing seat belts. (*Past perfect*)
3. Ms. Wilson _____ to the contest committee by Saturday. (*Future perfect*)
4. Our neighbors _____ to the construction crew about the noise. (*Present perfect*)
5. The newspaper reporter _____ to many witnesses before writing the story. (*Past perfect*)

Bring

6. Lila _____ oranges from Florida for me.
   (*Present perfect*)
7. The substitute mail carrier _____ the mail early.
   (*Present perfect*)
8. Before I realized it, the dog _____ mud into the
   house. (*Past perfect*)
9. He _____ the film projector before you return.
   (*Future perfect*)
10. Carol and Jody _____ their raincoats but not their
    umbrellas. (*Present perfect*)

Burst

11. Last winter the pipes under the house _____ before
    the renters moved in. (*Past perfect*)
12. After days of rain, the sun _____ through the clouds.
    (*Present perfect*)
13. Mysteriously, the soda bottles _____ during the
    previous night. (*Past perfect*)
14. The thinnest balloons _____ before they reach the
    ground. (*Future perfect*)
15. _____ your bicycle tire ever _____ before?
    (*Past perfect*)

Eat

16. I was surprised that the acid _____ a hole in my lab
    coat. (*Past perfect*)
17. Helena _____ three dozen sardines in the contest!
    (*Present perfect*)
18. Everyone in camp _____ breakfast before sunrise.
    (*Future perfect*)
19. Who _____ all the peanut brittle? (*Present perfect*)
20. The campers _____ the entire box of raisins by
    midnight. (*Future perfect*)

Choose

21. The government _____ the rose as the national flower. (*Present perfect*)
22. The boys _____ the chicken soup with rice, but they changed their minds. (*Past perfect*)
23. Everyone _____ geography projects by Friday. (*Future perfect*)
24. _____ they _____ Sancha as the new Safety Squad leader? (*Present perfect*)
25. The worms _____ the juiciest apples in the crate. (*Past perfect*)

Wear

26. That snowman _____ the same hat every day. (*Present perfect*)
27. The coach reported that the cheerleaders _____ their new uniforms to the rally. (*Past perfect*)
28. ____ he _____ that navy suit before graduation? (*Past perfect*)
29. They _____ their graduation gowns before the actual day. (*Future perfect*)
30. I _____ holes in all of my socks. (*Present perfect*)

Exercise 3

Complete each sentence by supplying the tense indicated in parentheses for each verb.

appear   1. Stars soon _____ in the gray twilight sky. (*Past tense*)

order   2. Doctor Chin _____ him to go to a warm, sunny climate. (*Past tense*)

gain   3. By the time she joined Buffalo Bill's Wild West Show in 1885, Annie Oakley _____ fame as a sharpshooter. (*Past perfect tense*)

lay   4. Grandmother's silver thimble _____ in her sewing basket. (*Past tense*)

finish   5. The artists _____ their work with oils. (*Present perfect tense*)

study   6. The astronomer _____ the distant planets through a powerful telescope. (*Present tense*)

drift   7. The lion cubs _____ to sleep beside their mother. (*Present perfect tense*)

fall   8. Snow _____ off and on during the skiing lessons. (*Past tense*)

win   9. Our team _____ the debate on which president was the greatest. (*Past tense*)

grow   10. Thousands of buttercups _____ around the abandoned log cabin. (*Present tense*)

take   11. My brother _____ a test to check his eyesight. (*Future tense*)

hide   12. The armadillo _____ behind the trash cans on T. J.'s property for a while before we noticed it. (*Past perfect tense*)

see   13. We _____ abstract paintings in the art gallery. (*Past tense*)

bring   14. The delivery person _____ the pizza in only thirty minutes. (*Past tense*)

place   15. Under his head, she _____ a blue and white striped pillow. (*Past tense*) build | 16. Wrens _____ a nest under the rusty tractor seat. (*Present perfect tense*)

close | 17. The grocery store _____ at eight o'clock. (*Present tense*)

teach | 18. Aristotle _____ his followers a clear method of reasoning. (*Past tense*)

tell | 19. I _____ him the unbelievable news by tonight. (*Future perfect tense*)

bake | 20. Vito _____ a delicious peach pie. (*Present tense*)

increase | 21. Michael _____ his pitching accuracy through practice. (*Past tense*)

celebrate | 22. People over the world _____ Pen Pal Day on September 23. (*Present tense*)

come | 23. Shetland ponies _____ from an island off Scotland. (*Past tense*)

give | 24. Gail, the zoo guide, _____ you directions to the aviary. (*Future tense*)

pack | 25. Explorers _____ eighty pounds of equipment on each burro. (*Present tense*)

Practice Power

The *synopsis* of a verb is a short way to practice using a verb in all the tenses. Any nominative case pronoun can be used. Study the example below, and then try to complete two on your own —one with the verb *land* and the personal pronoun *it* and the other with the verb *run* and the personal pronoun *they*.

Synopis for the Verb *See*

PRESENT TENSE	He sees
PAST TENSE	He saw
FUTURE TENSE	He will see
PRESENT PERFECT TENSE	He has seen
PAST PERFECT TENSE	He had seen
FUTURE PERFECT TENSE	He will have seen

Lesson 7 Agreement of Subject with Verb Part I

Verbs should agree with their subjects, both in person and in number.

A verb may be in the *first person*, the *second person*, or the *third person*. The first person refers to the speaker, the second person refers to the one spoken to, and the third person refers to the one spoken about.

In addition, the verb may be *singular* or *plural* in number. Singular refers to one; plural refers to more than one.

Note the changes in the verb in the sentences below as the subject changes from singular to plural or from first person to second and third persons. *The verb always agrees with the subject in person and number.* Note that all nouns are in the third person.

	SINGULAR NUMBER	PLURAL NUMBER
FIRST PERSON	I *am* his friend.	We *are* his friends.
SECOND PERSON	You *are* his friend.	You *are* his friends.
THIRD PERSON	She *is* his friend.	They *are* his friends.
FIRST PERSON	I *have* a two-dollar bill.	We *have* a two-dollar bill.
SECOND PERSON	You *have* a two-dollar bill.	You *have* a two-dollar bill.
THIRD PERSON	He *has* a two-dollar bill.	They *have* a two-dollar bill.
FIRST PERSON	I *walk* in the park.	We *walk* in the park.
SECOND PERSON	You *walk* in the park.	You *walk* in the park.
THIRD PERSON	It *walks* in the park. The child *walks* in the park.	They *walk* in the park. The children *walk* in the park.

Exercise 1

Name the subject and verb or verb phrase in each sentence. Tell the person and number of each verb or verb phrase.

1. Conifers are the only kind of tree near the top of a mountain.
2. We usually jog all the way home.
3. Your train has left!
4. The Mediterranean Sea contains a great amount of salt.
5. You have taped my finger to the box.
6. Louie flops on the couch with a bag of barbecue-flavored potato chips after football practice.
7. The twins often burst into laughter over their secret switches.
8. I was putting blue and green candles on Mia's birthday cake.
9. These albums contain photographs of early gold miners.
10. With every crash of thunder, the dog crawls farther and farther under my bed.
11. They speak softly in the library.
12. Grandmother has always kept a box of peppermints on a high shelf.
13. The trucks have come to clean the streets.
14. Huge caves lie under the earth's surface.
15. I have already taken the prescription to the pharmacy.

Singular and Plural Subjects

> A singular subject requires a singular form of the verb. A plural subject requires a plural form of the verb.

Notice the change in the form of the verb in each of the following sentences.

SINGULAR NUMBER	PLURAL NUMBER
A picture *hangs* on the wall.	Pictures *hang* on the wall.
She *sleeps* well.	They *sleep* well.
He *walks* to the park.	They *walk* to the park.
She *has* waited.	They *have* waited.

A noun or pronoun in the third person singular requires a verb that ends in *s* for the present tense.

Exercise 2

Find the subject in each sentence. Tell whether it is *singular* or *plural*. Then choose the correct verb.

1. My grandfather (sells, sell) antique furniture.
2. The logs on the truck (needs, need) a canvas cover.
3. The scouts (seems, seem) eager to leave for the mountains.
4. The starter (flags, flag) the cars to line up.
5. Noise (is, are) measured in units called decibels.
6. Seven Indian elephants (was, were) walking to the tent.
7. Those rockers (has, have) been repainted every summer.
8. The magician (show, shows) us a new trick at every performance.
9. Hail (has, have) ruined the corn crop this year.
10. The rolling hills (was, were) covered with purple and yellow wildflowers.
11. Do the avocados (looks, look) ripe enough for guacamole?
12. The sunset (has, have) beautiful shades of red and orange!
13. We (finds, find) quite a few fossils in rocky areas.
14. The most frequently sung song (is, are) "Happy Birthday to You."
15. Ms. Winston's miniature donkeys (has, have) been sold.

Exercise 3

Rewrite each sentence and change the italicized nouns from the plural to the singular. Then change the verb to agree with the new subject.

1. The *pictures* of sunflowers hang on the wall.
2. The *chalkboards* were full of sentences by students.
3. Have the *plates* been washed?
4. When left alone, the *puppies* climb up on the sofa.
5. Marge's front *teeth* are loose.
6. The *cookies* are cool enough to eat.
7. The *guards* direct traffic during rush hour.
8. There go the *trucks* to the fire!

Now change the italicized nouns from the singular to the plural. Then change the verb to agree with the new subject.

9. The *train* shakes the windows in our house.
10. The new *book* about outer space is on display in the library.
11. My *sister-in-law* swims a mile every day.
12. The silly *rooster* crows at sunset.
13. Does the *squirrel* bite?
14. Has the *wharf* been repaired?
15. The *messenger* brings us the daily report.

Sunflowers by Vincent van Gogh

There Is and *There Are*

There is or *there was* should be used when the subject, which follows the verb, is singular. *There are* or *there were* is used when the subject is plural.

> There (is, are) three windows in the room.

Here is the correct form: There *are* three windows in this room.

The subject *windows* is plural in number. To find the subject, omit the word *there* and rearrange the sentence: Three windows are in this room.

When a sentence begins with *there*, look for the subject after the verb.

Exercise 4

Find the subject in each sentence. Then choose the correct verb.
1. There (is, are) a thousand grams in a kilogram.
2. There (was, were) four robins eating.
3. There (is, are) many beautiful parks there.
4. There (were, was) seven wonders in the ancient world.
5. There (was, were) five kinds of flowers in this arrangement.
6. There (is, are) a group of baseball players warming up.
7. There (was, were) no key for this unusual box.
8. There (is, are) numerous groves of olive trees in Portugal.
9. There (was, were) a sudden knock at the door.
10. There (is, are) a beautiful rainbow in the sky.
11. There (was, were) several ripe peaches in the basket.
12. There (is, are) a box of saltwater taffy on the table.
13. There (is, are) thirty days in April.
14. There (was, were) ten gulls standing on the sandbar.
15. There (is, are) about one billion people in China.

Doesn't and Don't

If the subject of the sentence is in the third person, *doesn't* is the correct form in the singular. *Don't* is the correct form in the plural.

In the first and the second persons, the correct form is *don't*, whether the subject is singular or plural.

	SINGULAR NUMBER	PLURAL NUMBER
FIRST PERSON	I *don't* have a pet.	We *don't* have a pet.
SECOND PERSON	You *don't* have a pet.	You *don't* have a pet.
THIRD PERSON	He/She *doesn't* have a pet.	They *don't* have a pet.

Exercise 5

Complete each sentence with *doesn't* or *don't*.

1. Leta enjoys island life so much that she _____ want to leave Hawaii.
2. Why _____ Mr. McGregor wear his tartan kilt?
3. Leprechauns _____ really exist.
4. _____ Mrs. Rivera live northeast of the airport?
5. This _____ solve any of our problems.
6. They _____ know how to change a flat tire.
7. _____ a stalactite hang down from a cave ceiling?
8. If Kenny _____ watch out, he'll trip on the tree's roots.
9. Why _____ any of these letters have zip codes?
10. If you _____ want these photographs of old cars, let me have them.
11. Dad _____ believe in large allowances.
12. _____ you want a chance to break the piñata?
13. Apparently, I _____ know Morse code well enough.
14. This road _____ lead to the hollow oak tree.
15. Janet _____ eat red meat very often.

You as the Subject

Use the forms *you are* and *you were* whether the subject is singular or plural. Never use *is* or *was* when the subject is in the second person.

(Was, Were) you at the game today?

Here is the correct form: *Were* you at the game today?

The subject *you* is in the second person.

Exercise 6

Choose the correct form of the verb in each sentence.
1. (Is, Are) you looking for a four-leaf clover?
2. (Was, Were) you angry about the price of a hamburger?
3. (Was, Were) you frightened when the tree fell near your house during the storm?
4. You (are, is) welcome!
5. You (wasn't, weren't) there!
6. (Were, Was) you listening to the rock musician?
7. (Is, Are) you collecting rocks?
8. Where (was, were) you during vacation?
9. You (is, are) wrong about that.
10. You (are, is) late again!

Practice Power

Pretend you are a radio announcer in an age of dragons, knights, and princesses. Describe the action as a radio announcer would. Use the nouns listed below as subjects in your sentences and use strong action verbs in the present tense. Underline the subject and verb in each sentence.

dragons	a cave	a forest	knights
a castle	a princess	fire	horses

Lesson 8   Agreement of Subject with Verb Part II

Compound Subjects Connected by *And*

Compound subjects connected by *and* usually require a plural verb.

Janice and Marie (is, are) good friends.

Here is the correct form: Janice and Marie *are* good friends.

The subjects *Janice* and *Marie* are connected by *and*.

Exercise 1

Find the compound subject in each sentence. Then choose the correct verb.

1. King Arthur and Sir Galahad (was, were) friends.
2. The cat and her kitten (lie, lies) in the sun.
3. She and I (was, were) worried about the whimpering puppy.
4. Mr. Williams and his puppet (performs, perform) at the Red Globe Theater.
5. (Was, Were) your mother and father in the audience?
6. Tennis and golf (is, are) summer sports.
7. The lake and the river (was, were) covered with thin ice.
8. Hal and his staff (paints, paint) colorful designs on T-shirts.
9. Our stereo and television (are, is) both broken.
10. The parrot and the dog (sings, sing) in tune with the radio!
11. Longfellow and Whittier (were, was) early American poets.
12. The bison and the caribou (walk, walks) over eight hundred miles during migration.
13. Mathematics and history (is, are) my favorite subjects.
14. The woman and her daughter (writes, write) movie scripts.
15. Jason and I (make, makes) fancy envelopes from colorful pages out of magazines.

Special Pronouns

The distributive pronouns *each*, *either*, *neither* and the indefinite pronouns *anyone*, *no one*, *anybody*, *nobody*, *everyone*, *everybody*, *someone*, and *somebody* are always singular and require singular verbs.

Everybody (was, were) pleased with the result.

Here is the correct form: Everybody *was* pleased with the result.

The subject *everybody* is singular.

Exercise 2

Complete each sentence with the correct form of the present tense of the verb at the left.

know   1. No one _____ for certain why whales sing.

contain   2. Either of these books _____ information on Dutch holidays.

enjoy   3. I hope everybody _____ my sassafras tea.

agree   4. Neither of the students _____ with your theory.

like   5. Nobody _____ to get lost in a swamp full of snakes!

want   6. Here is a hoe if someone _____ to help with the garden.

buy   7. If our Indian corn isn't colorful, nobody _____ it.

admire   8. Everybody _____ Ada Harper's success in taming the wild raccoon.

carry   9. Neither lawyer _____ a briefcase.

know   10. Each of us _____ a shortcut to the Monroe Building.

leave   11. Someone always _____ the toothpaste uncapped.

fit   12. Neither of the jackets on sale _____ me.

ride   13. Anyone under age two _____ for free.

speak   14. Everyone _____ at once in these unorganized meetings!

believe   15. No one here _____ in mermaids.

Special Nouns

Such nouns as *deer, sheep, fish, swine, trout, salmon, cod, cattle, moose, corps,* and certain proper nouns, such as *Portuguese, Chinese, Swiss, Iroquois,* have the same form in the singular and the plural.

> This trout (is, are) twelve inches long.

Here is the correct form: This trout *is* twelve inches long.
The subject *trout* is singular.

> Many trout (is, are) caught in that stream.

Here is the correct form: Many trout *are* caught in that stream.
The subject *trout* is plural.

The sense of the sentence lets you know whether the subject is singular or plural.

Exercise 3

Find the subject in each sentence. Tell whether it is *singular* or *plural*. Then choose the correct verb.

1. There (is, are) several sheep grazing on the hillside.
2. This sheep (is, are) the only one that hasn't been sheared.
3. A male deer sometimes (scratch, scratches) his back with his antlers.
4. Many deer (ramble, rambles) through these woods.
5. A salmon (swim, swims) in the tank.
6. Salmon (are, is) found in the Columbia River.
7. The Swiss (has, have) four official languages: French, German, Italian, and Romansh.
8. That young Swiss (speak, speaks) four languages—and can yodel as well.
9. The Portuguese (were, was) great explorers.
10. Portuguese (is, are) a musical language.

Exercise 4 Review

Choose the correct verb form for each of the following sentences. Tell with which noun the verb agrees.

1. His directions (leads, lead) straight into the lake!
2. The first day of summer (was, were) June 21.
3. This watch (doesn't, don't) need to be wound.
4. Nobody (want, wants) to go and turn off the basement light.
5. Red and yellow (is, are) both primary colors.
6. Popcorn (is, are) a healthy and delicious snack food.
7. Each of these pieces (fits, fit) in the puzzle somewhere.
8. A zonkey (is, are) a cross between a donkey and a zebra.
9. (Was, Were) there any telephone calls for me today?
10. Everyone in our family (finish, finishes) dinner by seven o'clock.
11. Carla and Molly (collect, collects) old wooden toys.
12. Someone (is, are) bringing records to the party.
13. (Don't, Doesn't) you want to stay up until midnight?
14. There (was, were) a parking place on this side of the street two minutes ago.
15. Ricardo (ride, rides) his unicycle everywhere he goes.
16. (Is, Are) there a sports section in the newspaper?
17. The Japanese often (drink, drinks) ocha, a green tea, with their meals.
18. (Were, Was) you outside when it began to rain?
19. Chocolate and vanilla (is, are) the most popular flavors of ice cream.
20. There (are, is) no fish in the Dead Sea.

Practice Power

Write sentences using the following nouns as subjects. Choose action verbs in the present tense.

the moon and the sun
Japanese
everybody

sand crabs and starfish
flounder
no one

Chapter Challenge

Read this paragraph carefully and answer the questions.

¹Icebergs contain more than half the world's fresh water. ²Scientists have created a plan for the future to tow icebergs from the Antarctic to hot desert countries. ³The fresh water could irrigate the dry, thirsty land. ⁴Imagine it is the year 2050. ⁵The plan works this way. ⁶First, scientists choose a very large iceberg—at least five miles long and two miles wide. ⁷The iceberg itself actually becomes the ship. ⁸The crew members for the "ship" live on board the iceberg, which is driven by an engine. ⁹After the "ship" crosses the ocean, it is put into a giant plastic bag. ¹⁰The iceberg slowly melts, and water is piped into the fields to irrigate the land. ¹¹Scientists have estimated that one iceberg alone holds a supply of trillions of gallons of water. ¹²That is a big ice cube!

1. In sentence 1, is the verb singular or plural?
2. Name the auxiliary verb in sentence 2.
3. In sentence 3, name the receiver of the transitive verb *could irrigate*.
4. In sentence 5, is the verb *works* singular or plural in number? Why?
5. Name the verb in sentence 6. Give the past and past participle of this verb.
6. Name the linking verb and subjective complement in sentence 7.
7. In sentence 8, what person, number, and tense is the verb *live*?
8. In sentence 9, is the verb *crosses* transitive or intransitive? Why?
9. In sentence 10, is the verb *melts* transitive or intransitive? Why?
10. In sentence 11, which verb is present perfect tense?
11. In sentence 11, what person, number, and tense is the verb *holds*?
12. Name the linking verb in sentence 12. Does it link the subject with a noun, a pronoun, or an adjective?

Creative Space 4

Two Limericks

A fly and a flea in a flue
Were imprisoned, so what could they do?
Said the fly, "Let us flee!"
"Let us fly!" said the flea.
So they flew through a flaw in the flue.

There once was a pig that was thinner
Than the rest, so he thought, "What a winner!
They'll let me go free."
But mistaken was he.
The pig was the first to be dinner!

Exploring the Poem...

Do you recognize these poems as limericks? Most limericks are humorous. They are fun to read and write.

Read the limericks aloud. Can you hear the rhythm? In each limerick, which lines have the same rhythm?

Which lines rhyme? In these poems, the rhyme pattern is a-a-b-b-a. How are the rhythm and the rhyme connected to each other?

★ Try writing a limerick of your own. You can use one of the opening lines below to get started. As you write your limerick, the rhythm and rhyme pattern should help you to focus your ideas.

There once was a shoe that went walking...
There once was an elephant so thin...
A robot and its friends had a party...
Hot pizza's my favorite treat...
There once was a _____ in sixth grade...

Chapter 5

Adverbs

Lesson 1 Kinds of Adverbs

An adverb is a word that modifies a verb, an adjective, or another adverb.

The cowhand jumped on the horse *quickly*.

In this sentence, the adverb *quickly* modifies the verb *jumped*.

The bronco was *quite* wild.

In this sentence, the adverb *quite* modifies the adjective *wild*.

The cowhand rode the bucking bronco *very* skillfully.

In this sentence, *very* modifies *skillfully*, another adverb. *Skillfully* modifies the verb *rode*. *Very* is an *adverb of degree*. It tells *how much* or *how little*.

Adverbs may indicate time, place, manner, degree, affirmation, or negation.

Notice how the mountains are reflected in the water. What hobbies or talents are a reflection of your personality?

Adverbs of Time

Adverbs of time answer the question *when* or *how often*.

The old castle is *now* in ruins.   Gwen arrived *early*.
The plane left *already!*   I have *often* visited them.

Adverbs of time usually modify verbs. The following are adverbs of time:

again	before	finally	late	seldom
already	early	first	now	soon
always	ever	immediately	often	usually

Exercise 1

Complete each sentence with an adverb of time.

1. Professor Kent wants to start experiments with the robots _____.
2. I hope the power will _____ be restored.
3. Have you _____ seen such a huge gorilla?
4. Ellie answered the phone _____.
5. We have _____ heard that it is bad luck to spill the salt.
6. Trick-or-treaters _____ stop at the oldest house on Shadow Street.
7. _____, you preheat the oven.
8. Edward got up _____ on his twelfth birthday.
9. Tom Sawyer was _____ able to get someone else to do his work.
10. The earth _____ rotates around the sun.
11. We _____ play that old phonograph.
12. Tarantula bites are not _____ dangerous to people.
13. I liked that book so much I read it _____.
14. We were _____ for the movie so we ate a box of popcorn before it began.
15. I have never seen so many tulips _____.

Adverbs of Place

Adverbs of place answer the question *where*.

The rabbit hopped *forward*.   The giraffes roamed *far*.
Put your tuba *here*.   The chameleon crawled *away*.

Adverbs of place usually modify verbs. The following are
adverbs of place:

above	below	forth	in	there
away	down	forward	inside	up
back	far	here	out	within

Exercise 2

Complete each sentence with an adverb of place.
1. When the firecracker exploded, we jumped _____.
2. A whistling from the corner caused me to look _____.
3. _____ are all those missing socks!
4. When the tide moves _____, the beach is under water.
5. Jake stayed _____ because of the storm.
6. Wait _____ with the flashlight.
7. Claudia left her uncle's straw hat _____.
8. I opened the package, but there was nothing _____.
9. An army of black ants marched _____.
10. One lone hawk circled _____.
11. The skier lost her balance and fell _____.
12. I cannot go _____ this weekend.
13. When the doors opened, the shoppers rushed _____.
14. The balloons floated _____.
15. A boomerang always comes _____ to you.

Adverbs of Manner

Adverbs of manner answer the question *how* or *in what manner*.

A supersonic jet
travels *fast*.
The car stopped *quickly*.

The clerk wrapped the
box *expertly*.
Our band plays *well*.

Adverbs of manner usually modify verbs. The following are adverbs of manner:

bravely	eagerly	hard	resolutely	steadily
carefully	easily	honestly	slowly	truly
cheerfully	fast	neatly	smoothly	swiftly
clearly	gracefully	rapidly	softly	well

Exercise 3

Complete each sentence with an adverb of manner.

1. Male canaries sing _____.
2. Icicles hanging from the roof melted _____.
3. An architect has looked _____ at the house plans.
4. A hare can _____ outrun a tortoise.
5. You'll have to enter the cave _____.
6. He contributed _____ to the collection for needy families.
7. You can count on A. J. to brush the horses' coats _____.
8. Swans glided _____ along the banks of the Test River.
9. The famous scientist Albert Einstein did not do _____ in school when he was young.
10. The frog's tongue flicked _____ at the gnats.
11. Falcons are trained to return _____ to their handlers.
12. Andrea tore open the surprise package _____.
13. We could _____ see the comet in the sky.
14. The signatures on the Declaration of Independence were written _____.
15. The juggler tossed the oranges _____.

Adverbs of Degree

Adverbs of degree answer the question *how much* or *how little*.

Julia has *almost* finished the long novel. (*Modifies a verb*)
Steve drank the cold water *too* quickly. (*Modifies an adverb*)
Carol's handwriting is *scarcely* readable. (*Modifies an adjective*)

Adverbs of degree modify verbs, adjectives, or other adverbs.

almost	greatly	merely	quite	sufficiently
barely	hardly	much	rather	too
fully	little	partly	scarcely	very

Exercise 4

Complete each sentence with an adverb of degree.
1. This coffee is _____ hot to drink.
2. Kathryn, approach the fawn _____ slowly.
3. A dragonfly _____ landed on the end of my fishing pole.
4. It was _____ warm enough to go out without a jacket—and they were swimming!
5. The goats had _____ finished one stack of hay when they began on the other.
6. Stamps with errors are _____ rare and so are valuable.
7. I don't _____ understand the atom model.
8. The electric eel is a _____ long and skinny fish.
9. Jon has rehearsed _____ for the trombone solo.
10. Marie had _____ smothered the hamburger with pickles.
11. The history students were _____ happy that their test was postponed.
12. We came _____ close, but we did not finish the three-legged bag race.
13. To take a picture, you _____ press the red button.
14. The forecast is for a _____ cloudy day.
15. After getting braces, I could _____ chew gum.

Adverbs of Affirmation and Negation

> **Adverbs of affirmation or negation tell whether a statement is *true* or *false*.**

Alice will *not* go.   *Yes*, Neil is here.

Adverbs of affirmation are *yes, indeed, undoubtedly*.

Adverbs of negation are *no, not, never*.

Exercise 5

Find the adverbs in each sentence. Tell whether each shows *affirmation* or *negation*.

1. Yes, I have finished reading the sports page.
2. We do not know the answers to any of those trivia questions.
3. Shelby's advice to rub the plant leaves with milk was indeed strange.
4. Undoubtedly, baked potatoes have fewer calories than french fries.
5. Van's father never allowed him to mow the lawn without wearing safety glasses.
6. Mark Twain was indeed the inventor of suspenders.
7. No, I did not see the sand dollar.
8. Yes, a speleologist is a scientist who studies caves.
9. The peanut butter cookies are not ready yet.
10. We'll never know how that grand piano got through the door!

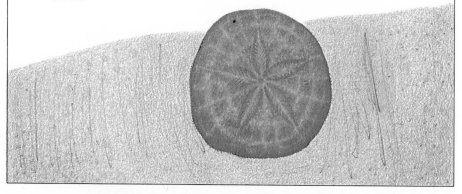

Exercise 6

Find the adverb or adverbs in each sentence. Tell whether each is an adverb of *time, place, manner, degree, affirmation*, or *negation*.

1. Scarlett tied the bow on her lace dress very neatly.
2. Yes, the sea is exceedingly rough, Meg.
3. There are too many hot peppers in these chimichangas!
4. Here are the dog biscuits Blue has been stashing away.
5. The astronauts float around weightlessly in space.
6. Do turtles walk slowly because their shells are heavy?
7. Two volunteers stepped forward for the magic trick.
8. The Senate sometimes hears rather long speeches.
9. Above, we could see the banner announcing a street fair.
10. There was barely enough birthday cake for everyone.
11. The audience immediately sat down when the music began.
12. Hearing the clock chime, I looked up.
13. We always keep a supply of cherry preserves in the pantry.
14. Pansies are quite hardy and grow well in cool temperatures.
15. I promise to count the bags of bagels very carefully.
16. The crowd laughed heartily at the bear's antics.
17. We did not know that the tire was flat.
18. Blue whales are the largest animals that have ever lived.
19. I almost knocked the ant farm over.
20. News travels fast!
21. We quickly wrote a menu for our hot-dog stand.
22. He secured the loose objects on deck and climbed below.
23. Mrs. Kellog complains that she seldom sees a blue jay at her bird feeder.
24. They were fully prepared for a sensational air show.
25. Searching for her photograph, Kelly flipped through the magazine rapidly.

Practice Power

Next to each verb in the list below is an adverb that modifies it. Write at least one synonym for each adverb. Write a sentence with the verb and the new adverb.

VERBS	ADVERBS
answer	immediately
gallop	briskly
sing	merrily
speak	honestly
drive	cautiously
act	courageously
move	quietly

Lesson 2 Comparison of Adverbs

Many adverbs can be compared. Like adjectives, they have three degrees of comparison: positive, comparative, and superlative.

Regular Comparison

Some adverbs form the comparative degree by adding *er* to the positive, and they form the superlative degree by adding *est* to the positive.

POSITIVE	COMPARATIVE	SUPERLATIVE
high	higher	highest
fast	faster	fastest
hard	harder	hardest
late	later	latest
soon	sooner	soonest
early	earlier	earliest

Adverbs ending in *ly* generally form the comparative degree by adding *more* or *less* to the positive, and they form the superlative degree by adding *most* or *least* to the positive.

POSITIVE	COMPARATIVE	SUPERLATIVE
swiftly	more swiftly	most swiftly
	less swiftly	least swiftly
bravely	more bravely	most bravely
	less bravely	least bravely
gracefully	more gracefully	most gracefully
	less gracefully	least gracefully

Irregular Comparison

Some adverbs are compared irregularly. It is necessary to learn the comparative and the superlative degrees.

POSITIVE	COMPARATIVE	SUPERLATIVE
badly	worse	worst
far	farther	farthest
late	later	latest, last
little	less	least
much	more	most
well	better	best

Most adverbs indicating time and place (*here, now, then, when, where, again, always, down, above*) and adverbs expressing completeness (*eternally, universally, never, forever, continually, entirely*) cannot be compared.

Exercise 1

Find the adverbs in these sentences. For those adverbs that can be compared, tell the degree of comparison: *positive, comparative,* or *superlative.*

1. We searched everywhere for the missing car keys.
2. The winner must stay on the bronco the longest.
3. During the thunderstorm, George acted more bravely than the rest of us.
4. The dog barked furiously at the passing cars.
5. Andy dove most courageously from the high diving board into the pool.
6. With the sudden gust of wind, the kite soared higher into the sky.
7. Our fire died sooner than we had expected.
8. That detective gathered clues the least patiently.
9. Read the poem in French slowly, Carole.
10. The carpenters need to work faster to meet their deadline.
11. This burro walks more steadily than a horse across rocks.
12. I always comb my hair this way.
13. Of all the rivers, the Amazon flows most swiftly.
14. October was an unusually warm month.
15. Henri arrived latest.

Exercise 2

One degree of the adverb is given below. Write out the complete comparison of each adverb.

POSITIVE	COMPARATIVE	SUPERLATIVE
quietly	_____	_____
_____	more slowly	_____
early	_____	nearest
_____	_____	most sincerely
_____	less harshly	_____
sharply	_____	most happily
_____	less accurately	_____
anxiously	_____	most probably
_____	less kindly	_____
well	_____	least firmly
_____	_____	soonest
sorrowfully	_____	_____
_____	more willingly	_____
late	_____	hardest
_____	_____	

Practice Power

From exercise 2, choose two adverbs in the positive degree, two in the comparative, and two in the superlative. Write sentences showing the correct use of each adverb.

Lesson 3 Using Adverbs Correctly

Adverbs and Adjectives

> **An adjective describes a noun or pronoun.**
> **An adverb modifies a verb, an adjective, or an adverb.**

Adverbs are often confused with adjectives that follow and complete verbs. Study the following examples.

> The gymnast stood on the beam (unsteady, unsteadily).
> The gymnast on the beam looked (unsteady, unsteadily).

The correct form for the first sentence is *unsteadily*: The gymnast stood on the beam *unsteadily*. *Unsteadily* modifies the verb *stood* and tells *how*.

The correct form for the second sentence is *unsteady*: The gymnast on the beam looked *unsteady*. *Unsteady* follows the linking verb *looked* and describes the subject *gymnast*.

To tell whether you use an adverb or adjective, try this: If some form of the verb *be* can be used in place of the verb in the sentence, the verb is a linking verb, and an adjective should follow it.

> This peach tastes *good*. (= *This peach* is *good*.)

The adjective form *good* correctly follows a linking verb.

> These peaches grow *well* in Georgia.

Well is an adverb. It tells *how* the peaches grow. If a form of the verb *be* is used in place of the verb *grow*, the sentence does not make sense.

Exercise 1

Choose the correct word to complete each sentence. Tell whether it is an *adjective* or an *adverb*.

1. Those red roses smell (sweet, sweetly) but have thorns.
2. The day grew (cool, coolly) as clouds hid the sun.
3. Nightingales sing (soft, softly) under the emperor's window.
4. Few people use a spinning wheel (good, well).
5. After sitting in the sun, Leo felt (warm, warmly).
6. Has he explained the directions (good, well)?
7. Your report on ethnic foods was (good, well).
8. The bobcat growled (fierce, fiercely) at an intruding dog.
9. Lamb's wool feels (soft, softly).
10. Without a rider, the bicycle bounced (aimless, aimlessly) down the hill.
11. Reel in the fish (careful, carefully)!
12. George Washington was (honest, honestly) in answering his father's question.
13. She answered the phone (cheerful, cheerfully).
14. Carmen paddled the boat against the current (smooth, smoothly).
15. Mr. Barlow's apple fritters always taste (good, well).
16. I'll sleep (good, well) after picking strawberries all day.
17. Your voice sounds (different, differently) over the phone.
18. After their parents fed them, the baby robins chirped (merry, merrily).
19. We closed the office door (quiet, quietly) behind us.
20. The twelve o'clock whistle blew (sharp, sharply).
21. A kudzu vine will grow (quick, quickly).
22. These lemon drops really do taste (sour, sourly).
23. Cows chew their cud (slow, slowly).
24. Your mattress should be (firm, firmly) if you have a bad back.
25. How (good, well) Patty imitates that famous singer!

363

Their and *There*

> ***Their*** is an adjective and shows possession or ownership.

The explorers lost *their* compass!

> ***There*** is an adverb that means *in that place*.

Put your dirty boots *there*.

> ***There*** is sometimes used as an introductory word, usually before a form of the verb *be*.

There are thirty-four countries in Europe.

Exercise 2

Complete each sentence with *their* or *there*.

1. Flying squirrels can glide through the air because _____ are skin flaps between _____ front and hind legs.
2. The Beatles became famous in the 1960s, and _____ songs are still popular.
3. The settlers named _____ new home Cranberry Lake.
4. _____ were three hundred fans standing in line for the rock concert!
5. _____ is a watering hole nearby, and the zebras usually gather _____.
6. _____ brother is at summer camp.
7. The electricians did _____ best work.
8. _____ are one hundred zeros in a googol.
9. The calico cat sat _____ to clean its paws.
10. Hockey players carried _____ skates into the arena.
11. People who live in deserts often cover _____ heads and faces.
12. Marie and Pierre Curie experimented with elements in _____ laboratory.
13. Adam, leave the lawn mower _____.
14. It was _____ first attempt at carving whistles for _____ grandchildren.
15. _____ was much excitement about the first snow of the season.
16. _____ prizes were movie passes.
17. We can't use the gym because the cheerleaders are practicing _____.
18. I've already looked _____.
19. _____ bus is coming.
20. _____ was a spider _____!

365

Two, Too, and *To*

Two **is a numeral adjective and refers to the number 2.**

There are *two* liters of water in that pitcher.

Too **is an adverb and has the same meaning as** *also,*
more than enough, **or** *besides.*

Todd can make omelets—and pancakes, *too.*

To **is a preposition and usually indicates motion**
toward some place or some person.

The entire school went *to* the gym for an assembly.

Exercise 3

Complete each sentence with *two, too,* or *to.*

1. A tiger is ____ ferocious to have as a pet.
2. Old Christmas trees are sent ____ the sand dunes to help in erosion control.
3. ____ students went ____ the science workshop.
4. At ____ o'clock in Chicago, it is three o'clock in New York.
5. My parents talk about the days when movie admission was ____ dollars.
6. Rocky sent a basketball ____ his nephew.
7. Matt, ____, likes this kind of watch.
8. We need ____ typewriters sent ____ the repair shop.
9. There are ____ sailors in that sloop.
10. It is ____ cold in Antarctica for many animals to survive.
11. Mom put the peanuts ____ far back on the shelf.
12. Which scientists are going ____ the rain forest?
13. We read the letters aloud ____ each other.
14. Nomads are people who move from place ____ place.
15. You may come ____.

Negative Adjectives and Adverbs

> If a sentence has one negative adverb such as *not*, avoid using another negative word, such as *no* or *never*.

I haven't (no, any) money.
No one (never, ever) goes there.

Here are the correct forms:

I haven't *any* money.
No one *ever* goes there.

The first sentence already has a negative word: *n't*, the contraction for *not*. The second sentence also has a negative word: *No one*. Another negative should not be used in either sentence.

Exercise 4

Choose the correct word to complete each sentence.
1. She didn't spend (no, any) time oiling the spinning wheel.
2. Marietta hasn't (any, no) time to start a new hobby.
3. We found (no, any) shells on this beach.
4. There hasn't been (no, any) rain for over a month.
5. Haven't you (ever, never) missed a day of school?
6. A two-year-old has (any, no) use for an encyclopedia.
7. I (never, ever) make the same mistake twice!
8. You have (no, any) excuse for letting the chickens loose.
9. Weren't you (never, ever) here before?
10. The detectives could not find (no, any) clues.
11. We thought the parade would (ever, never) start.
12. Opportunities (never, ever) wait.
13. There wasn't (ever, never) time to weed the garden!
14. I haven't written to (no, any) pen pals today.
15. Uncle Judd never had (no, any) money for ice cream.

Words Used as Adjectives and Adverbs

There are words that can be used either as adjectives or adverbs. Check to see how the word is used in a sentence. If it modifies a noun, it is an adjective. If it modifies a verb and tells how, where, or when, it is an adverb.

> That is a *fast* boat. (*Adjective—describes boat*)
> That boat travels *fast*. (*Adverb—answers the question* how)

Exercise 5

Tell whether each word in italics is an *adjective* or an *adverb*.
1. A *high* fence protects the old mansion.
2. The swarm of bees flew *high* into the air.
3. The geese are walking in one long *straight* line.
4. Hit that golf ball *straight*.
5. On the first day of band rehearsal, Jody awoke *early*.
6. An *early* frost will damage any late corn crops.
7. Diamonds are the *hardest* stones.
8. Believe it or not, Frankie works *hardest*!
9. The wheels of the bicycle went *round* and *round*.
10. Missie uses a *round* can lid to cut the biscuit dough.
11. The old portrait resembles his grandmother *very* closely.
12. President Washington ate in this *very* tavern!
13. Two dollars is the *best* price for this used book.
14. Some people work *best* in the early hours of the morning.
15. I think Joanne Allen is the *best* candidate for mayor.

Practice Power

Write original sentences showing the correct use of

> heavy (adj.), heavily (adv.)
> their (adj.), there (adv.), there (introductory word)
> two (adj.), too (adv.), to (prep.)

Chapter Challenge

Read this paragraph carefully and then answer the questions.

¹Two pioneers of the American West were Lewis and Clark, explorers of the Louisiana Territory. ²Asked by President Jefferson, these men organized a party and bravely undertook a difficult mission. ³They suffered many hardships on the extremely dangerous trip through unknown land. ⁴Very slowly and patiently they pushed up the Missouri to its source. ⁵Each day they traveled farther into the wild. ⁶The men often lost the way, but with the aid of a kind Indian woman they crossed the mighty Rockies. ⁷They descended the Columbia River and finally sighted the Pacific Ocean. ⁸Courageously, the explorers continued on until they reached their goal.

1. In sentence 2, name the adverb and tell what kind it is.
2. In sentence 3, which adverb of degree modifies *dangerous*?
3. In sentence 3, what part of speech does the adverb of degree modify?
4. Find two adverbs of manner in sentence 4.
5. In sentence 4, find an adverb that modifies another adverb.
6. Give the comparative and superlative degrees of the two adverbs of manner in sentence 4.
7. Name an adverb of place in sentence 5.
8. Write the positive and superlative degrees of the adverb in sentence 5.
9. In sentence 6, what kind of adverb is *often*?
10. In sentence 7, name the adverb of time.
11. Can the adverb in sentence 7 be compared?
12. Give the comparative and superlative degrees of the adverb of manner in sentence 8.

Creative Space 5

Noise

I like noise.

The whoop of a boy, the thud of a hoof,
The rattle of rain on a galvanized roof,
The hubbub of traffic, the roar of a train,
The throb of machinery numbing the brain,
The switching of wires in an overhead tram,
The rush of the wind, a door on the slam,
The boom of the thunder, the crash of the waves,
The din of a river that races and raves,
The crack of a rifle, the clank of a pail,
The strident tatoo of a swift-slapping sail—
From any old sound that the silence destroys
Arises a gamut of soul-stirring joys.
I like noise.

J. Pope

Exploring the Poem...

Do you like noise as much as this person does? Some people might describe noise as sounds that are *too* loud. Do you think the person in the poem would agree? What noises in the poem have you heard? What noises have you not heard? Use your dictionary if there are words in the poem you do not know.

What words in the poem rhyme? When two lines that follow each other have the same rhyme, the two lines are called *couplets*. Can you find a word in *couplet* that gives a clue to its meaning?

How does the poet begin and end his poem? Do you get a positive feeling from this sentence?

★ Think about some things that *you* like. Talk with a friend and see if you can agree upon a thing that you both like. Work together to write a group of *couplets*. Remember to begin and end your poem with "I like ...." Here is an example.

I like names.

The beauty of Mary, the sound of a Jim,
Peter and Jonathan, Susan and Kim.
A strong name like Sarah, a neat name like Matt,
Carolyn, Janet, Cornelius, and Pat.
I like names.

Chapter 6
Prepositions, Conjunctions, Interjections

Lesson 1 Prepositions

A preposition is a word placed before a noun or a pronoun. The preposition shows the relation of the noun or pronoun to some other word.

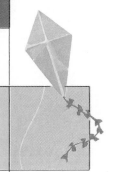

In each of these sentences, the preposition shows the relation between a noun or pronoun and some other word in the sentence.

The kite soared *into* the sky.

Into shows the relation between *soared* and *sky*.

The tail *of* the kite was long.

Of shows the relation between *tail* and *kite*.

The kite looked *like* a dragon.

Like shows the relation between *looked* and *dragon*.

The word *preposition* means "placed before." The noun or pronoun that follows the preposition is called its object.

When you are far away, you see *more* things, but *less* clearly. When you are close, you see *fewer* things, but *more* clearly. In which position would you rather be? Why?

373

The most commonly used prepositions are

about	around	by	in	through
above	at	down	near	to
across	before	during	of	toward
after	behind	except	off	under
against	beside	for	on	up
among	between	from	over	with

Exercise 1

Complete each sentence with an appropriate preposition.

1. Quite a few diseases are carried _____ insects.
2. The story _____ George Washington Carver's peanut studies is interesting.
3. She was leaning _____ a resin-covered pine tree.
4. We watched stars fall _____ the summer sky.
5. The red-haired baby toddled _____ me.
6. He spread peanut butter _____ the bread and topped it _____ bacon.
7. Gaining speed, the bowling ball rolled _____ the stairs.
8. Read the directions _____ the bottom of the box.
9. Aunt Edna had to sit _____ the mischievous twins.
10. Louie jumped _____ the only carousel giraffe.

Prepositional Phrases

> **A preposition and the noun or pronoun that follows it are separate words, but they do the work of a single modifier. This group of related words is called a *phrase*. Since it is introduced by a preposition, it is called a *prepositional phrase*.**

Washington, D.C., lies *on the Potomac River*.

In the sentence above, *on the Potomac River* is the prepositional phrase. It is introduced by the preposition *on*. The proper noun *Potomac River* is the object of the preposition. The entire phrase modifies the verb *lies*.

Exercise 2

Write a prepositional phrase for each preposition listed below.
Then name the object of each preposition. Follow the example.

PREPOSITION	PHRASE	OBJECT
through	through the fields	fields

1. with
2. for
3. down
4. across
5. in
6. between
7. of
8. around
9. during
10. about

Exercise 3

Find the prepositional phrases in each sentence. Name the
preposition in each phrase.

1. William Penn first landed at New Castle in Delaware.
2. The pear trees were white with blossoms.
3. Robin Hood lived in Sherwood Forest.
4. The field, with its rows of pineapples, was well kept.
5. Angry waves crashed over the dunes.
6. Farmers on nearby plantations supplied Savannah with
   cotton.
7. Books were once written on long rolls of parchment.
8. Tarzan clung to the vine above the thrashing reptiles.
9. What kind of animal made those strange tracks through the
   fresh snow?
10. There are no vitamins or minerals in sugar.
11. We heard the sound of trumpets.
12. *Treasure Island* was written by Robert Louis Stevenson.
13. With every step, she was growing thirstier.
14. The orphan had been living among wolves since infancy.
15. Watching for the hotel sign, the cabdriver slowed down.

Exercise 4

Complete each sentence with a prepositional phrase.
1. A laundry worker must have put too much starch _____.
2. When it began to hail, the picnickers ran _____.
3. We left our dog _____.
4. The silly cow just tried to jump _____.
5. In first-aid class, we will wrap gauze bandages _____.
6. That photograph _____ is very old.
7. Jonathan Earnestly likes to tell jokes _____.
8. The biggest mosquito I ever saw just flew _____!
9. Our class is saving money _____.
10. I can't believe that Vickie brought a monkey _____!
11. The ruins _____ are in Athens.
12. In the fairy tale, the witches cast a spell _____.
13. The first astronaut just stepped _____.
14. One cricket after another jumped _____.
15. The hikers place the log _____.

Practice Power

Use prepositional phrases to write a poem like the one below.
Think of an interesting topic.

A shadow
Slyly
Skipped
   across my window
   under my chair
   around my walls.
Should I try to catch it?

Lesson 2 Using Prepositions Correctly

Some sets of prepositions can be confusing. Each preposition may have a slightly different meaning and suggest a different idea. Carefully study the troublesome prepositions in this lesson. Learn how to use each one correctly.

At and *To*

> *At* shows presence in.
>
> *To* shows motion toward.

Toby and Tanya were *at* the party. (*Presence in*)
Toby and Tanya went *to* the door. (*Motion toward*)

Exercise 1

Choose the correct preposition to complete each sentence.
1. Vinnie is going (at, to) dinner.
2. About a hundred onlookers were (to, at) the farm auction.
3. Zod's pet stegosaurus comes (to, at) him when he whistles.
4. Yes, we were (to, at) the oyster roast.
5. The mummy couldn't come (at, to) the party because it was all wrapped up!
6. Were you (to, at) the last festival meeting?
7. Pedro sauntered (at, to) the gate.
8. The children are feeding apples (at, to) the horses.
9. Ricardo is (to, at) Robin's house working on the solar energy project.
10. Hazel is not (at, to) home right now.

Between and *Among*

Use *between* to speak of two persons or objects.
Use *among* to speak of more than two.

The king divided his fortune *between* the two princesses.
The king divided his fortune *among* his four children.

Exercise 2

Choose the correct preposition to complete each sentence.
1. There is an agreement (among, between) the two secretaries.
2. It might slither away (between, among) the many people in the crowd.
3. A music stand stood (between, among) the duo.
4. Watch for the helicopters (between, among) all of those dark clouds.
5. A ten-foot-tall sunflower stood (among, between) the twins.
6. Estelle Corinth-Walker's picture was (between, among) the two windows.
7. (Between, Among) the three, there was not one who knew how to say "hello" in Greek.
8. Many chestnuts are (among, between) the fallen leaves.
9. Skip a line (between, among) answers.
10. (Between, Among) the four students, there was a secret.

Beside and *Besides*

> *Beside* means *at the side of* or *next to*.
>
> *Besides* means *in addition to*.

Lisa walked *beside* me. (*Next to*)
Besides Lisa, Carla was also there. (*In addition to*)

Exercise 3

Choose the correct preposition to complete each sentence.
  1. Who is that (beside, besides) the traffic officer?
  2. Have you anything to drink (beside, besides) milk?
  3. Sit here (beside, besides) me.
  4. That railroad runs (besides, beside) the river for miles.
  5. Gwen has five dogs (beside, besides) this one!
  6. (Beside, Besides) french fries, we had fried onion rings.
  7. (Beside, Besides) the beaker sat a Bunsen burner.
  8. (Beside, Besides) birds, did you know that some kinds of butterflies also migrate?
  9. Mavis grows kale and turnips, (beside, besides) spinach.
  10. A small shark suddenly appeared (besides, beside) the shrimp boat.

In and *Into*

> Use *in* to show location within.
>
> Use *into* to show motion toward a place or change of position.

There are five students *in* the room. (*Location within*)
Five students ambled *into* the room. (*Change of position*)

Exercise 4

Choose the correct preposition to complete each sentence.
1. The storekeeper put the artichokes (in, into) the basket.
2. A cuckoo prefers to move (into, in) another bird's nest, rather than to build its own.
3. I'll put Arnie's books (in, into) my briefcase.
4. The clock (into, in) the kitchen keeps good time.
5. I can throw the paper (in, into) the basket from six feet away.
6. The ancient Incan civilization developed (into, in) South America.
7. She pushed the envelope (into, in) the mailbox.
8. Ray fell (in, into) the goldfish pond.
9. They have been (into, in) the hobby shop for an hour.
10. The game requires you to drop clothespins (into, in) the bottle.

Words Used as Prepositions and Adverbs

> **A preposition shows the relation between its object and some other word in the sentence.**
> **An adverb tells *how*, *when*, or *where*.**

Some words may be used either as prepositions or adverbs.

> *Below* us lay the beautiful valley. (*Preposition*)
> The captain went *below*. (*Adverb*)

HINT: A preposition is followed by an object—usually a noun.

Exercise 5

Tell whether the italicized word in each sentence is an *adverb* or a *preposition*.

1. All explorers left the Himalayas soon *after*.
2. I shall see you *after* the dance competition.
3. A couple skated *down* the ice-covered river.
4. The sun went *down*, leaving a dull red sky.
5. Weeds were springing *up* uncontrollably.
6. Sheep climb *up* the mountainside often.
7. Our school flag flies *above* the stadium.
8. What message was written *above*?
9. Ellen's Seeing Eye dog never has to wait *outside*.
10. The quarterback stood *outside* the huddle.
11. Have you visited this optometrist *before*?
12. Chi barely finished the assignment *before* school.
13. The bottom of a snail's body is a foot to help it get *about*.
14. Minstrels wrote songs *about* Princess Ella's long silver hair.
15. Jana wrote a paper *about* the explosion of Mount Vesuvius.

Practice Power

Use each one of the troublesome prepositions in a sentence.
Underline the prepositional phrases in your sentences.

Lesson 3 Conjunctions

A conjunction is a word used to connect words, phrases, or clauses in a sentence.

The bicycle *and* the car are in the garage. (*Connects words*)
Phil could not go to the game *nor* to the picnic. (*Connects phrases*)
The sky is blue, *and* the sun is shining. (*Connects clauses*)

Conjunctions that connect words and word groups of equal importance are called *coordinate conjunctions*. The principal coordinate conjunctions are *and, but, yet, or*, and *nor*.

Conjunctions Connecting Words

Coordinate conjunctions connect words that have the same *use* or *function* in a sentence. These words may be

nouns (subjects, objects, subjective complements)
verbs (predicates)
adjectives
adverbs

Subjects

Rita *or* Clare will play left field during the game.
Toothpaste *and* ice cream contain seaweed!

Objects

Brass is a mixture of copper *and* zinc.
Have you eaten the ham *or* the cheese?

Subjective Complements

Last Friday evening was bright *but* cool.
Was the painter of the *Mona Lisa* Leonardo da Vinci *or* Michelangelo?

Predicates

Sara tried *but* failed to stand up on her skis.
A telescope gathers *and* focuses light into a tiny, sharp point.

Adjectives and Adverbs

Bamboo plants make very light *and* strong building material.
Fill out the registration form quickly *but* accurately.

Exercise 1

Find the conjunction in each sentence. Tell what *words* each
connects.

1. Mowers and pens were patented by black inventors.
2. The United States sends cooking oil and powdered milk to
   third world countries.
3. Goodwin, the magician, needed a black cape and a rabbit.
4. On his tombstone was a long but interesting epitaph.
5. Ms. Garretto sells ponchos and serapes.
6. Children clapped and laughed at the puppet show.
7. The skillful but careless chess player lost her game.
8. Early peoples made ornaments and weapons of bronze.
9. Luciano finished the third plate of linguini surely but slowly!
10. Would you like lemon or milk in your tea?
11. The contestants worked quickly and quietly on the quiz
    questions.
12. Maybe a box of candy will surprise and please Mom.
13. Sailors steer their ships by the direction of the sun, moon,
    and stars.
14. Athletes walk or run around the larger track.
15. Agent 505's assignment is dangerous but important.
16. The White Sea, north of the Soviet Union, is covered with
    snow and ice.
17. Mexican food is tasty but spicy.
18. Water and wind do not exist on the moon.
19. Lucius whistles or sings in the shower.
20. Beth seems excited but nervous about moving to a new
    neighborhood.

Conjunctions Connecting Phrases

> Coordinate conjunctions connect prepositional phrases. These phrases may be adjectival or adverbial.

Adjectival Phrases

Carvings of ivory *and* of wood are for sale here.
Pineapples from the Philippines *and* from Hawaii are sold throughout the world.

Adverbial Phrases

The stream flowed across the field *and* under the bridge.
The cat ran under the bush *or* up the tree.

Exercise 2

Find the conjunction in each sentence. Tell which *phrases* each connects.

1. Shall I sit with you or with him?
2. Porcupines ran out of the field and into Mrs. Barrett's jeep.
3. Wild ponies on Assateague Island play happily on the beach and in the water.
4. There are strawberries in the refrigerator and in the cooler.
5. Silk from China and from Japan is imported through Western ports.
6. A honeysuckle vine is growing around the porch and across my window.
7. Will you send the package by parcel post or by express mail?
8. Flags of many colors and of many designs fly above the UN.
9. Huckleberry's raft swirled down the river and into the bay.
10. The Burmese child wore earrings of gold and of silver.
11. Our principal handed good citizenship awards to Denise and to Ollie.
12. We searched in the drawers and in the closet for my key.
13. You may play on the porch or in the yard.
14. We'll visit the zoos in New York and in San Diego.
15. A dog with a collar but without a name tag has been found.

Conjunctions Connecting Clauses

Coordinate conjunctions connect independent clauses.
An independent clause has a subject and a predicate and
expresses a complete thought.

California is on the West Coast, *and* New York is on the East
Coast.

Synonyms are words of similar meanings, *but* antonyms are
words of opposite meanings.

You may take the package with you, *or* we will deliver it.

Each conjunction in the above sentences connects a pair of
independent clauses. Each clause contains a subject and a
predicate, and it expresses a complete thought. Notice how the
two independent clauses in the first example can each stand as
a separate sentence.

California is on the West Coast.
New York is on the East Coast.

Exercise 3

Find the conjunction in each sentence. Tell which *clauses* each
connects.

1. The curtain rose, and the tumblers rolled onto the stage!
2. You may come on the camping trip, but you'll have to carry
   your own gear.
3. Erase a file from the computer disk, or use a blank disk.
4. The water was icy cold, but many people were swimming.
5. Sam must pass the lifesaving test, or he will have to take
   the class again.
6. The human arm has thirty-two bones, and the leg has
   thirty-one bones.
7. I got up at 6:00 A.M., but I didn't see the sun rise.
8. The band warmed up, and an audience gathered.
9. I thought I wrote a haiku, but it had too many syllables.
10. We must buy the tickets today, or they will be completely
    sold out.

385

Exercise 4

Find the coordinate conjunction in each sentence. Tell whether the conjunction connects *words*, *phrases*, or *clauses*.

1. Artemis and Jay are basketball guards.
2. I tossed the hook into the water, and something big jerked the cork under.
3. Rita laughed and cried at the same time.
4. Neil Armstrong and Edwin Aldrin took a walk on the moon.
5. His bike was in the attic, but Ed didn't know it.
6. Beth sells newspapers in the morning and in the evening.
7. The planets are divided into two groups—the inner and the outer planets.
8. Chalk or crayons were used in many famous pictures.
9. We were wary but curious in the laboratory.
10. Every country has a flag, and most have a national anthem.
11. A doomed egg rolled off the table and onto the brick floor.
12. I dropped the mirror on the floor, but it didn't crack!
13. Unicorns might have run through these woods or across this meadow.
14. Halley's Comet came into view, but then it quickly disappeared.
15. Will the craft fair be in the auditorium or in the gymnasium?
16. The construction crew worked quickly but carefully.
17. The dalmatian in front of the fire station leaped and barked.
18. Japan has a huge population but very little farmable land.
19. Diamonds are the most valuable and the strongest gems.
20. Did they run around the houses or through the park?

Practice Power

Write sentences that contain a coordinate conjunction to connect each of the word classes below. First, write six sentences with the examples given. Then write six sentences with examples of your own. Vary your choice of conjunctions.

1. nouns (muffins/rolls)
2. verbs (collects/labels)
3. adjectives (quick/easy)
4. adverbs (slowly/confidently)
5. phrases (from the country/to the city)
6. clauses (Mark read the map/Teresa drove the jeep)

Lesson 4 Interjections

An interjection is a word that expresses a strong or sudden emotion.

Oh! We are too late to enroll in the swimming class.
Sh! The baby is finally asleep.

The word *interjection* means "thrown in." What emotion do you think is expressed by the word *Oh*? It is not directly connected with any other word in the sentence, but from the idea of the sentence we understand that it expresses disgust or disappointment. The word *Sh* calls for silence.

Interjections may express *delight, disgust, pain, agreement, joy, impatience, surprise, sorrow, wonder*, and so on. They are not grammatically related to other words in the sentence. An interjection is usually set off from the rest of the sentence by an exclamation point. An entire sentence, however, may be exclamatory. If the sentence is exclamatory, the interjection is followed by a comma and the exclamation point is put at the end of the sentence. If the interjection expresses a mild feeling, a comma follows it.

Ah, there she goes again! (*Entire sentence is exclamatory.*)
Well, what should I do? (*Milder feeling*)

Some common interjections are

Ah!	Good!	Hooray!	Oh!
Aha!	Good-bye!	Hush!	Ouch!
Beware!	Hello!	Indeed!	Sh!
Bravo!	Hey!	O!	Well!

O and *Oh*

The interjection *O* is used only before a noun in direct address. It is not directly followed by an exclamation point.

Oh is used to express surprise, sorrow, or joy. It is followed by an exclamation point unless the emotion continues throughout the sentence. If the emotion continues, *oh* is followed by a comma, and the exclamation point is put at the end of the sentence.

> *O Helen*! I like your new bike. (*Direct address*)
> *Oh!* What do you think caused the trouble? (*Emotion does not continue.*)
> *Oh,* how happy I am! (*Emotion continues—milder feeling.*)

Exercise 1

Tell what idea or feeling is suggested by the interjection in each sentence.

1. Hooray! We won!
2. Oh! That can't be true.
3. Bravo! You passed the exam.
4. Oh! Have you heard the news?
5. Hey! It's raining again.
6. Hush! Wasn't that a sleigh bell?
7. Indeed! You did not know that a sponge was actually an animal.
8. Sh! We finally got the triplets to sleep.
9. Ah, what a close call!
10. Well, my homework is finally finished.
11. Hey! You should have seen the size of that bass!
12. Oh, I just used my last wish.
13. Ouch! I twisted my ankle.
14. Beware! The curve is dangerous at high speeds.
15. Hello! We're glad you made it!

Exercise 2

Write sentences using the following interjections. Tell what feeling each expresses.

　　Good!　Whew!　Hey!　Oops!

Write sentences using interjections that express

　　joy　annoyance　wonder　pain

Practice Power

You are shopping in a grocery store when you notice another shopper with a pet monkey on her shoulder. Suddenly, the monkey escapes from its leash! The monkey has a wonderful time exploring the store and causing mischief. Write a paragraph about what happens using at least three interjections. You may want to use dialogue to express the reaction of people in the store.

Chapter Challenge

Read this paragraph carefully and answer the questions that follow.

¹The trails were lined with redwood trees as we headed toward Indian Moccasin Lake. ²Ms. Hally, our guide, told us that these trees were the tallest and largest in the world. ³Some are so big," she said, "people put holes into them and drive cars through their centers." ⁴"Hooray!" we soon heard her exclaim. ⁵She had just found a soap plant beside a thick clump of bushes. ⁶Slowly and carefully, she pulled it from the ground. ⁷Its white, onionlike root made it look like real soap. ⁸"Sh!" whispered Ms. Hally as we neared the lake. ⁹She pointed to a turtle digging a hole in the mud to lay her eggs, and then we spied a water snake sunning itself on the rocks. ¹⁰What other wonders would Ms. Hally be able to show us before the day would come to an end?

1. In sentence 1, name two prepositional phrases.
2. In sentence 2, the conjunction *and* connects what two words?
3. These two words are what part of speech?
4. In sentence 3, the conjunction *and* connects *put* and *drive*. These two words are what part of speech?
5. Name any two interjections in the paragraph. What feeling or emotion does each express?
6. In sentence 5, name two prepositional phrases.
7. In sentence 6, what two words does the coordinate conjunction connect?
8. These two words are what part of speech?
9. Name a prepositional phrase in sentence 6.
10. In sentence 9, does the coordinate conjunction connect words, phrases, or clauses?

Review of the Parts of Speech

Tell the part of speech of each italicized word: *noun, pronoun, verb, adjective, adverb, preposition, conjunction,* or *interjection*.

1. Charlie, you will remember *these* stories in later years.
2. We returned home to find a "For Sale" *sign* on the house next door.
3. Would you please *sign* for that telegram?
4. Maybe the computer won't work because it's not plugged *in*!
5. Have you ever taken a ride *in* a submarine?
6. We'll need sharp saws when we *cut* that fifty-foot pine.
7. Is the dog obedience class going to be in the *park*?
8. *Park* your bicycle here.
9. Mr. Menlo marks *and* returns our papers every day.
10. I think my homework went into the *wash*, Ms. Talbert.
11. One more *brick* and you'll have a pair of bookends.
12. Early *brick* companies included their names on the finished products.
13. Ellie spoke to me *after* the bell.
14. I'm glad Saturday isn't a *school* day.
15. Each year, a *school* of humpback whales will migrate six thousand miles from Mexico to the Arctic.
16. Otters scoot down those *wet* rocks on their bellies.
17. The radio alarm always wakes *me* up.
18. Julius Caesar published the *first* newspaper in 60 B.C.
19. *Oh*, the view is beautiful from up here!
20. *Silver* is mined in Nevada.
21. Two *silver* bands glisten on the parrot's left foot.
22. *Forest* fires in California burn across many thousands of acres every year.
23. *Forests* surround the Hawaiian sugar fields.
24. I have *never* seen a famous movie star in person.
25. Did you decide to paint your bicycle red *or* leave it blue?
26. Jerry will only eat whole wheat *hamburger* buns.
27. I'll have a *hamburger* with tomato, lettuce, pickles, onions, mustard, mayonnaise, and extra cheese.
28. How many *stamps* do you have in your collection?
29. *Stamp* the book carefully.
30. We watched the swimmers' snorkels move *through* the water.

This Is Just to Say

I have eaten
the plums
that were in
the icebox

and which
you were probably
saving
for breakfast

Forgive me
they were delicious
so sweet
and so cold.

William Carlos Williams

Exploring the Poem...

"I'm sorry, I ate the plums." Do you think this sentence says the same thing that the speaker in the poem does? What information does the poem add that we don't get from the sentence?

What five things does the speaker tell the reader about the plums? Do you think eating the plums was an important part of the speaker's day?

Does the poem have any rhyme? How many sentences does the poem have? Where could you add punctuation marks? Why do you think they have been left out?

★ Write a simple sentence that begins "I'm sorry...." Add a piece of information—for example, "I'm sorry, the music was too loud." Then write a short poem that gives more information.

This morning
I played
my radio
too loud

and woke
everyone up
but
I couldn't sleep

The sun was so
bright and
the songs
so happy.

Chapter 7

Phrases, Clauses, Sentences

Lesson 1 Adjectival Phrases

A phrase is a group of words used as a single part of speech. A prepositional phrase consists of a preposition and a noun. Prepositional phrases may be adjectival or adverbial.

The pilot arrived *in an instant*. (*Adverbial phrase*)
Ellen has a pair of cloth shoes *from China*. (*Adjectival phrase*)

Each group of italicized words in these sentences takes the place of a single part of speech. In the first sentence, the phrase *in an instant* does the work of an adverb by telling *when* (*instantly*). The phrase *from China* in the second sentence modifies a noun and takes the place of an adjective (*Chinese*). Each phrase consists of a preposition and a noun. Each is a *prepositional phrase*.

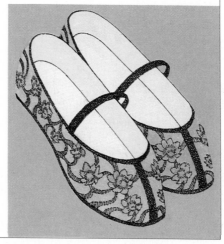

Temples or churches like this one have their own unique design. How does what you write express your uniqueness as a person?

Adjectival Phrases

> **An adjectival phrase is a phrase used as an adjective.**

Candlesticks *of silver* decorated the table.

The phrase *of silver* tells what kind of candlesticks. *Of silver* is an adjectival phrase modifying the noun *candlesticks*.

Note how adjectives may be replaced by phrases:

Snowy mountains could be seen in the distance.
Mountains *of snow* could be seen in the distance.
Janet found a *Brazilian* stamp.
Janet found a stamp *from Brazil*.

Exercise 1

Find the adjectival phrase in each sentence. Tell the *noun* that each phrase modifies.
1. The walls of the castle were colorfully decorated.
2. This is the workshop of a wood-carver.
3. One very strong natural fiber is silk from spiders.
4. The capital of Belgium is Brussels.
5. A flock of egrets is feeding here.
6. Vichyssoise is a cold soup with potatoes.
7. The author of this story is a young Panamanian.
8. The house across the street has always been painted green.
9. We all enjoyed her vivid account of ancient African customs.
10. The laughter of the amused crowd delighted the apes.
11. Sheena collects seashells from the Pacific.
12. The day after tomorrow will be my birthday.
13. Those joggers in the rear look fatigued.
14. He has told wonderful tales of King Arthur's knights.
15. The old clock above the fireplace slowly struck the hour.
16. Two ornaments on the tree caught the cat's attention.
17. Rafts of wood float easily.
18. The coach invited all the players on the baseball team.
19. The trees along the road are maples and oaks.
20. A basket of beach towels sat near the pool.

Exercise 2

Change each italicized adjective to an adjectival phrase.

Example: *Courageous* sailors sailed the ship.
Sailors *with courage* sailed the ship.

1. *Spring* blossoms are a welcome sight!
2. The *river* bank was steep and rocky.
3. We want an *intelligent* dog.
4. Lee trimmed the *garden* hedge carefully.
5. We watched a *cowboy* film.
6. *Musical* sounds could be heard across the lake.
7. Half the world's fresh water is in *Antarctic* icebergs!
8. *Dirt* roads wind between the squash and watermelon fields.
9. Many salmon are found in *Alaskan* waters.
10. This summer we are going to start a *bug* zoo.

Exercise 3

Complete each sentence with an adjectival phrase.
1. The postcard _____ took four weeks to arrive.
2. The first game _____ was played in this stadium.
3. Batteries _____ can be expensive.
4. A bowl _____ was placed in front of the cat.
5. We need two people to help carry this basket _____.
6. Many fans collect souvenirs _____.
7. That girl _____ is my cousin.
8. We took photographs _____.
9. Rugs _____ will be displayed.
10. A troop of kangaroos followed the path _____.
11. The center _____ is hot.
12. Aunt Jeanette keeps a vase _____ in the hall.

Practice Power

Use the following as adjectival phrases in sentences.

with curly red hair	of different sizes
in our path	with green skins
behind the orange sunglasses	of stones and twigs

Lesson 2 Adverbial Phrases

An adverbial phrase is a phrase used as an adverb.

The car crept *through the safari park*.

The phrase *through the safari park* tells *where* the car crept. *Through the safari park* is an adverbial phrase modifying the verb *crept*.

In the following examples, adverbs have been replaced by adverbial phrases.

At the assembly, Ben spoke *sincerely*.
At the assembly, Ben spoke *with sincerity*.
Carol waited in the line *patiently*.
Carol waited in the line *with patience*.
The meteor fell *there*.
The meteor fell *into the wheat field*.

Exercise 1

Find the adverbial phrase in each sentence. Tell the *verb* that each phrase modifies.
1. Pine logs blaze in the old fireplace.
2. On the steps stood a large black hog.
3. One twilight star glowed in the darkening sky.
4. On every corner, balloon vendors gathered.
5. The ice fishers made a hole in the thick ice.
6. Louis Braille was born in 1809.
7. We strolled through the Dutch tulip fields.
8. Early settlers came from many countries.
9. Sam's arrow whistled through the air swiftly.
10. In the tropics, the evenings are short.
11. The folded paper boat moved swiftly down the stream.
12. Leroy slid the muffins into the oven.
13. A baby cottontail scampered across the clover field.
14. Inside Mexican jumping beans wiggle tiny caterpillars.
15. The grapevine's tendrils coiled tightly around the fence post.

Exercise 2

Change the italicized word in each sentence to an adverbial phrase. An example has been done for you.

Example: Orchids bloom *there*.
    Orchids bloom *in the greenhouse*.

1. Our group built the model city *carefully*.
2. The ballet dancers leap *gracefully*.
3. He erased the pencil marks *hastily*.
4. *Faultlessly*, Keenan recited his poem.
5. She handed me the Swedish krona *immediately*.
6. Those chipmunks will disappear *instantly*.
7. *Formerly*, the Aztecs used chocolate beans as money.
8. Rain clouds travel *fast*.
9. Put your math books away *now*.
10. The audience listened *attentively* to the French fairy tale.

Exercise 3

Complete each sentence with an adverbial phrase. Tell whether each expresses *time, place*, or *manner*.

1. The dolphins leaped _____.
2. We shall leave _____.
3. A jogger ran _____.
4. The two toddlers swim _____.
5. _____ stands a very old barn.
6. The extinct pterodactyl once glided _____.
7. Carved vases were placed _____.
8. The art club will meet _____.
9. Carry the skateboard _____.
10. _____ the sun peeked.
11. Greyhounds race _____.
12. _____ the leaves fell.
13. Every book fell _____.
14. _____ the flag floated.
15. Jeremy walked _____.

Exercise 4

Find the phrase or phrases in each sentence. Tell whether it is *adjectival* or *adverbial*.

1. A baby robin with a broken wing fell to the ground.
2. Another name for the Eskimos is the Inuits.
3. Gary drives the bus with great care.
4. The checker rolled under the rocking chair.
5. The surface of the pond froze during the night.
6. My grandfather saw many deer among the hills.
7. After the spelling bee, Colleen sank into a chair.
8. Mr. Pernelli's building was destroyed in the fire.
9. I wanted to release the monkeys from their cages.
10. The strange color of the sky warns of a storm.
11. The largest signature on the Declaration of Independence was written by John Hancock.
12. The mice saw the cheese and climbed into the trap.
13. At the signal of the referee, the game began.
14. Dana keeps her cactus garden on a sunny shelf.
15. Usually each line of poetry begins with a capital letter.
16. The air was filled with the fragrance of pine.
17. A long line of covered wagons moved slowly into the valley.
18. Cleopatra was a powerful queen of Egypt.
19. Hungry bears waded through the stream.
20. Will Kelly climb to the top of the lighthouse?
21. Collections of coins were started many years ago.
22. Bumblebees were flying through the open window.
23. Ornaments of paper dangle from the reindeer's antlers.
24. Shadows of planes pass over our house.
25. The mobile of driftwood pieces was very unusual.

Exercise 5

Complete each sentence with a phrase. Tell whether each phrase is *adjectival* or *adverbial*.

1. A large lion prowled _____.
2. We listened to the noise _____.
3. _____ all contestants should walk quietly.
4. Long blue feathers were found _____.
5. A crate _____ is on our front porch.
6. _____ flew three squawking chickens.
7. The young knights searched thoroughly _____.
8. A small red car rolled _____.
9. Orange and red leaves danced _____.
10. The daisies _____ look like tiny stars.
11. I am carving a statue _____.
12. A giggling child sat _____.
13. _____ were jugglers, dancers, and singers.
14. The bottoms _____ were covered with mud.
15. Ralph, the dog, always jumps _____.

Practice Power

Use the following as adverbial phrases in sentences of your own.

on a T-shirt	from outer space
into the knapsack	across the boundaries
through the open window	over the doghouse

Lesson 3 The Essential Elements of a Sentence

Subjects and Predicates

> **The subject names the person, place, or thing about which a statement is made.**

To determine the subject of a sentence, place *who* or *what* before the verb to form a question.

> *Annabelle* picked flowers from our garden. (*Names a person*)

"Who picked flowers?" The answer is *Annabelle*, the subject of the sentence.

> The *garden* has many colorful flowers. (*Names a place*)

"What has many colorful flowers?" The answer is *garden*, the subject of the sentence.

> Those *flowers* are very beautiful. (*Names things*)

"What are beautiful?" The answer is *flowers*, the subject of the sentence.

The person, the place, or the thing about which a statement is made is called the *simple subject*.

> **The predicate states a fact about the subject.**

> The icicles on the roof *dripped*.

The subject of this sentence is *icicles*. What does this sentence state about the icicles? It states that the icicles *dripped*. The predicate of this sentence, therefore, is *dripped*.

The word that states what the subject is or does is called the *simple predicate*.

A simple predicate may contain more than one word. It may contain an auxiliary verb and a principal verb.

Few low plants *can grow* in a rain forest.

A sentence is a group of words that expresses a complete thought. A sentence contains a subject and a predicate.

Complete Thought	Incomplete Thought
The scientist designed a telescope.	The designer of the telescope
The sky is blue.	Blue as a summer sky
Sally went there.	There in the country

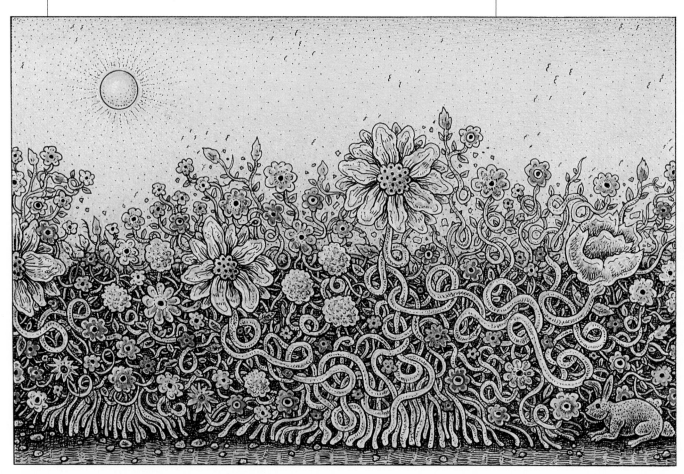

Exercise 1

Find the simple predicate and then the simple subject in each sentence.

1. Marbles bounced.
2. Multicolored marbles bounced noisily.
3. Marbles of many colors bounced all around the room.
4. The leaves rustled.
5. Dry amber leaves rustled occasionally.
6. Leaves of a reddish hue rustled in the breeze.
7. Anthony rode the subway into the city.
8. The city has many interesting museums.
9. These museums attract thousands of visitors every year.
10. My family visited the Parthenon in Athens, Greece.
11. Greece is home to many temples and statues.
12. The ancient temples appear particularly beautiful at dusk.
13. A blustery wind had disturbed the papers.
14. The last plums in the orchard are ripe.
15. A teaspoon of water has 120 drops!
16. Frogs jump with their strong hind legs.
17. Strange symbols blinked on the computer screen.
18. The Chinese invented the wheelbarrow.
19. The frosting stuck to my hands like glue!
20. Long yellow strips of flypaper hang from the ceiling.
21. White blocks of ice drifted nearer and nearer.
22. The quartet sang a song about a bicycle for eight.
23. A red stagecoach full of passengers creaked down the road.
24. An excited horse pranced in time to the music.
25. I will owe you a favor.

The Parthenon

Exercise 2

Tell if each group of words expresses a complete or an incomplete thought.

1. A flock of sparrows rose from the flowering thicket.
2. The musical but high-pitched laugh of the actress.
3. Two attempts at winning the election.
4. Cathryn wrote clues for the scavenger hunt.
5. Tinkling noises of small bronze bells.
6. I spotted a figure moving through the empty house!
7. Someone should help Lewis with his graphics program.
8. About the worst day in my diary.
9. A distinguished gentleman with a bowler hat and a cane.
10. All the postmasters had assembled.
11. On an unusual day with no wind.
12. The water of the Dead Sea is salty enough to keep you afloat on its surface.
13. Rose-colored castle turrets rose above the trees.
14. Clear across the yard and onto the street!
15. The Himalayas are the highest mountains in the world.
16. Five ballet dancers, already best friends.
17. One hundred centimeters equals one meter.
18. Bamboo serves many purposes for the people of the Orient.
19. To the sky without thinking twice.
20. On the next transit bus!

A bamboo forest

Exercise 3

Each group of words below does not express a complete thought. Add words or phrases to each to make a complete sentence.

1. A laughing hyena
2. Reeked of the skunk's scent
3. The pieces of the puzzle
4. A museum with exhibits
5. Clapped to the music
6. Will grow in desert regions
7. In a sailboat
8. Miles and miles of flooded plains
9. Stretching their branches skyward
10. Over a wooden bridge
11. Bright orange tents in rows
12. Amid the rolling waves
13. A shiny new penny
14. The telltale sign
15. Had scattered confetti everywhere

Practice Power

Read this short paragraph. Rewrite this paragraph so that each sentence expresses a complete thought. You can combine ideas into one sentence.

The trampoline was invented by a man named George Nissen. He had fun jumping up and down on a big bed. As a child. During high school. George began to work on designs. He experimented. And used old springs, rubber inner tubes, and scraps of iron. He tried out his invention at a YMCA camp. Kids loved it. An exciting activity. Now a person can jump high. As high as a kangaroo!

Lesson 4 Working with Subjects and Predicates

> **The subject with all its modifiers is called the *complete subject*.**

Marbles rolled across the pavement.

In this sentence, *marbles* answers the question *what rolled? Marbles* is the simple subject.

Large multicolored marbles rolled across the pavement.

In this sentence, the subject, *marbles*, is modified by the adjectives *Large* and *multicolored*. The subject with all its modifiers is the *complete subject*. The complete subject in the sentence is *Large multicolored marbles*.

Study the following examples. The simple subjects are underlined. The complete subjects are italicized.

The <u>athletes</u> on our team exercise.
The longest <u>bridge</u> is outside of New Orleans.

> **The predicate with all its modifiers and complements is called the *complete predicate*.**

The word that tells something about the subject is the simple predicate. The simple predicate may contain an auxiliary.

Summer has arrived!

In this sentence, the simple predicate is *has arrived*. It contains the auxiliary verb *has*.

The simple predicate may be modified by an adverb or an adverbial phrase. It may also have an object or complement to complete its meaning.

Look at the following sentences. The simple predicates are underlined. The complete predicates are italicized.

The caterpillar _moved gracefully_. (*Adverb*)
Tad _hid in the tree house_. (*Adverbial phrase*)
Pete _played the xylophone_. (*Object*)

In the sentences below, each simple subject and each simple predicate is underlined. Each complete subject is separated from the complete predicate by a vertical line.

Our choir|sings beautifully.
The archaeologists|had unearthed the fossils in the desert.

Exercise 1

In each sentence, separate the complete subject from the complete predicate by a vertical line. Then underline the simple subject and the simple predicate.

1. A pink ribbon fluttered in the breeze.
2. Broken shells cover the beach.
3. The Declaration of Independence was signed in the city of Philadelphia.
4. A large dragonfly whirled around the flowers.
5. The rusty key fit perfectly into the lock.
6. A snail's pace is actually about three hundredths of a mile an hour!
7. The sky darkened suddenly.
8. The chair fell with a crash.
9. Gertie joined the ostrich owners' club.
10. Waiters in the Alaskan restaurant were dressed as penguins.
11. This puzzle has two missing pieces.
12. Tall trees swayed in the warm tropical breeze.
13. The right side of the brain controls the left side of the body.
14. Workers heard the news of the holiday.
15. Jorge waxed the fiberglass surfboard eagerly.
16. A panel of students will test new games for the toy manufacturers.
17. Ms. Carlyle writes music scores with a computer.
18. The cover of the magazine showed a photograph of the newborn quintuplets.
19. You inhale about a gallon of air each minute of rest.
20. The Manx is a cat with no tail.

Compound Subjects and Predicates

A *compound subject* consists of more than one noun or pronoun.

A *compound predicate* consists of more than one verb.

Aldrin and *Armstrong* walked on the moon.
(*Compound subject*)
The astronauts *trained* and *planned* for their landing.
(*Compound predicate*)

In the first sentence, *walked* has two subjects, *Aldrin* and *Armstrong*. In the second sentence, *astronauts* is the subject of two verbs, *trained* and *planned*.

A sentence may have a compound subject, a compound predicate, or a compound subject and a compound predicate.

Jean and *Mike* enjoy poetry. (*Compound subject*)
Jean *reads* and *writes* poetry. (*Compound predicate*)
Jean and *Mike* read and *write* poetry. (*Compound subject and compound predicate*)

Exercise 2

Find the compound elements in each sentence.

1. I made sandwiches and put them into a picnic basket.
2. Gina and Gary told us a story, "How the Duck Got Its Bill."
3. The holidays came and went.
4. Football and baseball are my favorite sports.
5. Minneapolis and St. Paul are called the Twin Cities.
6. The wolf pups jumped and barked.
7. The photographer shoots and develops her own prints.
8. Oranges or lemons will make refreshing summer drinks.
9. Francis and Rosie are twin calves.
10. Dandelions and clover have overrun the herb garden.
11. In the Ice Age, people lived and hunted together.
12. Mosquitoes and bees come with the warm weather.
13. I read and reread *Romeo and Juliet*, a tragedy by William Shakespeare.
14. Sarah cracked the eggs and beat them with a fork.
15. Stevie Wonder composes his own music and performs it too.

Exercise 3

Complete each with a compound predicate to form a sentence.

1. The fireworks
2. My aunt and uncle
3. The trained seal
4. At the seventy-fifth floor, the window washers
5. For exercise, my friends and I

Complete each with a compound subject to form a sentence.

6. pedaled and pushed the tandem uphill
7. climbed to the top of the tower
8. will go to the street fair tomorrow
9. need oxygen and water
10. can tell time

Natural and Inverted Order in Sentences

> **A sentence is in the natural order when the complete predicate follows the complete subject.**

NATURAL ORDER   A fresh, cool breeze swept through the house.

In this sentence, the predicate is *swept*. You can find the subject by asking the question *who or what swept?* The answer is *A fresh, cool breeze* swept. The subject *breeze*, and all its modifiers, comes before the verb. Therefore, this sentence is in the natural order.

Who went with him?

The subject *Who* comes before the verb *went*. This sentence is also in the natural order.

> **A sentence is in inverted order when the complete predicate or *part of the complete predicate* comes before the subject.**

INVERTED ORDER   Through the house swept a fresh, cool breeze.

In this sentence, the predicate *swept* and the adverbial phrase *Through the house* come before the subject *breeze* with its modifiers. This sentence is in the inverted order.

Did you go with him?

In this sentence, the word *Did* in the verb phrase *Did go* comes before the subject *you*. This sentence is also in the inverted order.

Exercise 4

Change each sentence from the inverted order to the natural order.

1. Beside the lake stands a beautiful cottage.
2. In what state is Seattle located?
3. Enthusiastically the audience applauded the performance.
4. In that field, we will plant carrots.
5. Early in the evening, an unfamiliar ship appeared in the harbor.

Exercise 5

Change each sentence from the natural order to the inverted order.

1. A lemon meringue pie sat on the counter.
2. Trinkets from around the world were in the glass cabinet.
3. Many towering cathedrals were built in France during the Middle Ages.
4. The moon travels around the Earth in twenty-nine days.
5. Bread is probably the most common food throughout the world.

Exercise 6

Tell if each sentence is in the *natural order* or the *inverted order*.

1. Around the tiger's tail, the zoologists tied a small bell.
2. Coach Bremer planned a new line of defense.
3. Onto the yellow primrose climbed a ladybug.
4. Noah Webster published the first dictionary in America.
5. In the Torrid Zone, the climate is extremely hot.
6. Laurie will stop at the secondhand bookstore.
7. Under which tree did you find the four-leaf clover?
8. Delicately carved statues line the sides of the fountain.
9. In 1513, Ponce de Leon reached Florida.
10. Up the giraffe's neck crawled the green inchworm.
11. The missing ticket lay in the top drawer.
12. Ezra dragged the crate of chickens up the long hill.
13. The cheetah is the fastest animal on land.
14. In an orchestra, there are about one hundred musical instruments.
15. Through the ocean, currents race.

Practice Power

Make up three questions using information from social studies or science. Write your answers, first with a sentence in the natural order, and then write the same answer in the inverted order.

> What gift did Kublai Khan give Marco Polo?
> Marco Polo received the gift of a golden tablet from Kublai Khan. (*natural order*)
> From Kublai Khan, Marco Polo received the gift of a golden tablet. (*inverted order*)

Lesson 5 Sentences Grouped according to Use and Form

Division according to Use

> A *declarative sentence* is a sentence that states a fact.

Niagara Falls is on the border between the United States and Canada.

> An *interrogative sentence* is a sentence that asks a question.

Have you ever visited Niagara Falls?

> An *imperative sentence* is a sentence that expresses a command.

Look at this old painting of Niagara Falls.

In an imperative sentence, often the subject is not expressed. It is understood to be *you*.

> An *exclamatory sentence* is a sentence that expresses strong or sudden emotion.

How magnificent is Niagara Falls!

Exercise 1

Tell whether each sentence is *declarative*, *interrogative*, *imperative*, or *exclamatory*.

1. Southern Europe has mild winters.
2. Why did the chicken peck at you?
3. What a long snake that is!
4. Look in the yellow pages.
5. Was the rain dance successful?
6. Little League players wear safety hats.
7. Are we having spinach noodles for lunch?
8. Take the cat for a walk.
9. The peacock stared at its tail in the mirror.
10. *Shalom* in Hebrew means "hello" and "good-bye."
11. How many eggs does a sea turtle lay?
12. Oh, I can really see the craters on the moon clearly!
13. Avoid that dangerous road, Jerri.
14. Who broke the teapot?
15. Some weeds are just as beautiful as flowers.

Division according to Form

Sentences are divided according to form. Many sentences are *simple* or *compound*.

Simple Sentences

A simple sentence contains a subject and a predicate.
Either or both may be compound.

A simple sentence expresses one complete thought.

The bicycle had a flat tire.

This sentence contains a subject, *bicycle*, and a predicate, *had*.
Neither the subject nor predicate is compound.

The elephant raised its trunk and lifted one foot.

This simple sentence contains a subject, *elephant*, and a
compound predicate—*raised*, *lifted*.

The cymbal and the triangle are simple instruments.

This sentence contains a compound subject—*cymbal*,
triangle—and a simple predicate, *are*.

The wheels and the gears on the fantastic machine whirled
and hummed.

This sentence contains a compound subject—*wheels*,
gears—and a compound predicate—*whirled, hummed*.

Exercise 2

Find the subject and the predicate in these sentences.
1. The panda and its cub clutched bamboo leaves in their paws.
2. A quart of snow will not become a quart of water.
3. Ella and Warren designed and built a bird house for us.
4. Mares and their foals ran through the barn door.
5. White tables and chairs were under the yellow tents.
6. Licorice is made from the root of a plant.
7. Gymnasts run and somersault on a narrow beam.
8. Tony and I took photographs at the soapbox derby.
9. The Iliad tells the story of the war between the Greeks and
   the people of Troy.
10. Stephanie, your pencil fell and broke.

Compound Sentences

A compound sentence contains two or more independent clauses.

Tara decorated the gym, and Kelly helped with the food.

In this sentence, there are two complete thoughts. The first is *Tara decorated the gym*. The second complete thought is *Kelly helped with the food*. Each thought could be used as a separate simple sentence. These complete thoughts are called *independent clauses*.

An independent clause contains a subject and a predicate and expresses a complete thought. Any part of an independent clause may be compound.

Independent clauses usually are connected by a *coordinate conjunction*. The commonly used coordinate conjunctions are *and*, *but*, *or*, *nor*, and *yet*. When the clauses of a compound sentence have no connecting word, the connection is then indicated by a semicolon.

We often sail on Lake Michigan, but we never fish there. There are five Great Lakes; the largest is Lake Superior.

Exercise 3

Find the subject and the predicate in each independent clause of these compound sentences.

1. I like stories of adventure, but Marian prefers biographies.
2. Miska jiggled the weeds with a stick, and fireflies appeared.
3. He has not come, nor has he sent an excuse.
4. Wildflowers were abundant, and we decorated the house with them.
5. An inky blackness settled over the field, and we hurried for shelter.
6. Leonardo da Vinci was a man of many talents, but we remember him most as an artist.
7. The cage was open; the animal had escaped!
8. The little boy whistled, and the dog followed.
9. Charlemagne was a wise king, and during his reign his territories flourished.
10. Those mountains contained valuable timber, and the settlers found many uses for it.
11. The Phoenicians made dye from shellfish, and their traders carried the dye to the ports of the Mediterranean.
12. He opened the box, and a letter fell into his hands.
13. Tulips grow in many parts of the world, but we associate them most with Holland.
14. Tourists arrived at the wharf, and the guide was waiting there.
15. I take violin lessons, and my sister takes karate lessons.

Punctuation of Compound Sentences

1. The clauses of a compound sentence connected by the simple conjunctions *and, but, nor, yet* and *or* are usually separated by a comma.

> Fog and rain made driving difficult, but the flood made it impossible.

2. If the clauses are short and closely related, the comma may be omitted.

> The whistle blew and work began immediately.

3. Sometimes the clauses of a compound sentence have no connecting word. The connection is then indicated by the use of a semicolon.

> These are our duties; they are serious responsibilities.

Exercise 4

Add the correct punctuation to each of these compound sentences.
1. The dance-skating competition ended and the happy fans cheered the winners
2. Joseph had time but he didn't finish weeding the garden
3. King Arthur had many knights Galahad was the bravest
4. Betty is busy but she will help you
5. The yellow dress was pretty but Juanita didn't really like it
6. Bowling is an ancient sport cave people played it
7. Run quickly or you will miss the bus
8. The box held many old coins but they were unfamiliar to the collector
9. A sailor told exciting stories Mike eagerly listened to them
10. A snail weighs half an ounce but it can pull a pound of weight
11. The tourists were tired but they wanted to see the old fort
12. We had a heavy frost and the fruit was spoiled
13. Where did you go on your trip and would you recommend that place to me
14. No two snowflakes are alike but each has six sides
15. Madeline washed her father's car her sister waxed it

Exercise 5

Combine each pair of simple sentences to form a compound sentence.

1. Mr. Ashton designs cars. His wife builds them.
2. Millions of people put objects in their eyes daily. They wear contact lenses.
3. The first algebra problem was difficult. We solved the others rather easily.
4. Canada is north of the United States. Mexico is south.
5. The hamsters wanted to escape. They had not found a way.
6. Ottawa is the capital of Canada. Montreal is its largest city.
7. Isaac wanted a cloudless day. He waited for a long time.
8. I left my book outside in the rain. It was ruined.
9. Solar energy is being used. It is still rather costly.
10. You can fish from the boat. You can fish from the pier.
11. Animals with backbones are vertebrates. Animals without backbones are invertebrates.
12. Television was available in the 1930s. Not much was broadcast then.
13. The anchor is an emblem of hope. The heart is an emblem of charity.
14. New World monkeys have grasping tails. Old World monkeys do not have this kind of tail.
15. Hockey is a winter sport. Baseball is a summer sport.

Exercise 6

Tell whether these sentences are *simple* or *compound*. Explain why.

1. At the computer camp, we spent the morning doing nature activities, and we spent the afternoon working on the computer.
2. Along the river's edge lay alligators and turtles.
3. He stared up at the New York skyscraper for a long time, and he wondered about climbing it.
4. Marty cut oranges, cherries, and peaches for the fruit salad.
5. The Danube River flows into the Black Sea.
6. Nickels, pennies, and dimes rolled all over the sidewalk.
7. Do you have the correct time?
8. I heard the bamboo flute only once, but its music haunted me for years.
9. The far north is the home of the reindeer.
10. What did Mom say to you, and did she sound angry?
11. Tiny strawberry plants peeked out of the terra-cotta jar.
12. London is a commercial city; it is the largest city in England.
13. Penguins have wings, but they can't fly.
14. Encyclopedias, dictionaries, and atlases are in the reference section.
15. Singapore is called the Gateway to the East.
16. I can hear music; the parade must be starting.
17. About a thousand multicolored pigeons were strutting about the square.
18. Travel by stagecoach was slow and uncomfortable.
19. The wind jerked the door out of my hand and banged it against the side of the house.
20. The United States Naval Academy is located in Annapolis, Maryland; my sister hopes to attend it.

Practice Power

Write four compound sentences with the coordinate conjunctions *and, but,* and *or,* and one compound sentence with a *semicolon.* Use information from your social studies or science classes, or events that have happened at school or home.

Chapter Challenge

Read this paragraph carefully and answer the questions.

¹In the future, what will our cars be like? ²Probably, our cars will listen and will speak to us! ³For example, you will turn on the engine, lights, windshield wipers, defroster, heater, or radio with your voice. ⁴Cars of the future will be more convenient, and they will be safer. ⁵Automatic sensors will control the steering and the brakes. ⁶This automatic system will sense the nearby cars and guide your car through traffic. ⁷You will be able to drive faster, but there will be fewer accidents. ⁸Cars down the road will certainly be a breeze to drive!

1. Is sentence 1 in the natural or inverted order?
2. Find an interrogative sentence and an exclamatory sentence.
3. What is the compound element in sentence 2? What word helps you find it?
4. In sentence 4, is the prepositional phrase adjectival or adverbial?
5. Find one compound sentence in the paragraph.
6. Find a coordinate conjunction in sentence 4 that connects two independent clauses.
7. In sentence 5, name the simple subject and the simple predicate.
8. In sentence 6, name the adverbial phrase.
9. What are the two clauses in sentence 7?
10. Find the complete subject in sentence 8.

Creative Space 7

Haiku

Clouds curl their fingers
around the tall slim building
but the wind says, "No!"

The rabbits explore
the plow's thin ribbon-like paths
of newly turned earth.

Lonely winter trees
cast long shadows just to keep
themselves company.

Exploring the Poem...

Haiku is a kind of Japanese poetry. Each of the poems on the opposite page is a haiku. In pattern and content, what do each of these poems have in common?

These poems talk about clouds, the wind, rabbits, earth, winter, and trees. All these things are part of nature. A haiku poem usually describes or comments about some part of nature.

Haiku follows a specific pattern. Did you notice that there are five syllables in the first and third lines, and seven syllables in the second?

Which haiku is your favorite? Why?

★ Think of something in nature that you would like to write about. It could be something enormous like the sea, the sky, or a mountain. It could be something tiny like a grain of sand, a pebble in your shoe, or an ant crawling on your leg. First write one descriptive sentence. Break this sentence into three lines. Move words around and rearrange ideas until you have a 5-7-5 syllable pattern. Write your haiku in the present tense.

Chapter 8

Punctuation and Capitalization

Lesson 1 Periods and Commas

The purpose of punctuation and capitalization is to make the meaning of what you write clear. In speaking, the tone and inflection of your voice allow the listener to understand your thoughts. In writing, it is the use of punctuation marks and capital letters that help the reader to understand your thoughts.

If what you write is to be easily understood by your readers, you should learn how to use the marks of punctuation correctly. The rules taught in this chapter are the ones you will need to make your writing clear.

The Period

Use a period
  1. at the end of a declarative or an imperative sentence

     Plants need sunlight.
     Plant those seeds today.

  2. after an abbreviation or an initial

     Jan.   Joseph P. Cummings   C. A. Marcus

Stories are often told through pictures.
What story do you think this picture tells?

Study the following abbreviations:

B.C.	before Christ
A.D.	*anno Domini* (in the year of the Lord)
P.S.	postscript
N.B.	*nota bene* (note well)
U.S.A.	United States of America; United States Army
U.S.N.	United States Navy
Gen.	General
Dr.	Doctor
M.D.	Doctor of Medicine
Lt.	Lieutenant
D.D.S.	Doctor of Dental Surgery
gal.	gallon
qt.	quart
pt.	pint
l*	liter
g*	gram
m*	meter
Blvd.	Boulevard
E.	East
W.	West
C.O.D.	collect on delivery
Mt.	Mount, Mountain

*The symbols used in the metric system are *not* followed by periods.

Here is a list of the two-letter postal abbreviations for each state. Both letters in each abbreviation are capitalized, and periods are not used.

AL	Alabama	OK	Oklahoma
AK	Alaska	OR	Oregon
AZ	Arizona	PA	Pennsylvania
AR	Arkansas	RI	Rhode Island
CA	California	SC	South Carolina
CO	Colorado	SD	South Dakota
CT	Connecticut	TN	Tennessee
DE	Delaware	TX	Texas
DC	District of	UT	Utah
	Columbia	VT	Vermont
FL	Florida	VA	Virginia
GA	Georgia	WA	Washington
HI	Hawaii	WV	West Virginia
ID	Idaho	WI	Wisconsin
IL	Illinois	WY	Wyoming
IN	Indiana		
IA	Iowa	GU	Guam
KS	Kansas	PR	Puerto Rico
KY	Kentucky	VI	Virgin Islands
LA	Louisiana		
ME	Maine		
MD	Maryland		
MA	Massachusetts		
MI	Michigan		
MN	Minnesota		
MS	Mississippi		
MO	Missouri		
MT	Montana		
NE	Nebraska		
NV	Nevada		
NH	New Hampshire		
NJ	New Jersey		
NM	New Mexico		
NY	New York		
NC	North Carolina		
ND	North Dakota		
OH	Ohio		

Flamingos in Florida

Exercise 1

Add periods where they are needed.

1. Inez would like to visit Mexico someday
2. Mark Twain's real name was Samuel L Clemens
3. Mr and Mrs John A Kenneff are in charge of the sixth-grade magazine sale
4. "7 o'clock Oct 31—Come and see who's who at Helen's house," stated the invitation
5. Light the candles, Tony
6. Doctors use the letters M D after their names
7. We saw mysterious lights crossing Mt Holly
8. Mrs Frisby, a field mouse, is a character in a book by Robert C O'Brien
9. Listen to the sounds of the traffic
10. I ordered the tapes C O D
11. "Take Roosevelt Blvd and turn left" were the words written on the crumpled note
12. You'll need a D D S for that aching tooth
13. At the top of the list, the name Lt Jorge T Garcia appeared
14. Mr Nonniking had seventy hats, one for every birthday
15. Una did not know what *qt* and *pt* in the cookbook meant

Exercise 2

Give the postal abbreviation for each of these states, territories, or possessions of the United States.

Puerto Rico	South Dakota	Guam
Georgia	District of Columbia	Oregon
New Jersey	Delaware	Pennsylvania
Texas	Virgin Islands	Hawaii

Give the state for each postal abbreviation.

MA	UT	NH
SC	WA	AZ
KS	WY	OH

The Comma

Use a comma
1. to separate words or groups of words in a series

> This map shows countries, cities, rivers, seas, lakes, and mountains.
> Brenda likes going to plays, to movies, and to concerts.

2. to set off parts of dates, addresses, and geographic names

> Armstrong and Aldrin landed on the moon on July 20, 1969.

3. to set off *yes* and *no* when they introduce sentences

> Yes, I plan to cross the ocean in a sailboat.
> No, my sister has not returned from the mall.

4. to set off words of direct address

> Marco, have you used a ham radio?

5. after the salutation in a social letter and after the complimentary close in all letters

> Dear James,   Sincerely yours,   Yours truly,

6. to set off an appositive that is not part of the name

> The heart, a vital organ in the body, needs exercise.
> Today we studied about Richard the Lion-Hearted. (*Part of name*)

7. to set off short direct quotations

> If the quotation is at the end of the sentence, use a comma before the words of the speaker.

>> The teacher asked, "Have you completed your research work on Japan?"

> If the quotation is at the beginning of the sentence, use a comma after the quotation unless a question mark or an exclamation point is required.

>> "Tokyo is an important city in Japan," remarked the teacher.
>> "Who rules Japan?" asked the teacher.

> If the quotation is divided, two commas are needed.

>> "Richard," said the teacher, "locate Japan on the map."

8. to separate the clauses of a compound sentence connected by the conjunctions *and, but, or, nor,* and *yet*

>> The English settlers remained along the coast, but the French moved farther inland.

> If the clauses are short and closely connected, the comma may be omitted.

>> Go to the stand and buy a newspaper.
>> The bus jerked and my backpack slid off the seat.

Exercise 3

Give the number of the rule that applies to the use of the comma in each sentence.

1. Nina played volleyball, Ping-Pong, and soccer yesterday.
2. The witch warned her class, "You should never fly off the handle."
3. *Robinson Crusoe*, a novel by Daniel Defoe, was based on the real-life story of a shipwrecked sailor.
4. Come here, Spot!
5. Yes, I heard the owl call in the night.
6. A famous toy duck of the eighteenth century ate, drank, quacked, and walked.
7. It was too stormy to hunt, and so Tuk stayed inside the igloo.
8. The first person walked in space on March 18, 1965.
9. The limerick, a five-line poem, is often funny.
10. "The lettuce for the salad," said Mother, "is in the bin."
11. There is a circus-wagon museum in Baraboo, Wisconsin.
12. No, the fish aren't biting.
13. Contestants in the log-rolling contest balance on a floating log, and the winner is the one who stays on the longest.
14. A special dish of the South is gumbo, a thick soup.
15. The genie's address is 1705 Wishful Avenue, Brass Lamp, Land of Imagination.
16. "Enjoy yourself at the ball," said the fairy godmother, "but be back by midnight."
17. Umbrellas, bird cages, and tennis balls filled the hall.
18. Contact lenses were invented in the 1880s, but they became widespread only in the 1960s.
19. "Pita is a flat bread of the Middle East," explained Yul.
20. "Wake up, girls!" shouted Gail.

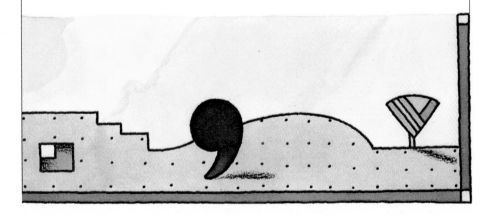

Exercise 4

Add commas and periods where they are needed in these sentences.

1. The flamenco dancers are from Madrid Spain
2. Benjamin Franklin said "A penny saved is a penny earned"
3. No I don't want to throw those magazines away
4. Orange green and purple stripes covered the toy zebra
5. We're going to ride the Ferris wheel the roller coaster and the bumper cars
6. Here is the answer Bruce
7. Thin air wind and wide temperature ranges make life on mountaintops difficult for insects
8. The ripe melons were picked and the workers carried them to the truck
9. Water from the cracked goldfish bowl had leaked onto the floor and Reba mopped it up before her parents got home
10. Charles P Tobias my great-great-uncle flew across India in a hot-air balloon
11. Yes our English papers are due today
12. Your cartoons are great Julie
13. The lion is a strong wild and ferocious cat
14. Icicles were forming on his eyebrows on his mustache and on his beard
15. "Please explain how the satellite works" requested Ann
16. Bruno went up the stairs but Thomas took the elevator
17. A baseball player on third base sang "There's no place like home"
18. Mr Carter shook the tree and the plastic ball fell out
19. The address on the envelope was 933 E Mayflower Blvd Decorah IA
20. No Christine I didn't watch the television last night
21. Thick white fog swirled across the lawn and I couldn't see my hand in front of my face

22. Buy cinnamon cloves and allspice for the pumpkin pies
23. Dr Erg's unusual invention the robot cat is shaking hands with a rat
24. Abraham Lincoln was born in Larue County Kentucky
25. The Declaration of Independence was signed on July 4 1776

Practice Power

Write one sentence to illustrate each rule for the use of a comma. Try to write a few sentences that would include abbreviations.

Lesson 2 Exclamation and Question Marks

The Exclamation Mark

Use an exclamation mark
  1. at the end of an exclamatory sentence

        Here comes the parade!

  2. after an exclamatory word or phrase

        Hurrah! The work is finished.
        Oh my! My pencil broke.

Exercise 1

Add exclamation marks where needed, and give the number of
the rule that applies
  1. What a noisy pet shop this is
  2. Halt Who goes there
  3. How blue your eyes are
  4. How unusual that lizard is
  5. Ready, set, go
  6. O Matt Don't step on that flower
  7. Wow Look at that ice-cream sundae
  8. Listen
  9. Hurry The bacon is burning
  10. What a nice surprise this is

The Question Mark

Use a question mark at the end of every interrogative sentence.

> Is their flight on time?
>
> Where can you find elephant seals?

Exercise 2

Add the correct mark of punctuation to end each sentence: an exclamation mark, a question mark, or a period

1. Do you know how the badger got its name
2. We will make spinach lasagna
3. How tired I was after cleaning the boat
4. How many pretzels have you eaten
5. At the age of fourteen, boys in the Middle Ages began training for knighthood
6. From whom did the United States purchase the Louisiana Territory
7. What a silly joke I heard
8. What does a milliner make
9. Many sheep are raised in Ireland
10. Can you name the largest insect in the world
11. What a convincing argument Tanya made for a bigger allowance
12. Where is the girls' softball team playing
13. How time flies
14. The geranium is a hardy plant
15. Look out the window at the snow

Practice Power

As a contest winner, you may spend fifteen minutes in the store of your choice selecting anything you would like. There will be no charge for any item! Write a short paragraph naming some of the things you would choose. Include an interrogative and an exclamatory sentence.

Lesson 3 Semicolons and Colons

The Semicolon

Use a semicolon
> to separate the clauses of a compound sentence when they are not separated by *and, but, or, nor,* or *yet*

> Al played the violin; Eileen played the piano.

Exercise 1

Add semicolons where they are needed in these compound sentences.

1. Vanessa cooked the spaghetti Michael made the sauce.
2. They followed every direction the experiment succeeded.
3. Angel Falls in Venezuela is the highest waterfall in the world it is about twenty times higher than Niagara Falls.
4. The sand was firm and not too wet it was perfect for building sandcastles.
5. Jean is a talented guitarist she also writes her own songs.
6. The people of India chewed pieces of Arāk roots a substance in the root whitened their teeth.
7. The first traffic signals appeared in London they were put up for horse-drawn buggies.
8. It would take much cheese to make a twelve-foot pizza it would also take many people to eat it.
9. Harry cut the wood he then built a fire.
10. New Guinea is the home for many birds of paradise these birds have magnificently colored feathers.
11. Two eyes appeared at the window my heart stopped.
12. Mount Vesuvius is an active volcano in Italy it erupts occasionally.
13. One of the stray cats disappears often it must have a secret hiding place.
14. The tickets for the finals went on sale at nine o'clock they were all sold by noon.
15. The book is new it even smells new.

Exercise 2

Below are simple sentences. Make each into a compound sentence by adding an independent clause and correctly using a semicolon.

Example: The old jalopy was sitting at the side of the road.
COMPOUND SENTENCE: The old jalopy was sitting at the side of the road; it had run out of gas.

1. The path on the right leads to the lake.
2. Alice goes to ballet class on Tuesday after school.
3. We ordered fish soup at the Chinese restaurant.
4. At the carnival, many people tried to knock over the stack of bottles with a ball.
5. Wendy brought a camera to the parade.
6. Asparagus are in season in the spring.
7. The dark clouds gathered quickly.
8. The elephant went down the street on roller skates.
9. The Statue of Liberty stands in New York Harbor.
10. Fred likes ketchup on his french fries.

The Colon

Use a colon
1. after the salutation of a business letter

   Dear Ms. Lee: Dear Sir or Madam:

2. before a list of items

   We ordered the following articles: charts, books, paper, pens, and rulers.

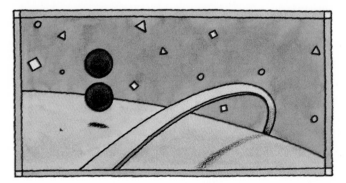

Exercise 3

Give the number of the rule that applies to the use of the colon in these items.

1. Dear Mrs. McKenna:
2. The dragon listed these items on the menu: fried leaves, rock candy, plates of armor.
3. Arrange these names in alphabetical order: Mozelle, Marcelle, Macelle, Estelle, Harry.
4. Dear Sir:
5. Provide the following: one bag of marshmallows, one box of graham crackers, ten chocolate bars.

Exercise 4

Add colons where they are needed in the following items.

1. We glued these together to make the nut ring pecans, peanuts, almonds, hickory nuts.
2. Dear Dr. Ray
3. Gwen wants to use these colors in her computer program turquoise, cyan, ocher, magenta.
4. The following beings just stepped off the UFO Zappies, Orks, Biddles, Urches.
5. The florist will use these flowers in the arrangement roses, pansies, carnations.

Practice Power

Write a short paragraph about your trip to a zoo. Make use of at least one semicolon and one colon to show that you understand how to use those marks of punctuation.

Lesson 4 Quotation Marks, Apostrophes, and Hyphens

Quotation Marks

Use quotation marks

1. before and after every quotation and every part of a divided quotation

> The teacher said, "The field day will be held next Friday."
>
> "Luke," questioned his friend, "have you ever seen a flying squirrel?"

2. to enclose titles of short stories, poems, magazine articles, newspaper articles, television shows, and radio programs

> I read Mona Gardner's short story "The Dinner Party," in which a snake is an unwelcome visitor at a dinner.
>
> Ogden Nash wrote the humorous poem "The Hippopotamus."

Titles of books, magazines, newspapers, movies, and works of art are usually printed in italics. In typing or handwriting, italics are indicated by underlining.

> *Wilderness Journey* is an exciting adventure story.
>
> <u>Wilderness Journey</u> is an exciting adventure story.

Exercise 1

Explain the use of the quotation marks and underlining in these sentences.

1. "My new neighbors," said Sally, "have three dogs, two cats, and a pet chameleon named Arnold."
2. "Let's go for a dip," said one potato chip to the other.
3. "The Lapps were probably the first skiers," replied Britta.
4. I've just finished "I, Hungry Hannah Cassandra Glen...," a clever short story.
5. An old proverb says, "Well begun is half done."
6. "Bob," he asked, "where did you put my tie?"
7. Who wrote the book The Wizard in the Tree?
8. "Who has my copy of the New York Times?" asked Dad.
9. "When I was a baby," explained John Henry, "I had a hammer instead of a rattle."
10. "The Pit and the Pendulum" is a classic short story.

Exercise 2

Add quotation marks and underlining where needed in these sentences.

1. Jackie, he called, why don't you answer?
2. On Friday afternoon, said the class president, we'll have a popcorn party.
3. Going out tonight? one candle asked the other.
4. Indeed, replied Rosa, that story is very interesting.
5. Be prepared is the motto of the Boy Scouts of America.
6. Please pass the hot sauce, said Gary.
7. I thought, remarked Tex, you were going to get TV Guide.
8. His hearing is fine, declared the doctor.
9. Browning wrote the poem The Pied Piper of Hamlin.
10. I enjoyed the biography Emma and I, the story of a girl and her Seeing Eye dog.

Change each direct quotation into a divided quotation.

11. "Please leave by the rear door," announced the usher.
12. "Henry, where are you?" shouted the upset parents.
13. "What is in your hand?" Agnes asked suspiciously.
14. "Don't move an inch," warned Todd.
15. "The trees are full of hungry vultures," said Brent.

The Apostrophe

Use an apostrophe
  1. to show possession

       John's uncle has a butterfly collection.

  2. with *s* to show the plural of letters

       a's   *d*'s   *i*'s

  3. to show the omission of a letter, letters, or numbers

       I'll   class of '90   o'clock

Study these contractions and note the letter or letters that have been omitted to form each contraction.

they're—they are   he'll—he will
let's—let us   don't—do not
there's—there is   we've—we have
mustn't—must not   aren't—are not

Exercise 3

Add apostrophes where needed in these sentences.
  1. Ill take this tomato soup next door to Mrs. Garza.
  2. Mens straw hats are on sale here.
  3. Wasnt Thomas Edisons most famous invention the electric light bulb?
  4. Shell help you put the horse costume on.
  5. My grandfather is a member of the class of 44.
  6. You mustnt make wishes carelessly; they might come true.
  7. The train pulled out of the station promptly at five oclock.
  8. The class of 60 donated this megaphone to the school.
  9. Eds *g*s look like *q*s.
  10. In one unusual contest, a contestants task is to ride down a 153-foot hill on a coal shovel.
  11. Theyve not yet returned.
  12. Arent the Jataka tales from India?
  13. Changs brother taught us to write our names in Chinese.
  14. Its so hot outside you could fry an egg on the sidewalk!
  15. Five-foot-tall cartoon characters decorate the childrens wing of the hospital.

The Hyphen

Use a hyphen

1. to divide a word at the end of a line whenever one or more syllables are carried to the next line

> Many unusual facts can be found in an encyclo-
> pedia, whether of one volume or of many volumes.

The dictionary shows how a word is correctly divided into syllables. Check the entry for a word in a dictionary when you have to divide the word at the end of a line.

2. in compound numbers from twenty-one to ninety-nine

> The ball cost ninety-five cents.

3. to separate the parts of some compound words

> brother-in-law   bright-eyed   self-respect

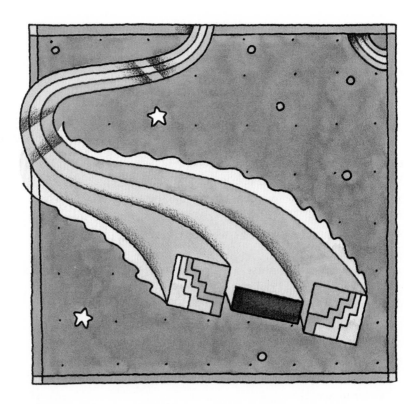

Exercise 4

Locate each of the following words in your dictionary. Use hyphens to show where the words could be divided at the end of a line.

Example: disorganize   dis-or-ga-nize

1. forgetful
2. lavender
3. parrot
4. affection
5. ingredient
6. hedgehog
7. unemployed
8. trustworthy
9. stepladder
10. catastrophe
11. embarrass
12. locomotive
13. needle
14. carousel
15. mosaic
16. sausage
17. dandelion
18. reverence
19. preparation
20. enlargement

Exercise 5

Add hyphens where needed in these sentences.
1. I can't believe my brother is twenty five years old.
2. That's a well known card trick.
3. The thirty one days of January often seem like a hundred.
4. Those guitar picks are seventy five cents each.
5. The cream colored pony was the one I wanted.
6. The baby seems good natured.
7. Farmer McGraw owns sixty five acres of prime farmland.
8. Just twenty four hours and school will be out for the summer.
9. Her mother in law owns the grocery down the street.
10. Purple forget me nots are embroidered across the quilt.

Practice Power

Add the correct punctuation to these sentences. Use any of the marks of punctuation taught in this lesson.

1. Are you going to your sister in laws cottage
2. The ladder just fell Ill need help to get down from the roof
3. Sue Ling enjoyed the unusual words in the poem Jabberwocky
4. Josefina signed this parchment on March 15 1818
5. Ms Iarusso are there enough peppermint sticks
6. Graham turned the yard light off and the skunks trotted toward his trash can
7. Our orchestra needs these instruments a harp a clarinet a tuba and a comb kazoo
8. All in a Summer Day by Ray Bradbury is a short story set in an imaginary world but its lesson applies to the real world
9. Lukes friend called Come to lunch
10. Members of an otter family tie seaweed around themselves and this keeps them from being separated
11. Help me said Gilberts dad gather pinecones for the wreath
12. Theyll learn how to use a hammer saw drill and planes
13. How hot the biscuits are
14. The scolded dog dashed around the corner down the alley and into the shed
15. Weve promised to return before eight oclock
16. The Black Sea is between Europe and Asia a deadly gas makes its seafloor black
17. Auguste the nimble French actor memorizes his lines standing upside down
18. Eunice Morgan bought sixty five acres of land near Salt Lake City Utah
19. Liza what a long shortcut this is
20. He makes his *ss* very carelessly

Lesson 5 Capital Letters

Capitalize

1. the first word in a sentence

    Scuba equipment is used by divers everywhere.

2. the first word of every line of poetry

    The day is coming to an end,
    The moon is coming 'round the bend,
    The stars are peeking out at me,
    I wonder what their bright eyes see?

3. the first word of a direct quotation

    The astronaut said, "Get off at the next planet."

4. proper nouns and adjectives

    The names of particular persons or groups of persons,
    religious denominations, political parties, institutions,
    buildings, cities, states, streets, months of the year, days of
    the week, and holidays are proper nouns.

    Christopher, Presbyterian, Catholic, Democratic party,
    Beaver College, Independence Hall, Baltimore,
    Maryland, Main Street, July, Thursday, Labor Day,
    Thanksgiving, Egypt, Hong Kong

5. titles of honor and respect when preceding the name

    Princess Caroline   Judge Quinn

6. *north, south, east,* and *west* when they refer to sections of the
    country

    My sister and her husband live in the South.

7. all names referring to the deity, the Bible, or parts of the Bible, and other sacred books

> In my church, we read the New Testament every Sunday.
> The Koran is the sacred book of the Muslims.

8. the principal words in the title of books, plays, poems, and pictures

> You'll enjoy the poem "Some Fishy Nonsense."

9. the pronoun *I* and the interjection *O*

> Tomorrow I will have my first subway ride.
> O Karen, how will we solve the mystery?

10. abbreviations when capitals would be used if the words were written in full

> Dr.   Rev.   U.S.A.

Do not capitalize
1. the seasons of the year

> winter   summer

2. the articles *a, an, the,* conjunctions, or prepositions in titles, unless one of these is the first word

> We have just read *The Prince and the Pauper.*

3. the names of studies, unless they are derived from proper nouns

> geography   history   English

4. the words *high school, college,* and *university,* unless they are parts of the names of particular institutions

> Kevin goes to college in Detroit.
> Kevin goes to the University of Detroit.

Exercise 1

Give the number of the rules that apply to the use of capital letters in each sentence.

1. Listen, my children, and you shall hear
   Of the midnight ride of Paul Revere...
2. The class recited Christina Rossetti's poem "Who Has Seen the Wind?"
3. Most ostriches live in Africa and western Asia.
4. On Wednesday, I'll begin working in the cafeteria.
5. There are Mexican, Chinese, and Italian restaurants near our school.
6. The West was a land of opportunity for the pioneers.
7. Curious Ursula asked, "Why does the old woman live in a shoe?"
8. Did Mr. I. B. Gone actually ride his amazing magic carpet all the way to Mars?
9. Tomorrow both King Paul and Queen Paula will attend the royal ball.
10. The first ice-cream cones were actually waffles; they were used in 1904 at the Louisiana Purchase Exposition in St. Louis, Missouri.

Exercise 2

Use capital letters where they are needed in these sentences.
1. a scandinavian student is visiting the wiesners.
2. florida is one of the states in the south.
3. i want to borrow *the pushcart war*, a book by jean merrill.
4. the insects are moving to locust avenue.
5. we'll lead the new year's parade with a chinese dragon.
6. the dentist, dr. tarcov, took one look at the alligator's teeth and shook her head.
7. twelve jesters twirl in front of king richard.
8. theresa will live on meeting street during august.
9. peter piper picked a peck of pickled peppers.
10. the smithsonian institution is in washington, d.c.
11. mel is an electrician for the copper lantern lighting company.
12. you'll have to make up that work by monday.
13. down in the south where bananas grow,
    a grasshopper stepped on an elephant's toe.
    the elephant said, with tears in his eyes,
    "pick on somebody your own size."
14. sally said, "don't forget the chili powder, bob."
15. during the civil war, the two johnson brothers fought on opposite sides.
16. yes, the wagon train leaves today for the west.
17. the message in the bottle is signed kim poe, u.s.a.
18. duluth is an important city on lake superior.
19. the computer tutor in franklin hall is willie days.
20. this summer i'll be pitcher for the dragons.

Practice Power

Write a sentence
1. naming three countries you would like to visit
2. about why you like a specific holiday
3. including the title of a book, a play, or a poem
4. giving the birthdays of two special people

Chapter Challenge

Below is part of a story about the day two legendary characters met: Pecos Bill and Paul Bunyan. Pecos Bill wanted the land for the grazing of his cattle, and Paul Bunyan wanted the mountain for its trees. Pecos Bill thought Paul Bunyan wanted the land, and Paul Bunyan thought Pecos Bill wanted the trees. Read about the battle that occurred. Then rewrite the selection on a separate sheet of paper, adding the correct marks of punctuation and capitalizing words correctly. Some punctuation is already given.

with the hundred men watching, the fight started. paul bunyan picked up his axe and hit at pecos bill so hard that he cut a huge gash in the earth. people call it the grand canyon of the colorado river.

then pecos bill swung his red-hot iron, missed paul bunyan, and scorched red the sands of the desert. that was the beginning of the painted desert out in arizona.

again paul bunyan tried to hit pecos bill and again he hit the ground instead. the scores of strange-shaped rocks that are piled up in the garden of the gods in colorado were split by paul bunyan's axe in that fearsome fight.

pecos bill's iron, instead of cooling off, grew hotter and hotter, until with one swing of his iron he charred the forests of new mexico and arizona. these trees, burnt into stone by the heat from pecos bill's running iron, are now the famed petrified forest.

neither man could get the better of the other. for the first and only time, pecos bill had met his match... it was the first and only time that paul bunyan's crew had seen a man that could stand up to him.

finally they paused to get their breath, and paul bunyan suggested, "let's sit down a minute."

"all right," agreed pecos bill, and they sat down on nearby rocks.

—From *Pecos Bill and Lightning* by Leigh Peck

Creative Space 8

Recipe

I can make a sandwich.
I can really cook.
I made up this recipe
That should be in a book:
Take a jar of peanut butter.
Give it a spread,
Until you have covered
A half a loaf of bread.
Pickles and pineapple,
Strawberry jam,
Salami and bologna
And ½ a pound of ham—
Pour some catsup on it.
Mix in the mustard well.
It will taste delicious,
If you don't mind the smell.

Bobbi Katz

452

Exploring the Poem...

Do you think you would like to eat the sandwich described in the poem? Which ingredients do you like in the recipe? Which don't you like? Why do you think some foods taste good together and some don't?

Name the sets of words that rhyme. Notice how the second and fourth lines rhyme. What other lines in the poem rhyme?

★ The title of the poem, "Recipe," is very simple, but the recipe itself is very original. Now work with a partner to write your own original recipe for a sandwich or a dish you both like. Start with the *same first four lines* that this poem uses, although you can change the word *sandwich.* Then use different ingredients for the next eight lines. Try to make your lines rhyme. Finally, end with the *same last four lines,* but change the words *catsup* and *mustard* to something else.

Would you like to eat what you just described? Would you serve it to anyone else?

Chapter 9

Model Diagrams

Diagrams show the relationships among the words in a sentence. Since there are simple sentences and compound sentences, and because sentences may contain various kinds of modifiers, no one form of diagram will serve for every type of sentence. The diagrams given here are those that will help you most in your work. When asked to diagram a sentence, look here for a sentence of the same kind and see how the diagram is made.

Nouns in Simple Sentences

Nominative Case

Subject: *Molly* will train for the marathon.

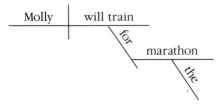

Subjective Complement: A junk is a wooden *sailboat*.

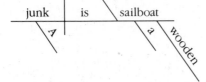

What do you see in this picture? Let your words help make this picture clearer.

455

Direct Address: Close the door, *Peter*.

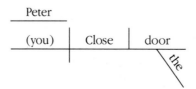

Appositive: Ms. Pucci, an *engineer*, designed a modern bridge.

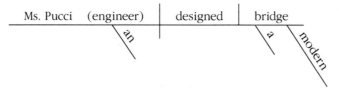

Possessive Case

Sally's mother works at a radio station.

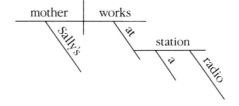

Objective Case

Direct Object: The hikers discovered an ancient *cave*.

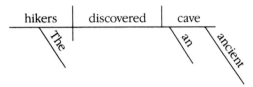

Object of a Preposition: The spacecraft landed on the *moon*.

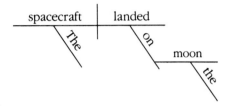

Indirect Object: The geologist showed *Chet* the limestone.

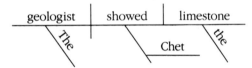

Appositive: We cannot see oxygen, a colorless *gas*.

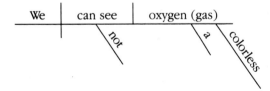

Kinds of Simple Sentences

Declarative Sentence

In the ocean, an aquanaut wears a wet suit.

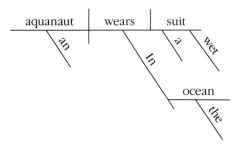

Interrogative Sentence

Have you read *Superfudge*?

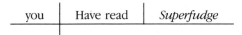

Imperative Sentence

Name two African countries.

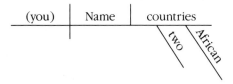

Exclamatory Sentence

How exciting the raft ride was!

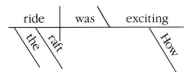

Compound Elements in Simple Sentences

Compound Subject: Laurie and Lynn take their own pictures.

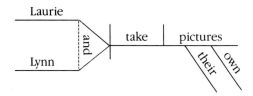

Compound Predicate: Laurie takes and develops her own pictures.

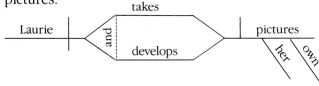

Compound Subject and Compound Predicate: Laurie and Lynn take and develop their own pictures.

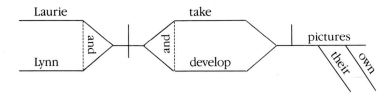

Compound Sentence

Max likes adventure stories, but Marian prefers biographies.

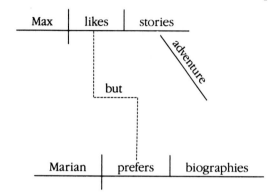

Index

Business letters
   folding, 136-137
   ordering a product, 128
   parts of, 124-127
   proofreading, 133
   reporting errors or defects, 131
   request, 130
   revising, 133
   types of, 128-132
But, for combining independent
   clauses, 33-35

C

"Camel's Complaint" (Carryl), 159
Capital letters, 447-450
Card catalog, 177-180
Carryl, Charles Edward, 159
Characters, 93-95
   for how and why tales, 108
   writing about, from books,
      102-104
   writing dialogue for, 99-101
Choral speaking, 153-161
Cinquain, 236-237
"City" (Hughes), 268
Clauses, independent, 33-35,
   385-386, 418
Climax, in plot construction, 96
co-, 26
Collective nouns, 199-200
Colons, 439
Commas, 431-435
   in appositives, 218-220, 231-233,
      431
   in dates, 431
   in quotations, 432
   in series, 431
   in social letters, 115-116, 431
   to join compound sentences, 33,
      420-421, 432
   with nouns in direct address, 217,
      431
Common adjectives, 272-274
Common nouns, 198-199
Comparative degree
   of adjectives, 289
   of adverbs, 359-361
Comparisons, use of, in writing,
   44-47

Complete predicates, 407-409
Complete subjects, 407-409
Complimentary close
   in business letters, 126
   in social letters, 116
   use of commas after, 431
Compound numbers, 444
Compound personal pronouns,
   244-245
Compound predicates, 410-411
   diagraming of, 459
Compound sentences, 33-35, 418-422
   diagraming of, 460
   use of commas to join, 432
   use of semicolons to join, 438
Compound subjects, 410-411
   diagraming of, 459
   and verb agreement, 342
Compound tenses, 329-334
Compound words, formation of, 444
Conclusion, in plot construction, 97
Concrete nouns, 203
Conjunctions
   coordinate, 382-386, 418
   definition of, 382
Consonant pronunciation exercise,
   154
Contractions
   pronouns in, 257-258
   usage of, 259-260
Coordinate conjunctions, 33-35,
   382-386, 418
Couplets, 371
Coupons, filling out, 138-141
Cross references, in encyclopedias,
   189

D

Dates, use of commas to set off, 431,
Declarative sentences, 415-416
   diagraming of, 458
Defects, letters reporting, 131-132
Degree, adverbs of, 355
Demonstrative adjectives, 283-285
Descriptive adjectives, 271-279
Descriptive paragraphs, 67-70
Descriptive writing, 80-81
Development, in plot construction, 96
Dewey Decimal System, 175-176

O

O, 447

O/ob, 388-389

Objective case
  diagraming of, 457
  nouns in, 225-235
  pronouns in, 250-255

Objects of prepositions
  diagraming of, 457
  pronouns used as, 252-255

Omission of letters, use of
  apostrophe to show, 443

Opinions, 71-74

Or, for combining independent
  clauses, 33-35

Order, writing letter to place,
  128-129

Outlines, 87-89

over-, 26

P

Paragraphs
  beginning sentences in, 7-10
  creating titles for, 22-23
  descriptive, 67-70
  ending sentences in, 14-17
  narrative, 59-63
  persuasive, 75-79
  supporting sentences in, 11-13
  topic selection for, 1-3
  topic sentence in, 4-6
  unity in, 18-21

Past perfect tense, 329

Past tense, 325

Periods, 427-430

Personal pronouns, 239-240
  case of, 246-255
  compound, 244-245
  gender of, 243
  number of, 242
  person of, 240-241

Persuasive paragraphs, 75-79

phono-, 82

Phrases
  adjectival, 395-397
  adverbial, 398-401
  conjunctions connecting, 384
  definition of, 395
  prepositional, 374-376, 395

Pitch, 148

Place, adverbs of, 353

Plot, 96-98
  for how and why tales, 108

Plurals
  of nouns, 205-209
  use of apostrophes in forming,
    443

Poetry, 392-393
  capital letters for first words in,
    447
  cinquain, 236-237
  couplets, 371
  haiku, 424-425
  limericks, 348-349
  metaphors in, 269
  prose, 50-51
  repetition in, 299
  rhyme in, 371, 453

Pope, J., 370

Positive degree
  of adjectives, 289
  of adverbs, 359-361

Possession, use of apostrophe to
  show, 443

Possessive adjectives, 286-287

Possessive case
  diagraming of, 456
  nouns in, 222-224

Possessive pronouns, 256-260

Predicates
  complete, 407-409
  compound, 410-411
  definition of, 402

Prefixes, 26-27

Prepositional phrases, 374-376, 395
  adding, 30-32

Prepositions, 373-374
  list of, 374
  objects of, 227-228
  usage of, 377-380
  words used as adverbs and, 381

Present perfect tense, 329

Present tense, 325

Pronouns
  compound personal, 244-245
  contractions containing, 257-258
  distributive, 264
  indefinite, 265-266
  interrogative, 261-263

in vs. *into*, 380
indefinite pronouns *anyone* or *anything* with negatives, 266-267
lie vs. *lay*, 312
O vs. *Oh*, 388
possessives vs. contractions, 259-260
pronouns as subjects and objects, 246-255
sit vs. *set*, 313
teach vs. *learn*, 316
the vs. *a* and *an*, 280-281
their vs. *there*, 364
this and *these* vs. *that* and *those*, 283-284
those vs. *them*, 284
two, too, and *to*, 366
who vs. *whom*, interrogative pronouns, 263

V
"Velvet Shoes" (Wylie), 156
Verb phrases, 304-307
Verbs
  agreement of subject with, 335-345
  definition of, 301-303
  intransitive, 319-321
  irregular, 308-316
  linking, 322-324
  synopsis of, 334
  tenses of, 325-334
  transitive, 317-318, 320-321
  words used as nouns and, 204
vid, 82
vis, 82
Vocabulary skills. *See also* Spelling, Word study
  homophones, 110-111, 170-171
  synonyms, 185-187

W
What, 261
Which, 261
Who/whom, 261, 263

Whom/who, 261, 263
Whose, 261
Williams, William Carlos, 392
"Wind Song" (Moore), 161
Word, choosing best, 41-43
Word division, use of hyphens in, 444
Word map, 12
Word study
  homographs, 144-145
  homophones, 110-111, 170-171
  misused words, 170-171
  prefixes, 26-27
  roots, 82-83
  suffixes, 52-53
World Almanac and Book of Facts, 190
Writing skills
  beginning sentences, 7-9
  book reports, 105-107
  business letters, 128-133
  combining sentences, 33-35
  descriptive paragraphs, 67-70
  dialogue, 99-101
  dividing sentences, 36-40
  ending sentences, 14-17
  expanding sentences, 29-32
  how and why tales, 108-109
  journal writing, 24-25
  narrative paragraphs, 59-63
  persuasive paragraphs, 75-79
  reports, 90-92
  revising, 48-49, 63, 70, 79, 92, 123, 133
  social letters, 118-123
  stories, 93-101
  supporting sentences, 11-13
  titles, 22-23
  topic sentences, 4-6
  word choice, 41-43
Wylie, Elinor, 156

Y
-y, 52
Yes, use of commas to set off, 431
You, as subject, 341

Acknowledgments

Text

Excerpts from *Across Five Aprils* by Irene Hunt. Copyright © 1964 by Irene Hunt. Reprinted by permission of Modern Curriculum Press, Inc. "Autumn Woods" from *A World to Know* by James S. Tippett. Copyright © 1933 by Harper & Row, Publishers, Inc. Renewed 1961 by Martha K. Tippett. Reprinted by permission of Harper & Row, Publishers, Inc. Excerpts from *The Black Stallion* by Walter Farley. Illustrated by Keith Ward. Copyright © 1941 and renewed 1969 by Walter Farley. Reprinted by permission of Random House, Inc. "Buffalo Dusk" from *Smoke and Steel* by Carl Sandburg. Copyright © 1920 by Harcourt Brace Jovanovich, Inc.; renewed 1948 by Carl Sandburg. Reprinted by permission of the publisher. "The Camel's Complaint" from *The Admiral's Caravan* by Charles Edward Carryl, in the public domain. "City" by Langston Hughes. Reprinted by permission of Harold Ober Associates, Inc. Copyright © 1958 by Langston Hughes. Copyright renewed © 1986 by George Houston Bass. "Fourth of July Night" by Dorothy Aldis, reprinted by permission of G.P. Putnam's Sons from *Hop, Skip and Jump!* by Dorothy Aldis, copyright © 1934, copyright renewed © 1961 by Dorothy Aldis. "Hector the Collector" (text only) from *Where The Sidewalk Ends: The Poems and Drawings of Shel Silverstein*. Copyright © 1974 by Evil Eye Music, Inc. Reprinted by permission of Harper & Row, Publishers, Inc. "It Couldn't Be Done" from *Collected Verse* by Edgar A. Guest. Copyright © 1934 by Contemporary Books, Inc. Reprinted by permission of Contemporary Books, Inc. Excerpt from *Man at Work: His Arts and Crafts* by Harold Rugg and Louise Krueger. Reprinted by permission of Silver, Burdett and Ginn. Excerpt from "May I Have Your Autograph?" by Marjorie Sharmat, from *Sixteen Short Stories by Outstanding Writers for Young Readers* edited by Donald R. Gallo. Copyright © 1984 by Marjorie Sharmat. Reprinted by permission of Delacorte Press. "Noise" by J. Pope. Reprinted by permission of *Punch*. Excerpts from *Pecos Bill and Lightning* by Leigh Peck. Copyright © 1940 by Leigh Peck. Copyright renewed © 1968 by Leigh Peck. Reprinted by permission of Houghton Mifflin Company. "Raccoon" excerpted from *Laughing Time* by William Jay Smith. Copyright © 1953, 1955, 1956, 1957, 1959, 1968, 1974, 1977 by William Jay Smith. Reprinted by permission of Delacorte Press/Seymour Lawrence. "Recipe" by Bobbi Katz, from *Faces and Places, Poems for You* selected by Lee Bennett Hopkins and Misha Arenstein. Copyright © 1971 by Scholastic Magazines, Inc. Reprinted by permission of Scholastic, Inc. Excerpts totaling approx. 175 words from pp. 27 and 29 from *Sounder* by William H. Armstrong. Copyright © 1969 by William H. Armstrong. Reprinted by permission of Harper & Row, Publishers, Inc. "Stop-Go" from *I Like Automobiles* by Dorothy W. Baruch. Permission granted by Bertha Klausner International Literary Agency, Inc. "Stopping by Woods on a Snowy Evening" copyright © 1923, 1969 by Holt, Rinehart and Winston. Copyright © 1951 by Robert Frost. Reprinted from *The Poetry of Robert Frost* edited by Edward Connery Lathem, by permission of Henry Holt and Company, Inc. "This Is Just to Say" by William Carlos Williams, *Collected Poems Volume I: 1909–1939*. Copyright © 1938 by New Directions Publishing Corporation. "Velvet Shoes" copyright © 1921 by Alfred A. Knopf, Inc., and renewed 1949 by William Rose Benet. From *Collected Poems of Elinor Wylie* by permission of Alfred A. Knopf, Inc. "Wind Song" from *I Feel The Same Way* by Lilian Moore. Copyright © 1967 by Lilian Moore (New York: Atheneum, 1967). Reprinted by permission of Atheneum Publishers. Excerpts from *The World Almanac & Book of Facts*, 1987, copyright © 1986, Newspaper Enterprise Association, Inc., New York, NY 10166.

Photographs

Fine Art

Illustrations

226(B), 314(B), 315(B), 362(B), 363(B);   Mary Jones, 16, 17, 22, 41, 46, 64(B), 65(B), 68, 69, 76, 77, 110, 113, 114(B), 166, 177, 180, 181, 188, 197, 198(M), 202, 203, 205, 228, 229, 239, 244, 245, 247(T), 255(B), 258(B), 259(B), 286(B), 301, 302(B), 320, 321, 324(B), 325, 340(B), 341(B), 348, 349, 384, 385, 403(T), 416, 417, 419(B);   G. Brian Karas, 34, 35, 78, 82, 97, 101, 108, 109, 118(B), 154(M)(B), 165(M)(B), 204(B), 222, 224(B), 230(B), 240, 241, 250(B), 251(B), 280(B), 281(B), 296, 297, 332, 333, 383, 386, 387(B), 410(B), 422, 423;   Carl Kock, 1, 6, 7, 8(T), 9(T), 15, 16(T), 17(T), 18(T), 19(T), 20, 21, 22(T), 23, 26, 32, 36, 37, 42, 43, 44(B), 48, 49, 52, 55, 58(T)(B), 59, 62, 63, 64(T), 65(T), 66, 70, 72, 73, 78(T), 79, 83, 90, 91, 92, 94(T), 95(T)(M), 98, 99, 100, 101(T), 114(T), 115, 116, 117, 118(T), 119(T), 120, 121, 122, 123, 125, 126, 127, 128, 129, 130, 131, 132, 133, 134, 135(T), 136(T), 137, 138, 139, 140(T), 141(T), 144(T), 161, 163(T), 170, 171(T), 174(T), 175, 178, 179, 182, 183, 184, 185, 186(T), 187, 189, 190(T), 191, 192(T), 193(T), 198(T), 199, 200, 201, 204(T), 208, 209, 210, 211, 216, 217, 218, 219(T), 220, 221, 224(T), 226(T), 227, 231, 232, 233, 234, 235, 248, 249(T), 251(T), 252, 253, 254, 255(T), 257, 258(T), 259(T), 260, 261, 262, 263, 265(T), 271, 272, 273, 274(T), 275, 279, 281(T), 282, 283, 284, 285, 288, 290, 291, 303(T), 310, 311, 312, 313, 318, 319, 326, 327, 328(T), 336, 337, 338, 339, 340(T), 343, 344, 345(T), 346, 351, 352, 353, 354(T), 355, 356(T), 357, 361, 365, 374, 375, 376(T), 378(T), 379(T), 380(T), 381, 387(T), 388, 389, 390, 391, 396, 400(T), 401(T), 404, 405, 408(T), 409(T), 410(T), 411(B), 420, 421(T), 427, 429, 430, 431, 432, 433, 434, 435, 436, 437, 438, 439, 440, 441, 442, 443, 444, 445, 446, 448, 449(T), 450, 451(T), 456, 457, 458, 459, 460;   Joan Landis, 364(B), 423;   April Uhlir Lemke, 345(B);   Eileen Mueller Neill, 38(T), 176(T), 238(set design);   Robert Post, 33, 38, 56, 57, 71, 354, 399(B), 428, 449(B);   Phil Renaud, 303(B), 376(B);   David Sheldon, 196;   William Seabright, 212, 421(B), 452, 453;   Lynn Westphal (handwriting), 12, 13, 24, 25, 86, 87, 114, 115, 116, 119, 120, 121, 124, 125, 126, 129, 130, 131, 139.

Editorial Staff

George A. Lane, S.J., Joseph F. Downey, S.J., Jeanette Ertel, Jane Guttman, and Laura Fries

Production Staff

Carol L. Tornatore, April Uhlir Lemke, David Miller, and Kristina Lykos

The type for this book was set by Jandon Graphics, Inc.; the film was made by H & S Graphics, Inc.; and the book was printed by R. R. Donnelley & Sons Company.